lonely planet

GREGOR CLARK & BRENDAN SAINSBURY

Contents

PLAN YOUR TRIP
Welcome to Italy 4
My Perfect Day Walk 6
Our Picks 8
When to Go 16
Get Prepared for Italy 18

THE ITALIAN LAKES 21
Orrido di Sant'Anna 24
Greenway al Lago di Como 26
La Strada del Ponale 30
Monte Isola Loop 32
The Slopes of Monte Grona 34
Monte Baldo:
Sentiero del Ventrar 36
Also Try 38

CAMPANIA &
THE AMALFI COAST 41
Passeggiata del Pizzolungo 44
Punta Campanella 46
Sentiero degli Dei 48
Valle del Sambuco 52
Le Tre Marine 54
Valle delle Ferriere 56
Santa Maria del
Castello Circuit 58
Also Try 60

ABRUZZO 63
Santo Stefano di Sessanio
to Rocca Calascio 66
Above Pescasseroli 68
Campo Imperatore Ridge 70
Rocca Ridge 72
Monte Mileto 76
Sentiero della Libertà 80
Also Try 84

TUSCANY 87
Panzano to Radda 90
Castellina to Radda 92
Certaldo to San Gimignano 94
Chianti Classico 96
Tuscan Hill Crests 100
Medieval Towns & Villages ... 104
Also Try 108

SICILY 111
Stromboli 114
Necropoli di Pantalica 116
La Rocca di Cefalù 118
Riserva Naturale
dello Zingaro 120
Oasi Faunistica di Vendicari ..124
Fossa di Vulcano 126
Punta Troia 128
Also Try 130

THE DOLOMITES
& STELVIO 133
Hans & Paula Steger Weg 136
Passo Gardena to Vallunga ...138
Sassolungo Circuit 142
Tre Cime di Lavaredo 144
Alpe di Fanes 146
Pragser Wildsee 150
Percorso delle Segherie 152
Adolf Munkel Weg 154
Also Try 156

SARDINIA 159
Cala Goloritzé 162
Gola di Gorropu 164
Tiscali 166
Cala Sisine to Cala Luna 170
Monte Corrasi 172
Also Try 174

UMBRIA & LE MARCHE 177
Passo del Lupo 180
Gola dell'Infernaccio 182
Monte Subasio 184
Around the Pian Piccolo 188
Bosco di San Francesco 190
Also Try 192

LIGURIA 195
Levanto to Monterosso 198
Portofino to San Fruttuoso ...200
Manarola a Corniglia 202
Sentiero Azzurro 204
Porto Venere to Riomaggiore 208
Also Try 210

THE WESTERN &
MARITIME ALPS 213
Tour du Mont Blanc 216
Sella-Herbetet Traverse 220
Gran Balconata del Cervino ..222
Vallone di Grauson 226
Rifugio Garelli 228
Also Try 230

TOOLKIT
Arriving 232
Getting Around 233
Accommodation 234
Hiking 235
Health & Safe Travel 236
Responsible Travel 237
Nuts & Bolts 238
Index 240

Welcome to Italy

From the ravishing coastlines of Sicily to the jagged spires of the Dolomites, and the terraced vineyards of Tuscany to the fragrant citrus groves of Campania, Italy is a walking destination straight out of central casting. Whatever your vision of bliss – a breezy beachside stroll or an adrenaline-pumping volcano climb – you've come to the right place.

Walking here means treading ancient Roman roads and medieval pilgrimage routes, wandering limestone gorges pockmarked by Bronze Age tombs, or strolling through the exuberant gardens of a neoclassical lakeside villa. It also means eating well. From Tyrolean dumplings and regional pasta dishes at a trailside *rifugio* to sweet temptations from the local *pasticceria* to the fresh produce, olive oil and wines gracing every market stall and restaurant table, Italy is an epicurean's delight.

So throw on your daypack, lace up your boots and hit the trail. *Buona passeggiata!*

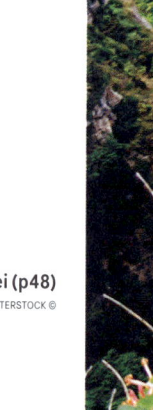

Sentiero degli Dei (p48)
NICOLE KWIATKOWSKI/SHUTTERSTOCK ©

My Perfect Day Walk

Gregor Clark

PASSO GARDENA TO VALLUNGA

P.138

Picking a single perfect walk is almost impossible in a country as varied as Italy. Stromboli, Mont Blanc and Sardinia's Cala Sisine all come to mind. But I'll go with the Passo Gardena to Vallunga loop, a walk that encompasses the Dolomites' full spectrum of natural splendour, from the knife-edged summits of Puez-Odle to the gentle green pastures surrounding Selva – with a built-in stop for alpine comfort food and companionship at a windswept mountaintop hut.

Passo Gardena (p138)

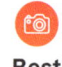

Best Scenic Walks

1 Cala Goloritzé
Weave through ancient oaks to one of Sardinia's most pristine beaches, punctuated by a dagger-shaped pinnacle.

2 Stromboli
Climb Italy's most hyperactive volcano at sunset to watch red-hot lava explode into a darkening sky.

3 Hans & Paula Stegerweg
Embark on an exhilarating stroll through vast alpine meadows at the foot of the Dolomites.

4 Portofino to San Fruttuoso
Pine-fringed headlands and translucent Mediterranean waters frame the path to a medieval monastery.

5 The Slopes of Monte Grona
Survey the convergence of lakes and alpine foothills from a jaw-dropping perch above Lake Como.

Best Village-to-Village Walks

1. Certaldo to San Gimignano
Meander between two iconic medieval hill towns amidst the splendour of the Tuscan countryside.

2. Gran Balconata del Cervino
Dip in and out of alpine villages, with the shapely Matterhorn providing a riveting backdrop.

3. Greenway al Lago di Como
Amble along Lake Como's elegant waterfront esplanade, taking in palaces, villas and wisteria-framed lake vistas.

4. Santo Stefano di Sessanio to Rocca Calascio
Cobbled streets and hilltop castles abound on this ramble connecting two of Abruzzo's loveliest stone villages.

5. Manarola to Corniglia
Savor stunning sea and vineyard vistas on this classic village-to-village hike in the Cinque Terre.

Brendan Sainsbury
MONTE MILETO
P.76

My favourite walk is the steep circuit around Monte Mileto, which starts in the village of Pacentro in Abruzzo and burrows deep into Majella National Park, a haunting domain of dome-shaped mountains, tumbledown stables and ancient beech trees where rarely spotted Marsican bears still roam. Despite being less than two hours from Rome, Mileto is one of Italy's forgotten corners where the only other hikers you're likely to see are whistling shepherds and their trusty Maremma sheepdogs.

Pacentro (p76)

Best Family Walks

1. Orrido di Sant'Anna
Stroll from Lago Maggiore to a scenic gorge where all ages can enjoy a cooling dip.

2. Adolf Munkel Weg
Dramatic Dolomites views, scrumptious trailside snacks and minimal exertion make this a family favourite.

3. Percorso delle Segherie
A water-powered sawmill and an enticing playground offer added diversion on this easy valley circuit.

4. Pragser Wildsee
Wheelchairs and buggies can navigate this broad, well-graded path along a stunning alpine lakeshore.

5. Fossa di Vulcano
Vulcano's smoking crater and sulphuric stench are sure to capture the imagination of young adventurers.

Our Picks

BEST COASTAL WALKS

Italy is a land of spectacular coastlines, from its treasure trove of offshore islands to the palm-fringed shores of Lake Como to the cliff-hugging villages of the Cinque Terre. Whatever your vision of coastal rapture – birdwatching in coastal marshes, zigzagging down through terraced lemon groves to the blue-green Mediterranean, or ambling along a perfect crescent of white sand – you'll find a walk to suit your fancy here.

COAST TO COAST

With 7600km of Mediterranean shores, Italy has the longest coastline of any country in continental Europe.

Sentiero degli Dei

Savour bird's-eye views of the Amalfi Coast from southern Italy's 'Path of the Gods'.

P.48

Oasi Faunistica di Vendicari

Mingle with flamingoes and explore an ancient tuna factory at this Sicilian wetlands reserve.

P.124

Sentiero Azzurro

Ply an iconic path above the Ligurian Sea, threading through terraced vineyards and olive groves.

P.204

Passeggiata del Pizzolungo

Capri's captivating coastline: lavish villas, turquoise seas and whimsical rock formations.

P.44

Cala Sisine to Cala Luna

Enjoy spellbinding vistas of secret coves and limestone highlands on Sardinia's rugged eastern shoreline.

P.70

Above: Monterosso, Sentiero Azzurro (p199); Right: Cala Luna (p170)

BLUE BEACHES
Nearly 500 of Italy's most pristine beaches are honoured with the coveted Blue Flag for environmental sustainability.

SEA SIDE
Italy is surrounded by the Ligurian, Tyrrhenian, Adriatic and Ionian Seas; bonus points if you can place them on the map!

VOLCANOES
Mt Etna and Mt Vesuvius are part of the same long chain of volcanoes, known as the Campanian volcanic arc.

PICTURE PERFECT
Long before modern mountaineering, Leonardo da Vinci scaled Monte Rosa in the Alps, studying fossils and sketching storm clouds.

Our Picks

BEST MOUNTAIN WALKS

Whether you're scaling the smoky slopes of Vulcano or gazing up at the Matterhorn from the Valle d'Aosta, Italy is a paradise for lovers of mountain scenery. The glacier-scoured peaks of the Alps and the jagged teeth of the Dolomites deserve every bit of their fame, but there are countless other summits worthy of a walker's attention, from Sardinia's Supramonte to the Apennine spine running the length of the Italian peninsula.

MOUNTAIN HIGH

Gran Paradiso (4061m) is the highest mountain entirely within Italy; Mont Blanc (4805m) spans Italy, France and Switzerland.

Tour du Mont Blanc

Gaze over glaciers and braided river valleys at the base of western Europe's highest peak.

P.216

Passo Gardena to Vallunga

Descend from the treeless expanses of the high Dolomites into the exuberant greenery of Val Gardena.

P.138

Tre Cime di Lavaredo (p144)

Monte Mileto

Climb through beech glades and wildflower-strewn meadows to the grassy summit of this Abruzzo peak.

P.76

Sella-Herbetet Traverse

Prowl the ethereal high country of Gran Paradiso National Park, then loop back along a rushing river.

P.144

Tre Cime di Lavaredo

Circumnavigate this classic trio of sawtooth spires in the Dolomites east of Cortina d'Ampezzo.

P.220

Mont Blanc (p216)

Our Picks

BEST WALKS FOR HISTORY

Italy's remarkable layer-cake of history encompasses so much more than the Renaissance and ancient Rome. As you ramble round the country, you'll stumble on countless other vestiges of Italy's past: an Etruscan necropolis, a megalithic water temple, a Norman palace. Corinthian columns get repurposed as baroque pillars; Byzantine mosaics shimmer alongside inscriptions in Latin, Hebrew and Arabic. Whatever your path, a walk here is a journey through time.

ANCIENT CIVILISATIONS

Before the Romans, other powerful civilisations ruled parts of modern-day Italy, including Etruscans, Greeks, Celts and Sardinia's Nuragic people.

1. Tiscali
Climb to a collapsed cave that shelters the enigmatic ruins of a prehistoric Sardinian village.
P.166

2. Necropoli di Pantalica
Gaping Bronze Age burial chambers punctuate the limestone cliffs on this hauntingly beautiful Sicilian circuit.
P.116

3. Medieval Towns and Villages
Steep yourself in Tuscan history, from San Gimignano's maze of medieval towers to Volterra's Medici palace. **P.104**

4. Sentiero della Libertà
Traverse the Apennines on this WWII escape route forged by Italian prisoners fleeing Nazi occupation.
P.80

5. La Rocca di Cefalù
Scale the slopes above Cefalù's cathedral to a megalithic temple and a ruined Arab-Norman castle.
P.118

UNESCO STAR
Italy has more UNESCO World Heritage sites (roughly five dozen at last count) than any other country in the world.

San Gimignano (p104)

Our Picks

BEST OFF-THE-BEATEN-TRACK WALKS

Despite Italy's perennial popularity, it's easy to find roads less travelled, especially when exploring on foot. Off-the-radar regions like Abruzzo and the Maritime Alps are delightful for walking, yet receive only a fraction of the visitors that flock to Tuscany and the Dolomites. Even in tourist hotspots like the Cinque Terre, escaping the crowds is often just a matter of branching off the main path and charting a slightly different course.

TRAVEL BY BOAT

Ride the ferry to the last stop to discover the tranquility of less-visited islands like Alicudi, Filicudi, Marettimo and Pantelleria.

Punta Troia (p128)

QUIET TIME

Visit Italy in April or October for quieter coastal trails, coupled with flamboyant Easter processions or autumn harvest festivals.

❶ Punta Troia

Hike to Marettimo's fortress-crowned northern tip, a dreamy end-of-the-line outpost in Sicily's remote Egadi Islands.

P.128

❷ Tuscan Hill Crests

Trace the less-travelled ridges south of San Gimignano, traversing sleepy rural hamlets, vineyards and olive groves.

P.100

❸ Around the Pian Piccolo

Prowl through grasslands ablaze with June wildflowers on this Umbrian plateau ringed by lonesome mountains.

P.188

❹ Porto Venere to Riomaggiore

Leave the crowds behind on this alternate high-altitude approach to the world-famous Cinque Terre.

P.208

❺ Rifugio Garelli

Ascend past stone shepherds' huts to a mountaintop oasis in northwestern Italy's lesser-known Maritime Alps.

P.228

BEST DAY WALKS: ITALY

Our Picks

BEST WALKS FOR FOODIES

At least half the joy of walking in Italy is the culinary cornucopia awaiting at trail's end. Regional cuisine is as dazzling and varied as the country's landscapes, and everything – from the familiar to the unexplored – is fabulous. Whether you're crunching on cannoli in Sicily, sampling dumplings in the Dolomites or cooling off with gelato in an Umbrian piazza, it's impossible to imagine a more appetising place to walk.

FOOD FOR THOUGHT

Biscotti, cannoli and *panini* are plural nouns in Italian; if you want just one, ask for *un biscotto, un cannolo, un panino.*

❶ Chianti Classico
Wander among the vineyards, olive groves and farmsteads of Tuscany's most renowned wine-growing region.
P.96

❷ Alpe di Fanes
Dig into dumplings, sauerkraut and apple strudel on the sunny terrace of an Austrian-themed Dolomites lodge.
P.146

❸ Rocca Ridge
Descend from the heights of Parco Nazionale d'Abruzzo to feast on truffles, roast pork and Montepulciano.
P.72

❹ Valle del Sambuco
Refuel from your ramble through the citrus groves with a *delizia al limone,*, featuring fragrant Amalfi lemons.
P.52

❺ Riserva Naturale dello Zingaro
Dine family-style on Sicilian seafood, produce and olive oil following this exhilarating coastal walk.
P.120

Above: Truffle pasta (p74); Right: Fruit, Amalfi (p43)

CHEAPER COFFEE
Under Italy's two-tier price system, drinking coffee at the bar costs less than ordering from a table served by a waiter.

SNAIL'S PACE
Italy's Slow Food movement certifies dozens of standout regional eateries each year; look for the snail logo out front.

When to Go

Italy is a three-season walker's delight. Depending on your destination, you'll find prime conditions anytime between April and October.

To make the most of your Italian adventure, tailor your itinerary to the season. In the Alps, Dolomites and Apennines, prime conditions prevail from June through September, when melting snow yields to long, warm days and mountain huts offer trailside sustenance. Elsewhere, especially along the southern coast, spring and fall are ideal for walking, with a profusion of wildflowers in April and May, and pleasant weather without the crowds in September and October.

Accommodation

Throughout Italy, you'll find best value for money in spring and autumn, when fewer Italians are on the road. In the mountains, where the walking season is shorter, June and September are

I LIVE HERE

Fabiana Mariotti, owner of Agritur Il Tempo delle Mele

I'm lucky enough to have been born in the mountains. Whenever I have a free moment, I put on my trekking shoes and within minutes I'm out on the forest paths. In summer I'm drawn to the peaks of the Adamello Brenta and Stelvio parks. I leave at dawn with my backpack on my shoulders and start hiking in the fresh air, leaving the woods behind and climbing above treeline. The satisfaction of reaching the summit and gazing over a splendid panorama is worth the effort. I feel free.

Palio di Siena

Weather Watch

JANUARY	FEBRUARY	MARCH	APRIL	MAY	JUNE
Avg. daytime max: **12°C**. Days of rainfall: **11**	Avg. daytime max: **12°C**. Days of rainfall: **8**	Avg. daytime max: **15°C**. Days of rainfall: **9**	Avg. daytime max: **19°C**. Days of rainfall: **13**	Avg. daytime max: **24°C**. Days of rainfall: **9**	Avg. daytime max: **28°C**. Days of rainfall: **8**

Fiera Internazionale del Tartufo Bianco d'Alba

> **ALTITUDE & LATITUDE**
>
> Italy's orientation and topography create microclimates, affected as much by altitude as latitude. Temperatures in the south are more sultry, yet snow often crowns Mt Etna's summit, while palm trees rise defiantly against the pre-Alps on Lake Como's shores.

MAIN FESTIVITIES

Carnevale Held 40 days before Easter, Carnevale is celebrated in various forms. **February/March**

Settimana Santa The Pope leads Good Friday worshippers to the Colosseum and delivers the Easter blessing from St Peter's Square, while processions fill the streets from Sorrento to Sardinia. **March/April**

Giro d'Italia There's no event more iconic than this three-week international bike race up and down the Italian peninsula. **May**

Fiera Internazionale del Tartufo Bianco d'Alba Held every weekend during autumn celebrating Alba's white truffles. **October/November**

LOCAL FESTIVITIES

Sciacchetrail Runners flock to Italy's mythical Cinque Terre in early spring for this challenging 47km race. **March/April**

Fioritura di Castelluccio Photographers swoon over the technicolour explosion of Umbria's Piano Grande plateau near Castelluccio. **June**

Palio di Siena Daredevils thrill the crowds with this chaotic horse race around Siena's medieval piazza. **2 July and 16 August**

Corsa degli Zingari Centuries-old footrace in Abruzzo, where runners hurtle barefoot down a path, cross the Vella River and finish in Pacentro. **September**

the best months for bargains. Accommodation prices soar and availability gets tight countrywide in mid-summer, when most Europeans take their annual holidays. Book well in advance if traveling in July, and try to avoid August altogether, especially the mid-August national holiday Ferragosto, when prices skyrocket.

Timing Travel to Your Tastebuds

Seasonal cuisine is one of Italy's great pleasures. Time your itinerary to coincide with regional specialities – from spring strawberries and artichokes in Sicily to autumn truffles and chestnuts in Piedmont – to make a walking vacation even more memorable.

MOUNTAIN WEATHER

Weather conditions can change abruptly in Italy's mountains, with sudden downpours, gusty winds and even early September snow. Plan ahead and travel prepared with multiple layers of moisture-wicking clothing, a warm hat, wool socks, a lightweight winter jacket and dependable rain gear.

JULY	AUGUST	SEPTEMBER	OCTOBER	NOVEMBER	DECEMBER
Avg. daytime max: **31°C**. Days of rainfall: **5**	Avg. daytime max: **31°C**. Days of rainfall: **6**	Avg. daytime max: **27°C**. Days of rainfall: **9**	Avg. daytime max: **21°C**. Days of rainfall: **12**	Avg. daytime max: **15°C**. Days of rainfall: **14**	Avg. daytime max: **11°C**. Days of rainfall: **13**

Get Prepared for Italy

Useful things to load in your bag, your ears and your brain

WATCH

Il Postino
(*Michael Radford/ Massimo Troisi; 1994*) Love story set against the stunning backdrop of Procida and the Aeolian Islands.

The Talented Mr Ripley
(*Anthony Minghella; 1999*) Psychological thriller with scenes filmed in locations throughout Italy.

Il Commissario Montalbano
(*Alberto Sironi/Luca Zingaretti; 1999–2021*) TV series combining detective drama and Sicilian cuisine.

Un Passo Dal Cielo
(*Jan Michelini; 2011–2023*) TV drama about a climber who retreats to the Dolomites following a personal tragedy.

Le Otto Montagne
(*Felix van Groeningen/Charlotte Vandermeersch; 2022*) Epic tale of a four-decade friendship in the Italian Alps.

Clothing

Sun hat: The Italian sun can be strong, even on overcast days. A wide-brimmed or billed hat offers protection for your scalp, ears and neck.

Footwear: Comfortable, well-made footwear is the single most important element of any walking vacation. Lightweight walking shoes may be perfectly suitable for easier day walks, but if you're tackling the more challenging hikes in this guide, consider sturdy hiking boots with full ankle support and mountain-tough tread. Choose a reputable brand and field-test it extensively at home before you hit the trail. When hiking in rainy or chilly weather, at high altitude or on trails with stream crossings, wool socks will keep you warm, even when wet; better yet, bring a dry extra pair.

Hiking pants, shorts and shirts: Bring at least two sets of quick-drying, lightweight garments to cover your torso and legs on the trail. Convertible pants with zip-off legs compensate in versatility for what they lack in style.

Rain gear: Keep comfy and ward off hypothermia with lightweight, breathable rain gear.

Outer layers: Especially when walking in the mountains, bring extra layers of clothing, including a windbreaker, fleece, lightweight winter jacket and/or warm hat to accommodate unexpected changes in weather.

Rocca Calascio (p67)

Words

Buongiorno Good morning/day
Buona sera Good evening
Ciao Hi / Bye
Sì Yes
No No
Grazie Thank you
Per favore Please
Dov'è...? Where is...?
Vorrei... I would like...
Quanto costa? How much does it cost?
Aiuto! Help!
a destra to the right
a sinistra to the left
sempre dritto straight ahead
sentiero trail
bivio crossroads, fork in the trail
rifugio mountain hut
acqua water
colazione breakfast
pranzo lunch
cena dinner
sorgente spring
zaino daypack, backpack
scarponi da trekking hiking boots
bastoncini hiking poles
mappa map

LISTEN

L'Orfeo (*Claudio Monteverdi; 1607*) Late Renaissance opera depicting the ancient legend of Orpheus and Eurydice.

Miss Sarajevo (*Passengers; 1995*) Renowned Italian tenor Luciano Pavarotti teams up with U2 and Brian Eno in this tribute.

Ciao Bella (*Erica Firpo, 2019-2024*) Podcast celebrating Italian culture, art, cuisine and heritage through conversations with contemporary innovators.

The Story of Art Without Men (*Katy Hessel; 2023*) Bestselling audiobook, including wonderful profiles of artists Artemisia Gentileschi and Elisabetta Sirani.

READ

The Decameron (*Giovanni Bocaccio; 1353*) 100 tales told by noblemen and ladies villa-hopping through the Tuscan countryside.

The Name of the Rose (*Umberto Eco; 1980*) Engaging mystery in a medieval monastery, interwoven with philosophical musings.

My Brilliant Friend (*Elena Ferrante; 2011*) First volume of Ferrante's tetralogy in a Neapolitan neighbourhood.

The Land Where Lemons Grow (*Helena Attlee; 2015*) A travellwer's window into Italian culture seen through its citrus crops.

Villa Balbiano (p27)

The Italian Lakes

01 **Orrido di Sant'Anna**
Short valley circuit on the Piedmontese shores of Lago Maggiore. **p24**

02 **Greenway al Lago di Como**
A 'best of' Lago di Como's villages, incorporating villas, gardens and ancient Roman lanes. **p26**

03 **La Strada del Ponale**
Spectacular path cut into the cliffs above Lago di Garda. **p30**

04 **Monte Isola Loop**
Get to know the largest lake island in southern Europe. **p32**

05 **The Slopes of Monte Grona**
Short, sharpish ascent to a refuge perched above Lago di Como, with options to continue higher. **p34**

06 **Monte Baldo: Sentiero del Ventrar**
A wild botanical 'garden' hidden on the exposed slopes of Lago di Garda's sentinel ridge. **p36**

Explore

The Italian Lakes

The Lakes! Where Germanic precision meets Italian passion and gothic alpine peaks collide with the colours and cacophony of the Mediterranean. This is a land of posh yachts and placid fishing harbours, extravagant villas and hill-hugging villages, well-combed gardens and wild mountain slopes. Choose your lake – historic Maggiore, deluxe Como, or sporty Garda (or perhaps the smaller Iseo or Orta) – and choose your path. Trails fan out in all directions and, unlike most things in this lavishly decorated region, you don't have to pay wads of euros to use them.

Lago di Como

Set in the shadow of the snow-covered Rhaetian Alps and hemmed in on both sides by steep, verdant hillsides, Lago di Como is perhaps the most spectacular of the three major lakes. Shaped like an upside-down Y, measuring around 160km in squiggly shoreline, it's littered with villages, including exquisite Bellagio and Menaggio. Where the southern and western shores converge is the lake's main settlement, Como, an elegant, prosperous Italian city that echoes with history.

Lago Maggiore

Lago Maggiore is the most demure of the three main lakes. While Lago di Garda hosts theme parks and Como breeds billionaires, tourism is much less pervasive here – you'll see people going about their everyday lives, growing vegetables, cutting grass, and coppicing chestnut trees. There are mountains too, less dramatic than Como's stash, but eye-catching all the same with their steep tree-covered slopes extending well into Switzerland on the lake's northern extremity. Maggiore's best walks cover its western Piedmontese slopes, departing from quiet Cannobio (the entrance to the Valle Cannobina and a network of age-old paths) and handsome Stresa, whose grand belle-époque buildings recall an age of bygone decadence.

Lago di Garda

Poets and politicians, divas and dictators: they've all been drawn to captivating Lago di Garda.

WHEN TO GO

May to September is the Lakes' best weather window, when the temperature is mild to warm and the forecast is most likely to be settled. July and August are usually hot, and the area is very crowded with tourists. Whatever the weather, lake ferry services are substantially reduced in autumn and winter.

In fact, 7% of all tourists to Italy head for this lake's shores, taking to its wind-ruffled waters in the north and village- and vineyard-hopping in the south. Surrounded by three distinct regions – Lombardy, Trentino Alto-Adige and the Veneto – the lake's cultural diversity attracts a cosmopolitan crowd. Mitteleuropeans colonise northern resorts such as Riva del Garda and Torbole, where restaurants serve air-dried ham and Austrian-style *carne salada* (salted beef), while in the south, French and Italian families bed down in Valtenesi farmhouses and family-friendly spa towns such as Sirmione and Bardolino.

Lago d'Iseo

Less than 50km from both Bergamo and Brescia, Lago d'Iseo (aka Sebino) is one of the least known Lombard lakes. Shut in by soaring mountains, it's a magnificent sight. About halfway along the lake, a mountain soars right out of the water forming the hump-backed island of Monte Isola, nexus for the region's best trails. The gateway to the area is the eponymous town of Iseo on the lake's eastern shore, with fast train links to the city of Brescia. From here, boats depart multiple times daily for Monte Isola.

TRANSPORT

The Italian Lakes are all best accessed through the northern Italian hub city of Milan. Efficient and regular trains run from Milan to the southern lake shores of Maggiore, Como and Garda. From here, you're better off travelling by bus or, better still, boat. Public ferries run on all three main lakes, although services are cut back between October and April.

WHAT'S ON

Rockmaster Festival
Arco, near the tip of Lago di Garda, is one of Europe's most popular climbing destinations and is the location of the Rockmaster festival and climbing competition in late summer. (*rockmaster.com*)

Settimana del Tulipano
In the last week of April, tens of thousands of tulips erupt in magnificent multicoloured bloom in Verbania's Villa Taranto on the shore of Lago Maggiore.

WHERE TO STAY

The Lakes have a good range of accommodation. In summer, you should book at least a month in advance, and in popular places such as Como and Bellagio a minimum two-night stay may be required. The best-value accommodation is in B&Bs and some of the more luxurious versions border on boutique hotels. For the flush, the region is renowned for its exclusive lakeside villas turned five-star hotels. Stresa is a good gateway town for Lake Maggiore; Como (city) anchors Lago di Como. From a walking perspective, Riva del Garda is the best base on Lago di Garda.

Resources

Gestione Navigazione Laghi (*navigazionelaghi.it*) Covers ferry services on the three main lakes (Maggiore, Como and Garda). The website includes timetables and pricing.

360gardalife.com
Information portal for activities around Lago di Garda including a full list of walks on Monte Baldo.

01

Orrido di Sant'Anna

DURATION	DIFFICULTY	DISTANCE	START/END
2hrs	Easy	5km	Cannobio

TERRAIN	Flat riverside paths and paved roads

The walk to Orrido di Sant'Anna is a perfect excuse to decamp to Cannobio, home of Lake Maggiore's most splendorous waterfront esplanade. Sitting on the cusp of the forested Valle Cannobina, the Orrido itself is a narrow gorge guarded by a medieval church above a diminutive beach and pool ideal for summer swimming.

From Cannobio's unusual lake-facing main square, **Piazza Vittorio Emanuele III**, stroll north passing waterside bars and restaurants until you reach a roundabout near the town lido.

Pick up a paved walking path behind the lido, which goes under a road bridge and follows the Cannobino River inland. Cross the river at the second bridge (a bouncy pedestrian-only suspension bridge), and take the well-marked trail along the northern bank. This skirts woodland (meandering paths lead closer to the rushing mountain stream), and finally reaches tranquil shallows at the base of a cliff topped by a small church, the **17th-century Chiesa di Sant'Anna**. The pebbly beach here makes a fine spot for a dip on warm days. Just past the church is the **Orrido di Sant'Anna**, a tight ravine where the rushing water has carved a path through the mountains on its descent to the lake. The gorge is crossed by two stone bridges, one dating from the 12th century.

From here, loop back to Cannobio by taking the road on the opposite side of the bridge. You'll quickly merge with a wider road (SP75). Follow it for 1km before veering right onto a **cycling trail** near the Camping Valle Romantica. Follow this trail through suburban streets back to the southern end of Cannobio.

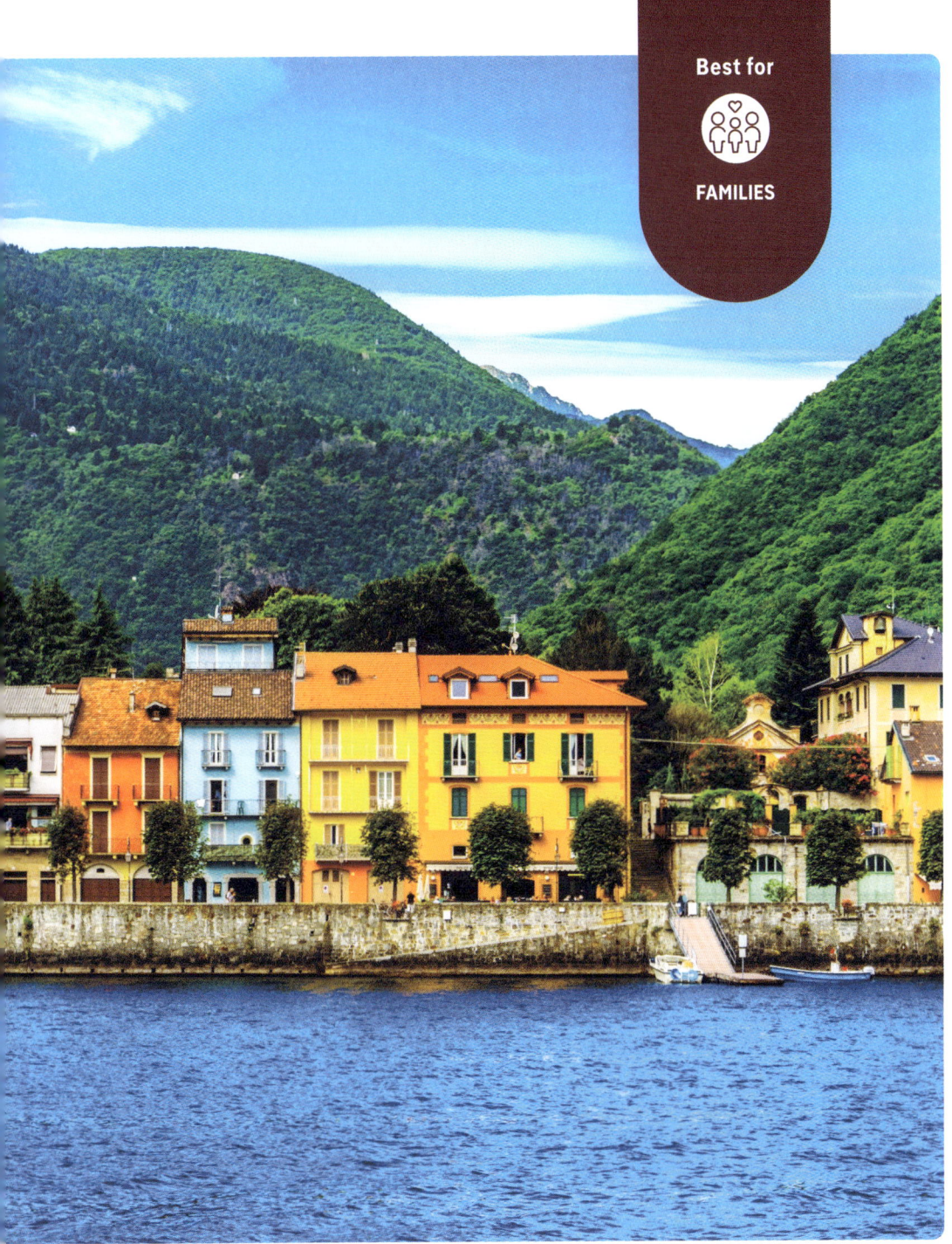

Cannobio

02

Greenway al Lago di Como

Best for

QUAINT VILLAGES

Ossuccio

DURATION	DIFFICULTY	DISTANCE	START/END
3hrs	Easy	10km	Colonno/Cadenabbia

TERRAIN	Quiet paved roads and lanes through lakeside villages

Following the Strada Regina, an old Roman road that linked Milan and Switzerland, this refreshingly well-signposted path winds its way along Lago di Como's western shore between Colonno and Cadenabbia, avoiding the traffic-choked highway and dipping into plenty of *belli* villages along its course. The trail meanders along lakeside esplanades draped in wisteria and cobbled lanes empty save for the odd cat. Minor climbs are rewarded with Como-esque views over red-tiled roofs and distant villas.

Getting Here

The ASF (*asfautolinee.it*) bus C10 from Como will get you to the start of the walk in Colonno. It runs roughly hourly throughout the day.

Starting Point

Begin on the main lakeside road at the south entrance to the village of Colonno. Next to the bus stop, a green sign pointing up Via Cappella marks the start of the Greenway.

01 Walk up Via Cappella, following it around a tight bend before forking right into Via Civetta. The street descends into the medieval heart of Colonno, crossing a stream and exiting the red-roofed settlement on an old cobbled Roman road, the Via Vecchia Regina. Running roughly parallel to the main SS340 below, the narrow lane heads north, past olive terraces and private gardens to the adjacent village of **Sala Comacina**.

Villa Carlotta

The star of the show on a lake shore not bereft of elegant touches, the **Villa Carlotta** (villacarlotta.it) is a fusion of neoclassical architecture and harmonious garden design. The botanic gardens are filled with colour: orange trees are interlaced with pergolas next to rhododendrons, azaleas and camellias. The 8-hectare gardens also contain a fern valley, a bamboo grove, a rock garden, cedars and a lookout.

The 17th-century villa adds a human touch to the surroundings, with bright rooms embellished with sculptures, paintings and tapestries.

02 Forking left onto a cobbled path just past the **San Rocco chapel**, the Greenway descends to the main road just north of Sala Comacina. As you head down you can admire the **Isola Comacina**, Lago di Como's only island, shimmering below. Once the site of a Roman fort and medieval settlement, it today protects the ruins of two **Romanesque churches**.

03 Walk briefly along the main road past the **San Giacomo church** before turning left up Via Santuario and entering Ossuccio, a tiny village with a few Romanesque vestiges and an archaeological museum hiding in its narrow lanes. For those seeking some extra exercise and a little spiritual enlightenment, it's worth making a diversion to the **Sacro Monte di Ossuccio** (the Sacred Mountain of Ossuccio), a chapel-lined walking route that has been a pilgrimage destination for centuries. The church at the top, the **Santuario della Madonna del Soccorso**, was built over various periods from 1537 until 1719, and its ceiling is swirling with richly hued frescoes depicting the coronation of the Virgin Mary and her assumption into heaven. To reach it, continue straight (away from the lake) on Via Santuario. It's a 1.5km one-way walk.

04 Otherwise, turn right off Via Santuario around 200m from the lakefront onto Via Castelli, cross a roundabout and cut right at a T-junction by a church to rejoin the SS340 by the impressive entrance to the stately Villa Balbiano.

05 Here the path veers off the main road again, crosses a bridge, snakes past a campground and the entrance to the glorious **Villa Balbianello** (worth an elongated side trip; see p29) to dispense you on the lakeshore at **Lido di Lenno** where ice cream awaits. It's worth lingering awhile on this deluxe promenade with its **11th-century church** and **free-standing octagonal baptistery** complemented by a **tiny artificial beach**.

BEST DAY WALKS: ITALY 27

06 Continue along the lakeshore, crossing a stream and turning left up an alleyway to reach the SS340. Cross the road and head uphill on Via della Piana to a four-way junction where a right turn puts you on Via Pola in the village of **Mezzegra** perched on the hill slopes overlooking the lake.

07 After 300m, veer left at a fork into Via Pola Vecchia (if you continue on Via Pola for another 300m, you'll come to the spot where Mussolini was shot by Italian partisans in April 1945, marked by a black cross). Turn right at a T-junction, pass the **Chiesa di San Giuseppe** and, after veering left at a second junction, you'll reach the much larger **Parrocchia di Sant'Abbondio**. From here there are extra-special lake views over towards Bellagio and the so-called Larian Triangle.

08 After curving through the narrow streets of the hamlet of **Bozzanigo** and its **17th-century Brentano palaces**, pitch downhill, turning left into Via delle Gere, right into Via Fabio Sala and left again into Via Monte Grappa to descend back to the lakeside on the western edge of **Tremezzo**. The ritzy town sits opposite Bellagio on the villa-lined Riviera della Tremezzina at the point where the three arms of Lago di Como meet. Recalling older more combative times is the **Torre Rogaro**, a medieval watchtower that once formed part of an elaborate lakeside defence system.

09 From Tremezzo it's a straightforward, but hugely attractive, lakeside walk alongside the main SS340 (equipped with a protected pavement) to the ferry dock at Cadenabbia. Along the way you'll pass **grand hotels**, **handsome Liberty facades** and the crème de la crème of Como's stately houses, the art-packed **Villa Carlotta**. From Cadenabbia, regular ferries will take you back to Como.

☕ Take a Break

The word *fabbrica* (factory) takes on a whole new meaning when you stick the words 'ice cream' after it. Out go thoughts of smoky factories and in come ideas of artisan gelato served in generous dollops right on Lenno's waterfront. On busy summer days, the owners at **La Fabbrica del Gelato** dispense cones from a cute little ice-cream van that looks like a polished relic from a black-and-white Fellini movie.

Villa Balbianello

Villa Balbianello

A 1km walk along the partially wooded lake shore from Lenno's main square, **Villa Balbianello** (*fondoambiente.it*) has cinematic pedigree: this was where scenes from *Star Wars Episode II* and the 2006 James Bond remake of *Casino Royale* were shot. The reason? It is one of the most dramatic locations anywhere on Lago di Como, a genuinely stunning marriage of architecture and lake views. Though the grounds are lovely, it's well worth joining a guided tour to view the villa's interior.

03

La Strada del Ponale

DURATION	DIFFICULTY	DISTANCE	START/END
2.5hrs	Moderate	6.5km	Riva del Garda/ Pregasina

TERRAIN	Gently ascending old road – a mixture of dirt, gravel and asphalt

Once the main (and only) road linking Riva del Garda with Limone, the Ponale has been reborn as a dedicated cycling and walking path that cuts into the cliff face like a horizontal crevasse close to Lago di Garda's northern tip. From a distance it looks like a via ferrata, but up close it's wide enough for mountain bikers and hikers to share the road.

Getting Here

Riva del Garda is accessible by ferry from most points around Lago di Garda.

Starting Point

Get orientated at the boat dock of Tyrolean flavoured Riva del Garda on the windy northern tip of Lago di Garda.

01 Head south from **Riva del Garda's waterfront** using the pavement that parallels the main lakeside road (SS45). Pass a hydroelectric plant and, after around 700m, veer left where the SS45 disappears into a long tunnel. In another 50m, turn right, go under a bridge and turn right again to circle back over the same bridge.

02 You're now – as various signboards and markers will announce – on the **Strada del Ponale**. Mostly unpaved in its early stages, the vehicle-wide track ascends gently past old WWI emplacements and through numerous tunnels dynamited out of the rock. Much of the road is split in two with separate lanes for cyclists and walkers, but you'd still

A Palace to Stay

If you're flush with euros, Riva's captivating **Lido Palace** (*lido-palace.it*) is the place to offload them. The exquisite building dates back to 1899 when it opened as a resort for holidaying Austrian royalty. A renovation means super-modern bedrooms with muted colour schemes now embellish the grand Liberty-style villa, offering peerless views over lawns and lake.

Lago di Garda

be wise to watch out for fast-moving mountain bikes that come hurtling around blind curves. Etched into Lago di Garda's massive cliffs, the Ponale commands views that are extravagantly expansive (and a little vertigo-inducing).

03 The first main stop and turnaround point, comes after 3km at **Ponale Alto Belvedere**, a spectacularly sited bar-restaurant where waterfalls are visible from the deck.

04 Around 250m past the *belvedere*, the now paved (but car-free) road splits. A right turn – the Strada del Ponale proper – takes you inland, zigzagging up the slopes of the Valle di Ledro to a car park just outside Biacesa. It's more rewarding to take the **left fork,** which crosses a gully and snakes back towards the coast en route to the village of Pregasina (532m).

05 While still offering fabulous **lake views**, the road soon begins to switchback through tight hairpin bends as it climbs 300 vertical metres up the cliff side.

06 The car-free strada ends north of **Pregasina** where it joins a main road at the mouth of a tunnel. Turn sharp left (away from the tunnel) and you'll soon be in Pregasina where you can replenish your appetite before heading back on foot – or by catching bus B214 – to Riva.

☕ Take a Break

Perched high above Lago di Garda on the La Strada del Ponale, the **Ponale Alto Belvedere** lures in large consortiums of walkers and cyclists either because they're too knackered to go any further, or because they can't resist the view. There's been a bar here for over a century, but the current incarnation comes equipped with a modern wooden deck offering views over the lake and two nearby waterfalls.

04

Monte Isola Loop

DURATION	DIFFICULTY	DISTANCE	START/END
3hrs	Moderate	11km	Peschiera/Maraglio

TERRAIN	Hill paths, mule tracks and a flat paved section at the end

Hiking (or biking) is practically obligatory on Monte Isola, an island in Lago D'Iseo where cars are mercifully banned, so you might as well go the whole hog and aim to conquer the island's highest point, crowned by the beautifully weathered Santuario Madonna della Ceriola.

Getting Here

Trains from Brescia run once or twice hourly to the lakeside towns of Iseo (€3.60, 30 minutes) and Sulzano (€4, 40 minutes). Ferries operated by **Navigazione sul Lago d'Iseo** (*navigazionelagoiseo.it*) cross at least twice hourly to Peschiera Maraglio on Monte Isola from Iseo (€3.60, mid-Jun-Aug) and Sulzano (€2.60, year-round).

Starting Point

Peschiera Maraglio is an attractive lakeside village on the southeastern shores of Monte Isola. A signposted trail starts behind the information centre.

01 After climbing some stairs and crossing a paved road, a well-defined hill path leads steeply out of Peschiera Maraglio and winds up through woodland. Following an abrupt ascent, the trail levels off and contours around the south side of the island. As the trees thin out you'll get fabulous views of the southern part of **Lago d'Iseo**.

02 Within around 2.5km you'll reach the hamlet of Cure set high on the hillside. Here the path forks, presenting two options to reach the Ceriola sanctuary. We recommend the longer route accessed by turning right just before you enter the village. A mule path switches back south, passes a house and then curves north, finishing with a series of steps

Santuario Madonna della Ceriola

Monte Isola

The towering island at the south end of Lago d'Iseo is easily the lake's most striking feature, its beauty magnified by the lack of any four-wheeled traffic (cars are banned). With a population a little under 2000 spread over 11 separate hamlets, the island has been furnished with the EU-sponsored EDEN award for sustainable tourism. The erstwhile Duke of Milan, Francesco Sforza, granted the people of Monte Isola special fishing rights in the 15th century. Its people, whose ancestors may have lived here in Roman times, became known for their handmade fishing nets. Nets and hammocks are still made here in smaller numbers, while locally caught lake fish are hung out in the sun to dry.

that ascend to the **Santuario Madonna della Ceriola** perched at the island's highest point (600m).

03 At the top, you can admire the heady lake views, genuflect before the chapel's surprisingly ornate **altarpiece** and grab a toasted panino from an industrious gentleman who operates a small cafe adjacent to the church.

04 From the church, descend past 15 chapels dedicated to the rosary to a pleasant mule track that snakes through olive groves and fields down to the hamlet of **Massa** on the island's northern slopes.

05 In Massa, proceed past the village **church of San Rocco**, turn right in the square and then right again onto a paved road signposted Olzano.

06 The paved road quickly ends in the hamlet of **Olzano**, from where a well-used path descends lake-ward to a cluster of houses known as Nocelle, 1km below. From here steps drop down to the larger lakeside settlement of **Carzano**.

07 From Carzano, it's a sedate 2.7km stroll along a **car-free lakeside esplanade** back to Peschiera Maraglio. The flat paved path runs the full eastern length of the island and is popular with cycling tourists and the odd local on a moped.

Take a Break

The Soardi family has been serving up local dishes at **Locanda al Lago** (*locandaallago.it*) in Carzano since 1948, perfecting deceptively simple treatments of lake fish. It means you can sit on the waterside terrace and feast on fish lasagna or the day's catch combined with *trenette* (a flat pasta) and lashings of extra virgin Monte Isola olive oil.

05

The Slopes of Monte Grona

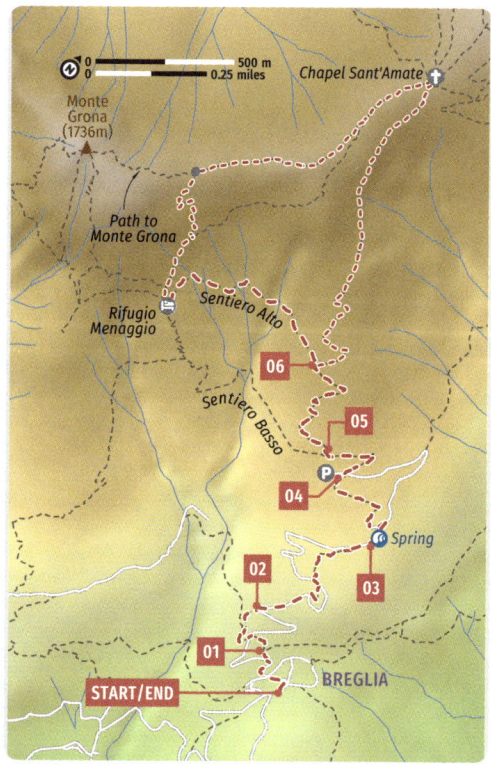

DURATION	DIFFICULTY	DISTANCE	START/END
5hrs	Hard	8km	Breglia

TERRAIN	Mostly on mountain paths with some steep ascents

Steep-sided Monte Grona glowers like a craggy faced old man above Menaggio and Lago di Como. While its tree-filled lower reaches are innocuous enough, the upper sections are precipitous and narrow. This walk to Rifugio Menaggio is relatively straightforward, while easy passage to the Sant'Amate chapel can be enjoyed by continuing along a grassy ridge.

Getting Here

Breglia can be reached on bus C13 from Menaggio (30 minutes, nine daily except Sunday). Menaggio has regular ferry service to other towns on Lago di Como, including Como itself (€10.60, 2½ hours).

Starting Point

Breglia is a small mountain village situated 7km from and 550 vertical metres above Menaggio. This walk starts at the main bus stop.

01 Walk up the **narrow paved road** marked Rifugio Menaggio. After a couple of bends, turn right and ascend a path signposted to the *rifugio*.

02 The path soon rejoins the paved road, crosses it and ascends a track for 50m before turning right by an electricity pylon. Within minutes you'll join the road again. Follow it up for approximately 300m before turning left by a **red and white marker**.

03 Climb up past some small houses and meet the road twice more. On the first occasion, cross it; on the second, turn right into an open

Best for

MOUNTAIN VIEWS

Lago di Como

Sant'Amate

Directly above the *rifugio*, prominent red and yellow signs indicate the way up to a rugged saddle called Forcoletto and, above it, Monte Grona. Ignore the Grona signs and head north towards Sant'Amate, along a clear path on a smooth ridge. The simple stone chapel stands on a grassy windswept ridge at 1623m with romantic views over two lakes – Como and Lugano – and two countries (Italy and Switzerland). From the chapel, take the descent path, signposted to Breglia. It crosses the steep grassy eastern flank of the ridge. About 30 minutes walk brings you back to the path you took up to the *rifugio*. Head downhill for Breglia.

area replete with **sorgente** (spring) and picnic tables. A sign behind the sorgente directs you uphill on a path that crosses the contact zone between greyish crystalline rocks and the smooth, grey-white limestone (dolomite).

04 After reaching a rough parking area at the end of the narrow road, take the path to the **rifugio** leading off to the left (uphill).

05 A path junction soon after gives an option of two routes to the refuge: the *sentiero basso* (low path) and the *sentiero alto* (high path). Weather permitting, take the *sentiero alto*

that sallies upwards as **lake views** unfold like a widescreen cinema epic below you.

06 Within 15 minutes, you'll come to a junction where the return path from Sant'Amate rejoins the main route.

Keep left and the path will soon leave the spur and make a fine rising contour around a valley, up to the **Rifugio Menaggio** (1¼ to 1½ hours from Breglia) where you can relax, drink and even stay over.

 Take a Break

Magnificently set amid the rocky heights at 1383m, the **Rifugio Menaggio** (*rifugio menaggio.eu*) makes a fine base camp with its clean, simply set rooms and sweeping views. If you're stopping by during a hike, you can refuel on hearty mountain meals, including vegetable soup and plates of polenta with meat or cheese (meals around €20).

06

Monte Baldo: Sentiero del Ventrar

DURATION	DIFFICULTY	DISTANCE	START/END
2hrs	Hard	5km	Tratto Spino

TERRAIN	Mostly on mountain paths with some mildly exposed sections with cable support

The high grassy meadows and narrow ridgelines of Monte Baldo dominate the northeast shores of Lago di Garda and engender a true top-of-the-world feeling. Accessible by cable car from the lakeside town of Malcesine, the ethereal domain hides plenty of high-country surprises, including this exhilarating cliff walk amid a botanical array of mountain flora.

Getting Here

Malcesine is on the northeastern shores of Lago di Garda. Regular express ferries connect to Desenzano and towns on the lower lake. A cable car heads up to Tratto Spino.

Starting Point

The *funivia* (cable car) deposits you at Passo Tratto Spino, a saddle atop the Monte Baldo ridge where numerous trails converge.

01 Exit the upper station of the *funivia*, turn left and head uphill towards La Capannina restaurant. Pass the restaurant building on your right and follow the narrow trail (path 651) across the smooth grassy ridgetop of **Colma di Malcesine**. Fabulous viewpoints open up on both sides. The ridge is a popular launch site for paragliders utilising the thermals that caress the exposed slopes on this part of Lago di Garda.

02 After around 2km, the path reaches a **belvedere** (viewpoint) where the ridgeline ends. To the north and northwest, the tip of Lago di Garda plunges like a knife into the Trentino region with the Brenta Dolomites in the background.

Monte Baldo

Monte Baldo

Monte Baldo is the name of a long mountain ridge rather than an individual peak. Ironically, the name doesn't refer to its baldness (although the upper slopes are treeless); rather, it comes from the German word 'wald', meaning forest. Monte Baldo reaches its highest point at Cima Valdritta (2218m), one of five significant summits that punctuate the ridge. Baldo is a hiking paradise thanks to a combination of lake views, well-maintained trails and easy access to high alpine terrain via the Monte Baldo cable car, located at 1760m. It is also intensely popular with mountain bikers who revel in the tumbling single-track descents that head down towards the base terminus in Malcesine.

The mountain immediately to the north is Altissimo di Nago (2079m), part of the Monte Baldo range. From the *belvedere*, the path swings to the right and heads steeply downhill to meet a road.

03 From the road, path 3, aka the **Sentiero del Ventrar**, veers off to the left. Though not particularly steep or technical, the trail has narrow and exposed sections that wrap around the gullies and rock walls at the north end of the Colma di Malcesine. Cables are provided in places for safety and support. It's not recommended for vertigo sufferers.

04 As you progress along the ledges and bluffs, you'll notice both long-range and short-range views. Omnipresent in the background is the Alpine majesty of Lago di Garda and its surrounding peaks. Adorning the crags and ledges at close range is a botanical bonanza of flowers and plants, including the red and pink **dwarf alpenrose** and the haunting **devil's claw** (pinky-blue with black tips).

☕ Take a Break

Several eating options are available at the upper station of the cable car. Arguably, the best is **La Capannina,** located around 200m north of the main buildings. Choose from a sunny terrace with sunloungers or a woodsy alpine interior. The mountain-flavoured menu emphasises polenta, mushroom tagliatelle, strudel and the like.

05 The end of the main section of the 1km-long Sentiero del Ventrar is marked by a **signboard**. Turn left on narrow trail 16 that ascends on a long diagonal back south along the Colma di Malcesine.

06 The return trail cuts lightly into the grassy hillside and will eventually deposit you back at the **upper funivia station**.

Also Try...

Orta San Giulio

Monte Mottarone

DURATION	DIFFICULTY	DISTANCE
10hrs	Moderate	11km

The 1492m-high peak behind the Lago Maggiore town of Stresa is known as Monte Mottarone and can be ascended by cable car or by a moderately graded trail labelled as L1. Thanks to the cable car you can opt to either hike up or down – or both!

Trail L1 starts near Stresa's train station and ascends up through the villages of Somerano and Levvo to the Alpina botanical garden at the halfway station. It's worth stopping here to view more than 1000 species of subalpine plants. From here, it's a fairly straightforward ascent through woodland and, later, grassland to Mottarone's summit, home to a winter ski area and a summer amusement park. There are superb views of Lago Maggiore's Borromean Islands with their privately owned palaces below.

Sass Corbée

DURATION	DIFFICULTY	DISTANCE
3hrs	Moderate	10km

A medium-length walk with historical twists, this easy-ish ramble near Lago di Como incorporates the resort of Menaggio, the villa-sprinkled Loveno, plus a foray into the Senagra River valley with its broad-leafed foliage and rather interesting milling history.

The walk is straightforward save for a scramble up a small gorge on the north side of Sass Corbée (steps and some handrails are provided). The section along the river is furnished with a number of interactive signs that provide explanations on the various sights, including a mill, a chapel, an old lime kiln and a former nail-making factory. From Piazza Garibaldi in Menaggio, take Via Calvi inland through Loveno and Pianure to the Val Sanagra Park. From here the path loops back round via Barna to Pianure.

Monte Mottarone

Cannobio–Carmine Superiore

DURATION	DIFFICULTY	DISTANCE
1.5hrs	Moderate	3.5km

This combo of paths and lanes meanders to the semi-abandoned hamlet of Carmine Superiore, perched 100m above Lago Maggiore (no road access).

Take Via Cuserina followed by Casali Bagnara to link with the path south out of Cannobio. It ascends through chestnut woods, briefly joins a road and winds past old farmhouses on its way to the hamlet of Mulinesc (Mollineggi). From here, follow the path down to the lakeside eagle's perch of Carmine Superiore with its 14th century Romanesque church.

Orta San Giulio

DURATION	DIFFICULTY	DISTANCE
1hr	Easy	3km

Overlooking the banks of shimmering Lago d'Orta, the village of San Giulio (pictured) has abundant allure.

The village and the adjacent hill topped by the Sacro Monte di San Francesco occupies a kidney-shaped peninsula and can be circumnavigated on a series of delightful walking paths. You'll be close to the water for two-thirds of the route, ambling through the cobbled streets of Orta San Guilio and along a narrow waterside esplanade that creeps past lake-lapped gardens, family vegetable plots and private fishing jetties.

Marina di Praia (p54)

Campania & the Amalfi Coast

07 **Passeggiata del Pizzolungo**
Capri's greatest hits are squeezed into 4km of coastal splendour. **p44**

08 **Punta Campanella**
Admire a protected marine reserve on the rugged tip of the Sorrento peninsula. **p46**

09 **Sentiero degli Dei**
The 'Path of the Gods' is one of Italy's most heavenly trails. **p48**

10 **Valle del Sambuco**
Ruined mills, fat lemons, hidden hamlets and a medieval convent atop a forested hillcrest. **p52**

11 **Le Tre Marine**
A coast-hugging extravaganza linking three contrasting Amalfi coves. **p54**

12 **Valle delle Ferriere**
A shady sojourn through a coastal river valley speckled with waterfalls. **p56**

13 **Santa Maria del Castello Circuit**
Spectacular climb above Positano to an ancient mountain crossroads. **p58**

BEST DAY WALKS: ITALY   41

Explore
Campania & the Amalfi Coast

Looked at through the prism of its often frenetic travel industry, Italy's most densely populated region can sometimes feel more like a tourist conveyor belt than a temple to history and art. But the outward mayhem belies a curious inner calm. Away from the busy towns and cities, Campania hides a parallel universe of ancient stone stairways and deserted trails crowned by the steep-sided Amalfi Coast, an irresistible melange of terraced gardens and plunging escarpments dotted with priceless medieval heirlooms.

A Maze of Trails

The Amalfi Coast is laced with ancient footpaths, many of them dating back to the 10th and 11th centuries and the era of the *ducato* (independent city state). Until the coastal road was built in the 1850s, the trails were the primary means of getting around. Today, they're still frequented by a mix of hikers on holiday and locals who use them to access their terraced lemon groves and outlying farm buildings. Italy's main hiking body, the CAI (Club Alpino Italiano), maintains a list of 124 numbered trails in the region, all marked with distinctive red-and-white paint. Between them, they measure out a total distance of 530km. The longest trail is the arterial Via dei Monti Lattari (trail 300), a 70km west–east romp that's rarely done in its entirety. The most popular by far is trail 327, aka the Sentiero degli Dei (Path of the Gods), a lofty cliffside traverse between the villages of Bomerano and Nocelle with unbroken coastal views. With the coastline mainly made up of plunging cliffs and craggy mountains, the paths are notorious for their steps (there is little flat ground in these parts). Additionally, some of the narrower, higher trails are mildly exposed. If you're out of shape and/or acrophobic, plan your route carefully before setting out. Although the area is heavily populated and the paths well used, it's wise to take a map. The complexity of the trail network and often erratic signage can hinder navigation. While you'll rarely be lost for long, needlessly adding 500 steps to the 1000 you've already scaled can weaken the steeliest resolve.

WHEN TO GO

The Amalfi Coast is strictly seasonal, with the majority of hotels, restaurants and bars pulling down their shutters from late October to Easter. April to June and October are less crowded periods, with June usually offering proper summer heat. The best time for hiking is April and May, when colourful wildflowers bloom and the weather is pleasantly temperate, albeit occasionally wet.

Amalfi

Pretty little Amalfi, with its sun-and-shade piazzas and diminutive beach, was once a maritime superpower that ruled over a de facto independent state. Today, the tightly packed coast-hugging community is significantly smaller but continues to exude plenty of history and culture, spearheaded by its oversized Byzantine-influenced cathedral and unusual Paper Museum. Amalfi gets congested with tourists in season, but – fear not, solitude-seeking hiker – 95% of visitors rarely leave the town's compact medieval grid, meaning the surrounding trails are gloriously serene.

Sorrento

A small resort with a big reputation, Sorrento is a town of lemons, high-pedigree hotels and plunging cliffs that cut through the heart of the historical core. The town's longstanding popularity stems from its proximity to Naples and location at the western gateway to the Amalfi. Tourism has a long history here. It was a compulsory stop on the 19th-century 'Grand Tour' when a long line of holidaying literary geniuses – including Byron, Goethe, Dickens and Tolstoy – came to sample the Sorrentine air. The romance persists.

TRANSPORT

Campania is easily accessible from most other parts of Italy via Naples, its biggest city. Trains connect Naples with Sorrento and Salerno, but the rest of the Amalfi region is only accessible by bus.

 WHAT'S ON

Settimana Santa (Holy Week)
Sorrento's holy week is famed throughout Italy for its atmospheric processions of robed and hooded penitents on Holy Thursday and Good Friday.

Ravello Festival
In July and August, the Ravello Festival – established in 1953 – turns much of the town centre into a stage. Events range from orchestral concerts and chamber music to ballet performances, film screenings and exhibitions (*ravellofestival.info*).

Resources

Cart&guide (*carteguide.com*) Publishes a series of six excellent 1:10,000 Amalfi hiking maps with marked routes and written descriptions in English and Italian. Most local bookshops or newsagents sell them for €5 each.

CAI Monti Lattari (*caimontilattari.it*) Club Alpino Italiano website with marked routes and descriptions of all CAI trails in the Amalfi-Sorrento region.

 WHERE TO STAY

If you're planning on exploring beyond the coast, Sorrento has the best transport connections, making it a convenient base. Positano, Amalfi and Ravello offer some of the most atmospheric and sophisticated accommodation in Italy, ranging from sumptuous palazzi (mansions) to humbler B&Bs with knockout coastal views. Always book ahead in summer and remember that most hotels close over the winter.

07

Passeggiata del Pizzolungo

DURATION	DIFFICULTY	DISTANCE	START/END
1hr	Moderate	4km	Capri Town

TERRAIN	Paved pathway with ascending and descending steps

This fine walk can be done as a circuit from the centre of Capri Town. It's spectacular even by Capri standards, taking in a necklace of west-coast sights including the Arco Naturale, Faraglioni and several grottoes and *belvederes* (lookouts). Most of the path is paved and there are quite a few steps, though it is not inordinately difficult.

Head east out of Capri Town on the Via Le Botteghe and the Via Matermania to the **Arco Naturale**, a curious eroded-limestone arch dating back to the Palaeolithic period and formed by millennia of natural wear and tear.

At the end of Via Matermania, backtrack to **Le Grottelle restaurant** and take the set of stairs beside it (Passeggiata del Pizzolungo). About halfway down you'll pass the **Grotta di Matermania**, a giant natural cave used by the Romans as a nymphaeum (shrine to the water nymph). You can still see traces of the mosaic wall decorated with shells.

At the bottom, continue down the path as it follows the rocky coastline south. The striking flat-roofed red villa you eventually see on your left, on the Punta Massullo promontory, is **Villa Malaparte**, the former holiday home of Tuscan writer Curzio Malaparte (1898–1957). Carrying on, the sea views become increasingly impressive as the path continues westward around the lower wooded slopes of **Monte Tuoro**. A few hundred metres further along you will arrive at a staircase on your right, which leads up to the **Belvedere di Tragara**, a prime viewing point for the pointed **Isole Faraglioni**. From here, follow Via Tragara back to the town centre.

Arco Naturale

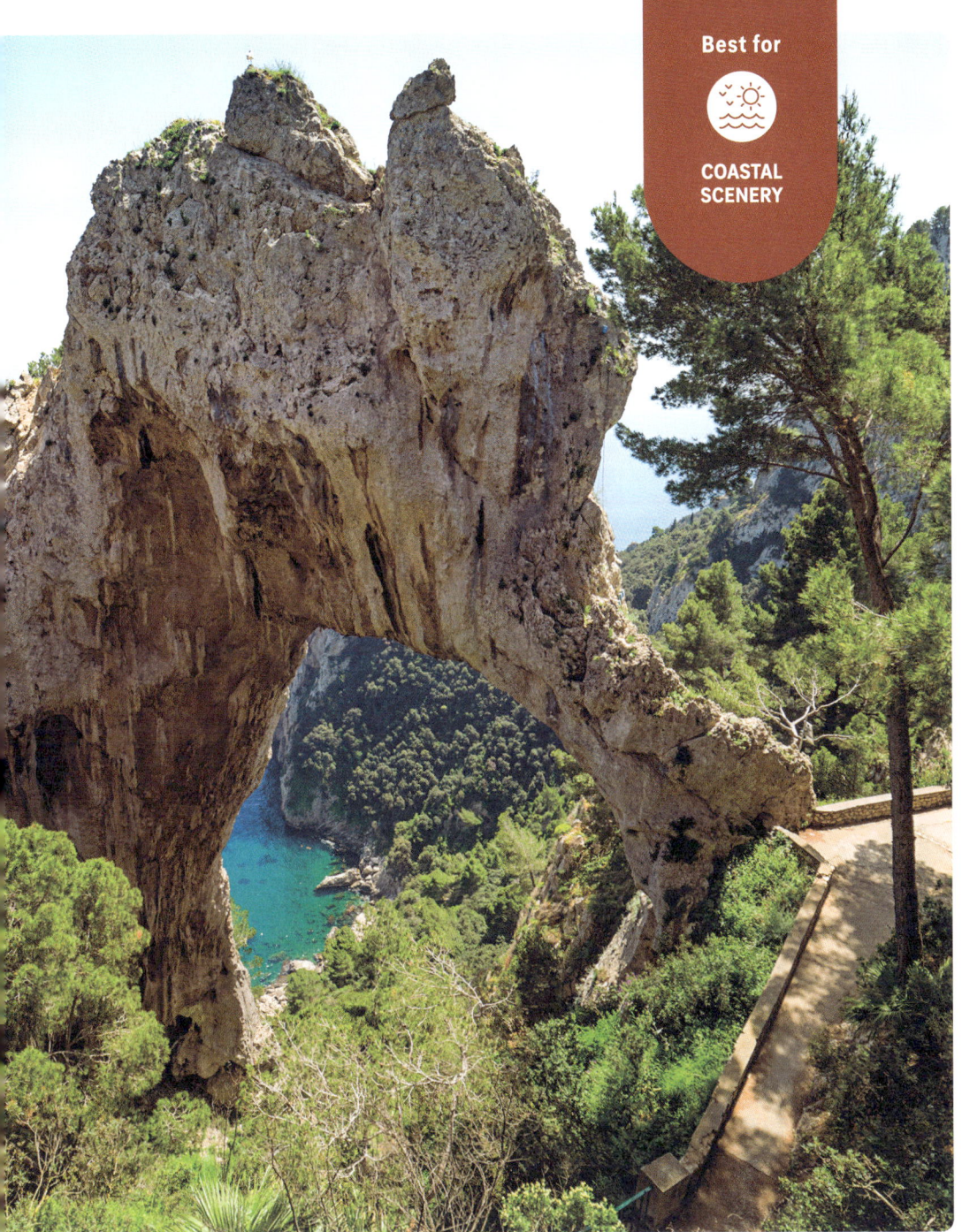

08

Punta Campanella

DURATION	DIFFICULTY	DISTANCE	START/END
3hrs	Moderate	8km	Termini

TERRAIN	Good paved path juxtaposed with a moderate hillside ascent over stonier ground

Sorrento has seduced many an enamoured North European visitor and this hike on a rocky uncultivated peninsula with spectacular views across the Bay of Naples to the island of Capri will do little to sully its lofty reputation.

Getting Here

SITA Sud (*sitasudtrasporti.it*) runs buses roughly hourly to Termini from the Circumvesuviana train station in Sorrento.

Starting Point

Get your bearings in the diminutive Piazza Santa Croce in the village of Termini, 8km southwest of Sorrento.

01 From the Piazza, follow Via Campanella to the left as it zigzags downhill, following signs for Punta Campanella. The minor road soon becomes a wide track and takes you all the way to the **headland**.

02 Punta Campanella makes a spectacular endpoint for the peninsula with **magnificent views** of Capri westwards and across the Bay of Ieranto to the mountains beyond. The modern light beacon stands close to the crumbling ruins of a Saracen tower dating from the 1300s, about 250m beyond the one and only fork in the path (where you keep right).

Punta Campanella

Baia di Ieranto

A spectacular beach at the tip of the Punta Penna peninsula just southeast of Punta Campanella, the Baia di Ieranto is reached via a path that starts in the village of Nerano about three-quarters of the way around this hike. The walk takes about 45 minutes one way and there are several steep downhill sections to negotiate. The small pebbly beach with crystalline water is sheltered by headlands and perfect for swimming, but can get crowded in summer.

03 Walk back along the track to the junction and turn right following the stone path up and across the steep slope to the **ridge crest**.

04 Here you turn sharp left onto an indistinct but relatively well-marked path that ascends steeply close to the **ridge**, through thick, low scrub and rock outcrops.

05 The building at the summit of **Monte San Costanzo** (497m) is a fenced-off military installation. The path skirts the southwestern (right) side of the compound just shy of the summit and then descends to a minor road on a bend; turn right.

06 About 50m just past the bend at a small parking bay on the right, turn off and follow the widest path through a pine grove. From the far (eastern) edge of the pines, go up steps to the plain white **chapel of San Costanzo**, another superb viewpoint.

07 Retrace your steps from the chapel (200m) and go down to the left at the edge of the pine grove on a faint path across a grassy slope. Contour the slope past a vegetable garden and a stone hut on the right. Then swing left to pass a cleft on the right and immediately, at the corner of a stone wall, turn diagonally right along a path and descend through woodland. Eventually, two flights of steps take you down to the cobbled **Punta Penna** path; turn left to reach **Nerano**. From the Via Rotabile di Nerano (in Nerano) go up beside Olga's *alimentari* and pass between **houses** and olive groves back to Termini.

 Take a Break

If you're passing through Nerano, it's practically obligatory to try the local pasta dish, spaghetti alla Nerano (with fried courgettes and cheese), as well as the seafood. The best restaurants hug the seafront in Marina del Cantone, 1.5km from Nerano, and include **Lo Scoglio**.

09

Best for

COASTAL SCENERY

Sentiero degli Dei

DURATION	DIFFICULTY	DISTANCE	START/END
3.5hrs	Moderate	9km	Bomerano/Positano

TERRAIN	Narrow hillside paths, some paved sections, lots of (downhill) steps towards the end

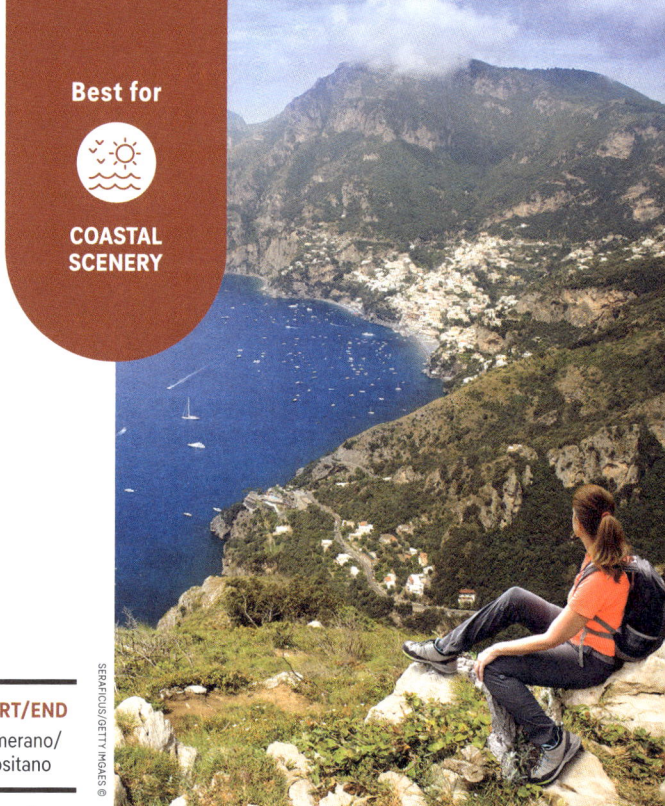

View of Positano from Sentiero degli Dei

Sentiero degli Dei translates as 'Path of the Gods' and this high-level coastal hike certainly has a celestial quality. This is by far the best-known walk on the Amalfi Coast, and for good reason. Not only is it spectacular from start to finish, but unlike most Amalfi treks, it doesn't involve Olympian amounts of stair-climbing.

Getting Here

Take a **SITA Sud** (*sitasudtrasporti.it*) bus from Amalfi town up to the village of Bomerano.

Starting Point

The walk starts in the main square (Piazza Paolo Capasso) in the village of Bomerano (a subdivision of Agerola), where several cafes supply portable snacks.

01 Follow the **red-and-white** signs southwest along Via Pennino. Pass under a bridge and, within a minute or two, you'll come to a signboard directing you right over a wooden bridge and up a staircase to a paved road. Turn left.

02 The start of the walk proper is marked by a **monument** inscribed with quotes by Italo Calvino and DH Lawrence. Views of terraced fields quickly open out as the path contours around a cliff-face and passes beneath the overhanging **Grotta del Biscotto** (Biscuit Cave).

Nocelle

A tiny, still relatively isolated mountain village, located 2km southeast of Montepertuso, Nocelle (450m) commands some of the most spectacular views on the entire coast. A world apart from touristy Positano, it's a sleepy, silent place where not much ever happens and where the small population of residents are happy to keep it that way. The Sentiero degli Dei officially ends here. Handy as you stumble off the Sentiero degli Dei with wobbly legs, **Villa della Quercia** (villaquercia.com) is a delightful B&B in a former hilltop monastery. It comes armed with a tranquil garden and spectacular, goat's-eye views of the coast.

03 From here, the trail continues its traverse of the mountainside with some minor undulations. Periodically it dips into thickets of trees and sometimes you'll be required to negotiate rockier sections, but, in the main, the going is relatively easy.

04 The first main landmark after the *grotta* is a path junction at Colle Serra. Just below Colle Serra, a path from the Sentiero degli Dei's alternative start in Praiano joins the main trail. Bear in mind that starting in Praiano involves a thigh-challenging climb up 1000 steps before you reach the trail proper. Here you get a choice between a low route or a high route. The **low route** (left turn) threads its way through vineyards and rockier sections with magnificent views of Praiano below. Roughly 800m along its course, it is possible to make a short diversion south to the San Domenico Monastery. The more popular **high route** (327a), accessed by turning right, sticks to the rocky heights with broad, sweeping vistas. Both paths are moderately exposed but not dangerous if handled with care.

05 The two paths converge at a point called Cisternulo, 1.5km beyond Colle Serra. After **Cisternulo**, the path kinks around some half-obscured *grotte* (caves) and descends into the **Valle Grarelle** before climbing back up to the official finish point in the tiny village of **Nocelle**.

06 A small kiosk selling cold drinks and coffee, served on a charming terrace with fresh flowers, greets you as you enter the village. Alternatively, head a little further through the village to **Piazza Santa Croce**, where a stall dispenses fantastic freshly squeezed orange and lemon juice. Although this is the end of the Sentiero degli Dei proper, it makes sense to carry on to Positano with its beach, restaurant and transport links. Some people take the stairs (around 1500 of them!) down through the village to be deposited, via a succession of olive groves, on the coast road 2km east of Positano; others catch a bus from Nocelle to Positano (minibuses run by **Mobility Amalfi Coast** depart 10 times a day). A much nicer option, especially if you're weary of steps at this point, is to continue along the path that leads west out of Nocelle towards Montepertuso.

07 Turn right off Via Pizzillo in the centre of Nocelle and follow **pedestrian Via Cercola** as it winds round to join the terminus of the village's main paved road.

08 From here, follow the quiet road for 2km as it contours around a large ravine. Don't miss the huge hole in the centre of the cliff at **Montepertuso** where it looks as though an irate giant has punched through the slab of limestone.

09 You'll know you've reached Montepertuso when you see a soccer field below. Follow the main road as it wraps around the western end of the pitch and turn left on a bend into Via Pestella that cuts below the **church of Santa Maria delle Grazie**. Just past the church continue along Via Pestella as it turns right and descends the semi-rural hillside, utilising a long narrow *scala* (stairway).

10 On the northern fringes of **Positano**, just above the town **cemetery**, the stairway pitches right and becomes Via Santa Croce. Soon after passing several impressive **villas**, you'll be deposited on SS163, the main Amalfi Coast road on the eastern side of Positano. Save a little time to explore the town with its vertiginous houses tumbling down to the sea in a cascade of sun-bleached peach, pink and terracotta. No less photo-worthy are its steep streets and steps, flanked by wisteria-draped hotels, smart restaurants and fashionable retailers. There are two beaches. Spiaggia Grande probably isn't anyone's idea of a dream beach, with greyish sand covered by legions of bright umbrellas and loungers that cost around €20 per person per day. A gentle walk west, with an acceptable number of steps (hooray!), is **Spiaggia del Fornillo**: more laid-back than its swanky neighbour and home to a handful of summer beach bars, which can get quite spirited after sunset.

Positano

☕ Take a Break

Nocelle's modest **Trattoria Santa Croce** has spectacular views over the coast and is located just past the 'official' finishing post on the Sentiero degli Dei in Nocelle. The menu is short and traditional, with dishes such as rustic lentil soup, *tagliatelle alla genovese* (pasta with a rich, onion-based Neapolitan sauce) and freshly caught fish with local herbs.

Need to Know

The Sentiero degli Dei is not advised for acute vertigo sufferers. Although sunny days are the norm in spring and summer, it can be cloudy in the dizzy heights, but somehow that adds to the drama, with cypresses rising through the mist like dark, shimmering sword blades and shepherds herding their goats through fog-wreathed foliage. Bring a rucksack and plenty of water, and wear proper walking shoes as the going can be rough. You may want to pack swimming gear too and end the walk with a refreshing plunge into the sea. Inclement weather and/or landslides can sometimes lead to trail closures. Check ahead. The tourist office in Bomerano can provide more guidance and details.

10

Valle del Sambuco

DURATION	DIFFICULTY	DISTANCE	START/END
4.5hrs	Moderate	10.5km	Maiori/Minori

TERRAIN	Mix of good, clear paved and dirt paths; steps and staircases in some sections

This citrus-scented circuit explores the hills and valleys behind the Amalfi town of Minori, circumnavigating lemon groves and the ruins of old paper mills. Its peak is the 13th-century Convento di San Nicola, perched high atop the coastline amid pine and oak trees.

Gettig Here

Maiori is linked by year-round **SITA Sud** (*sitasudtrasporti.it*) buses to all other Amalfi towns. From April to October **TraVelMar** (*travelmar.it*) ferries also jockey between the towns.

Starting Point

Diminutive Piazza D'Amato is the main square in the Amalfi beach town of Maiori and is the launch site for this walk.

 From the square, climb up the staircase to the left of the fountain to reach Maiori's main church, the 13th century **Collegiata di Santa Maria**. After admiring its bell tower and majolica-tiled dome take another stairway up to the popular paved pathway on Via Fuori Tuoro, better known as the Sentiero dei Limoni (Path of the Lemons).

 The path heads west with broad over Maiori's **harbour**. Small terraced plots packed with lemon trees characterise the hillsides: the fragrant lemons are known as *sfusato amalfitano*.

 After around 700m, take the staircase on the right (CAI path 315c) signposted 'Convento San Nicola' and start ascending, first through

Minori

Alternative Ending: Ravello

From Sambuco it is possible to divert via a relatively quiet paved road to the refined hilltop town of Ravello (2km). With its weighty arts festival and luxuriant villas, Ravello has long had a metamorphic effect on artistic celebrities. This is the town that cured Richard Wagner's writer's block, provided inspiration for DH Lawrence as he nurtured the plot of *Lady Chatterley's Lover*, and impressed American writer Gore Vidal so much that he stayed for 30 years and became an honorary local. Don't miss the **Villa Rufolo**, famed for its exquisite cascading gardens.

gardens and then through oak and **pine forest**. Soon after a junction with path 315a, the trail becomes less steep as you traverse the hillside below the ridge of Monte Forcella with the Convento San Nicola occasionally visible.

04 To reach the **Convento San Nicola**, take a trail on the right, following it for 300m to the chapel (489m), thought to date from the 12th century, and a spectacular viewpoint.

05 Return to the main path and turn right. Within 400m, it emerges briefly from the trees and hangs left at a rocky mountain pass before heading down to the small agricultural hamlet of **Sambuco**.

06 After passing slightly north of the village, the path crosses the **Sambuco River**, swings back around and climbs via steps, up to the paved road to Ravello. Turn left and follow this road through Sambuco, branching left after 400m and taking steps down to the western side of the Sambuco river valley.

☕ Take a Break

Pasticceria? Yes. Cafe? Yes. Gelateria? Yes. **Sal de Riso** (*salderiso.it*) on Minori's seafront is all these things and more: an emporium of edible sweetness that will make your eyes pop out and your blood sugar shoot up in the same bite. The ample glass display cases are like an art gallery of avant-garde desserts crammed with delicate cheesecakes, eclairs, sponges and pastries.

07 From here, the path parallels the river, skirting past a scattering of old **paper mills** before meeting a paved road just shy of a bend.

08 Turn left, go around the bend and continue through the outskirts of **Minori**, finishing up on the beachfront.

11

Le Tre Marine

DURATION	DIFFICULTY	DISTANCE	START/END
3hrs	Moderate	7km	Marina di Praia/Conca dei Marini

TERRAIN	Narrow hillside paths, steps, some paved sections

This coast-hugging walk incorporates three of the region's most secluded coves: Marina di Praia, the Fiordo di Furore and Conca dei Marini. But don't be lulled into a false sense of security by its proximity to the water: the precipitous hillsides require plenty of ascending and descending on sometimes indistinct paths. The views are rarely less than magnificent.

Getting Here

SITA Sud buses stop on SS163, the main Amalfi Coast road, just above Marina di Praia.

Starting Point

The path starts just east of Praiano at Marina di Praia, the village's minuscule beach.

01 Climb up behind the beach, cross the SS163 coast road and take the path up the west side of the Vallone di Praia. As the path climbs and circumnavigates the dry, scrubby valley, it becomes narrow and hard to identify before reappearing as the **Sentiero dell'Agave** in Fiori.

02 This path soon metamorphoses into the paved **Passeggiata dell'Amore**, inscribed with poetic quotes, before finally emerging opposite the **San Elia church** in Furore.

03 Take the steps heading downhill directly behind the church on what is now called the **Sentiero della Volpe Pescatrice** to come out

Fiordo di Furore

The Fiordo di Furore, a deep and narrow cleft in the coastline 6km west of Amalfi, is a misnomer. Fjords are formed by glaciers, whereas the Furore 'fjord' is a drowned river valley carved by the Schiato stream. The mouth of the *fiordo* is crossed by an arched stone bridge, the site of an international high-diving tournament in July. A tiny beach at the bottom of the cleft, accessible by a stone staircase, is backed by a few abandoned houses. Despite the lack of sun, this is a popular bathing and boating spot in the summer. There's a simple, seasonal bar-restaurant too.

Fiordo di Furore

next to the **famous bridge** across the Fiordo di Furore.

04 Cross the bridge and take the so-called **Sentiero dei Pipistrelli Impazatti** (Path of the Crazy Bats) glued to the cliff on the east side. Opposite you'll see the **Marina di Furore**. The tiny fishing and milling community was once a busy little commercial centre, although it's difficult to believe today. In medieval times, its unique natural position protected it from the threat of foreign raids and provided a ready source of water for its flour and paper mills.

05 Leaving the water, the path pitches inland into woodland. Veer left at a fork, pass some artificial water channels and you'll soon encounter an **old paper mill** (supposed home of said bats). Soon after, by a small waterfall, the path pitches right and climbs steeply out of the trees to **Punta Tavola**, a lofty viewpoint. Here it joins a paved road, the Via Maggio, on the western outskirts of **Conca dei Marini**.

Take a Break

Seafood lovers should head for the widely acclaimed, no-frills **Da Armandino** (*daarmandino.it*) restaurant located in a former boatyard on the beach at Marina di Praia. It's great for fish fresh off the boat. There's no menu; just opt for the dish of the day – it's all excellent. The holiday atmosphere and appealing setting round things off nicely.

06 Follow the paved path on the south side of the road, the Via San Michele, passing a church of the same name. The path briefly rejoins the main road before veering right again onto the pedestrian Via Pali, guarded by the vanilla-ice-cream-coloured **church of San Giovanni** clinging to the hillside.

07 Continue along Via Pali. After the church, it joins wider Via Miramare. Turn right and take the stairs down to the centre of **Conca dei Marini**.

12

Valle delle Ferriere

DURATION	DIFFICULTY	DISTANCE	START/END
5hrs	Moderate	11km	Amalfi

TERRAIN	Mix of wooded and mountain paths with lots of stairs at the start and end

The Valle delle Ferriere is a subtropical wooded valley behind Amalfi town crossed by the Canneto river and punctuated by several waterfalls. In times of old, it hosted an ironworks (*ferriera*) and various paper factories (*cartiere*). Today the factories are mossy ruins and the whole area has been turned into a reserve known for its orchids and other flora.

Getting Here

Amalfi town is the hub of the region and linked to other coastal towns by SITA Sud buses, and from April to October by TraVelMar ferries.

Starting Point

The *sentiero alto* (high route) around the Valle delle Ferriere starts on the main north-south street in Amalfi town, just south of the Museo della Carta.

01 Around 250m south of the Museo della Carta, take the Via Casamare uphill, continuing as it turns into a gravelly path studded with multiple steps – thus begins a long climb to the village of **Pogerola** perched on a crag 252m above. The stairs lead directly into Pogerola's main square, overlooked by the **church of Madonna delle Grazie**.

02 From here, take the road on the right (standing with your back to the church). After 150m divert right again onto a path (Via Riulo), passing houses, fields and more steps, before entering a more forested domain. This is the Valle delle Ferriere proper, a nature reserve replete with **ferns** and a refreshing array of **waterfalls** (some up to 20m high).

Museo della Carta

Amalfi's **Paper Museum** (*museo dellacarta.it*) is housed in a rugged, cave-like 13th-century paper mill (the oldest in Europe). It lovingly preserves the original paper presses, which are still in full working order, as you'll see during the 30-minute guided tour (in English). The tour explains the original cotton-based paper production and the subsequent wood-pulp manufacturing. Afterwards you might be inspired to pick up some of the stationery sold in the gift shop, including calligraphy sets and paper pressed with flowers.

Valle delle Ferriere

The mainly flat trail sets out on the wooded west side of the valley and is blissfully peaceful compared to the frenzy of the coast.

03 Veer right at the turnoff for Agerola (which heads left) and cross two streams with small cascades before arriving at the main crossing over the **Canneto River** and the largest of the waterfalls.

04 Ford the river (there's no bridge) and return on the more open, craggy east side of the valley. Increasingly **impressive views** of Amalfi town reveal themselves as you contour the steep valley slopes.

05 After passing through a **tunnel** high above Amalfi town, the path cuts briefly north before reaching a crossroads.

06 Turn sharp right and take the steps down to the village of **Minuta**, hitting it just shy of a bend in the road to Scala. Swivel right down Via San Giovanni, passing two **churches**.

07 After a left turn at a T-junction, you'll arrive at a third **church**, dedicated to Santa Maria del Carmine, in the village of **Pontone**. Take the steps to the right, cross the road and let gravity and a long staircase help you back to Amalfi.

 Take a Break

Fuel up for the trail at the marbled and mirrored **Pasticceria Pansa** (*pasticceriapansa.it*), a fifth-generation pastry shop where black-bow-tied waiters serve full-bodied espresso, frothy cappuccino, fresh-baked cornetti and standout pastries like the *coda di aragosta*, a lobster tail-shaped concoction filled with rich lemon-custard cream.

13

Santa Maria del Castello Circuit

DURATION	DIFFICULTY	DISTANCE	START/END
3hrs	Moderate	9km	Positano

TERRAIN	Steep cliff paths, paved lanes, lots of stairs

For those travelling on foot, there's no real way out of Positano that doesn't involve climbing steep stone staircases – lots of 'em! The advantage of this particular circuitous route is that it enjoys a bit of shade in its early stages as you plod heavenward amid a thick and gnarly holm-oak forest.

Getting Here

Regular SITA buses patrol the Amalfi Coast road, connecting all the major towns and providing easy access to the start and finish points of this walk.

Starting Point

The walk starts on the main coast road (SS163) above Positano by a ruined building adjacent to the turnoff for Montepertuso.

01 A marked path – known locally as the **Capo d'Acqua trail** – starts beside the road, climbing steeply through ever-thickening oak trees up the mountainside.

02 Pass a rustic walk-in-only **rifugio** and continue the upward climb, using the steps. The oak forest breaks into drier Mediterranean scrub as you ascend high above Positano and **coastal views** open out as the path (333a) traverses the dry craggy hills above Positano, with the hulk of **Monte Sant'Angelo** standing sentinel in the background.

03 Turn left 2km up the ascent and then right at the top to join a wider trail. This track heads northeast **traversing the hillside**, passing

BEST DAY WALKS: ITALY

Church of Madonna delle Grazie

At a Snail's Pace

Positano is one of more than 85 towns in Italy, and nearly 300 worldwide, to have gained Slow City status (an extension of the Slow Food movement, established in northern Italy in 1986). In order to be considered, certain criteria must be met: towns need to have fewer than 55,000 inhabitants, no fast-food outlets or neon-lit hoardings, plenty of cycling and walking paths, and neighbourhood restaurants serving traditional cuisine with locally sourced ingredients. For more information, check *cittaslow.org*.

first through scrub, then skirting the edge of a wood, before morphing into a paved road by a house with a red-tile roof.

04 Just past the house, the track bends left by an electricity pylon, cuts up a narrow walled lane and reaches a crossroads. Turn right along another paved lane and in around 300m you'll be in the 'village' of **Santa Maria del Castello**, perched at 670m above the Mediterranean.

05 The village **church** is on the right and accessed by a short circular road. On the left is a small bar-restaurant called **Zi Peppe** that's good for a drink. Santa Maria del Castello was an ancient crossing point between Sorrento and the Amalfi Coast. A fort once stood here in medieval times. Take the narrow lane back down to the hill crest where you hiked up earlier. This time take the main path straight ahead (trail 333) by the electricity pylon.

06 The trail bends immediately to the left, proceeds around the headland and then switches right, becoming what is known as the **La Tese trail**. This path leads steeply down via a series of well-constructed staircases to Positano, visible in all its glory directly below.

07 Follow the steps down until you meet the main Positano–Montepertuso road (Via Corvo). Cross the road and head down narrow Via Chiesa Nuova. After circumnavigating the **church of Madonna delle Grazie**, you'll be deposited on the SS163 coast road next to the Bar Internazionale in upper Positano.

 Take a Break

Calling like a siren to any cash-poor budget traveller who thought Positano was for celebs only, **C'era Una Volta** is an authentic trattoria at the top of town specialising in honest Italian grub. No need to look further than the *gnocchi alla sorrentina* (gnocchi in a tomato and basil sauce) and *insalata caprese*. Pizzas start at €4.50; beer €2.

Also Try...

Sentiero dei Fortini

Monte Epomeo

DURATION	DIFFICULTY	DISTANCE
1hr	Moderate	2.5km

For anyone of average fitness, an ascent of the slumbering volcanic peak on the island of Ischia is practically obligatory.

The quickest way to climb Epomeo is from the village of Fontana, on the mountain's southern flank. The route (signposted from a bend in the road where the CS and CD buses stop) weaves up a paved road, diverts onto a track and finishes on a steepish path. For a more gradual and pleasant ascent, opt to start in the village of Serrara Fontana, 2km south of Fontana, where a road/track winds up through vineyards, terraced fields and scrubby brush. Just shy of the summit there's a lovely rustic restaurant, behind which you can climb a steep tower of volcanic rock to reach the actual 789m peak (aided by steps and railings), beneath which lies a 15th century chapel.

Croce della Conocchia

DURATION	DIFFICULTY	DISTANCE
6hrs	Hard	12km

This is the westernmost peak (1314m) on the long, dramatically rugged chain of huge lumps of limestone called Sant'Angelo a Tre Pizzi – the highest part of the Amalfi's Monti Lattari Range.

Unlike the main summits, it's accessible from the coast. Take the step-aided path 329 (steep at first before easing) from Montepertuso up to Caserma Forestale, a stone barracks and major path crossroads. From here, waymarked CAI path 300 ascends north through woodland and out into open ground with views of cliffs and the coast. Croce's crucifix-topped summit is easily gained, although the waymarked path bypasses it to the left in hazel woodland. The view embraces the sprawling city of Naples, Vesuvius, the isles of Ischia and Capri and mountains to the northwest. Descend via the same route.

Ravello

Sentiero dei Fortini

DURATION	DIFFICULTY	DISTANCE
3hrs	Moderate	5.25km

Snaking its way along Capri's oft-overlooked western coast, the Sentiero dei Fortini (Path of the Small Fortst) is a wonderful if somewhat arduous walk that's about as remote as the island gets.

Named after the three coastal forts (Pino, Mesola and Orrico), the path starts at Punta dell'Arcera near the Grotta Azzurra and heads south to Punta Carena at the island's southwestern tip, where it is possible to go for a refreshing swim. Along the way, it passes through some of Capri's most unspoilt countryside. Carry plenty of water.

Atrani–Ravello–Maiori

DURATION	DIFFICULTY	DISTANCE
2.50hrs	Moderate	6km

Ravello is a beautiful old town, clustered on a narrow plateau rising steeply between Atrani and the coastal town of Maiori.

The town can provide the focus for an easy day out from Atrani or can be one of the highlights in a moderate walk from Atrani up to Ravello, then down to the coast again at Minori (the site of an ancient Roman coastal resort) and on to Maiori. The 6km route follows old paths and laneways through olive and citrus groves and quiet villages with extensive coast and mountain vistas.

BEST DAY WALKS: ITALY

Rocca Calascio (p66)

Abruzzo

14   **Santo Stefano di Sessanio to Rocca Calascio**
A historic hike between two recently reinvigorated medieval villages. **p66**

15   **Above Pescasseroli**
Short, steep but sweet climb above national park hub. **p68**

16   **Campo Imperatore Ridge**
A close-up look at the imposing peaks atop Abruzzo's high mountain plateau. **p70**

17   **Rocca Ridge**
Contrasting mix of ancient beech forests and breezy mountain ridges. **p72**

18   **Monte Mileto**
A spirit-reviving circuit around the ethereal Majella mountain massif. **p76**

19   **Sentiero della Libertà**
Track the course of an erstwhile WWII escape route. **p80**

BEST DAY WALKS : ITALY   **63**

Explore

Abruzzo

Abruzzo's spinal mountains, the Apennines, are also its least crowded. Indeed, at times, a visit here feels like a trip back to the 1950s; a world of wheezing trains, buzzing Vespas (motor scooters), ruined farmhouses and fields splashed with blood-red poppies. All this is good news for prospective hikers who share the region's ample trails with sheep dogs, mountain goats, abundant birdlife and the odd – rarely sighted – human being. A major national park building effort in the 1990s has created an almost unbroken swathe of protected land across Abruzzo, protecting rare wildlife and Italy's highest mountains outside the Alps.

L'Aquila

From tragedy springs hope. More than a decade after a powerful earthquake killed 308 of its citizens and toppled copious historic buildings, L'Aquila is – just about – back in business. It's certainly ready to welcome a new wave of out-of-town travellers, not just to admire the durability of its churches and fountains, but to study the meticulous renovation work that has returned many of them to their former glory – and in some cases even surpassing it.

Sulmona

An underappreciated city of traditional trattorias, narrow medieval streets and half-discovered mountain magic, Sulmona sits strategically on a plateau surrounded by three national parks, making it the ideal base for outdoor excursions in Abruzzo. It's easy to reach from Pescara or Rome, and simple to navigate once you arrive (trails fan out from the city limits). The city can trace its history back to the Roman town of Sulmo, where the poet Ovid (of *Metamorphoses* fame) was born in 43 BC. It is also known within Italy for its *confetti* – the almond sweets, not the coloured paper scattered at weddings.

Parco Nazionale d'Abruzzo, Lazio e Molise

Italy's second-oldest national park is also one of its most ecologically rich. Established by royal decree in 1923, it began as a modest 5-sq-km reserve that, little by little, morphed into the 440-sq-km protected area it is today. The evolution wasn't easy. The park was temporarily abolished in 1933 by the Mussolini government. It returned to the fold in 1950, only to face further encroachment from housing construction, road building and ski developers. The park has managed to remain at the forefront of Italy's conservation movement, reintroducing

WHEN TO GO

Fickle weather in the Apennines can bring both early- and late-season snow – although the region enjoys a slightly longer walking season than the Alps. It's best not to attempt the higher mountains before mid-June. The first snows often arrive in late September. Lower-level trails are generally good from mid-May to mid-October.

and protecting wild animals such as the Abruzzo chamois, Apennine wolf, lynx, deer and – most notably – Marsican bear (the park has Italy's largest surviving enclave of these threatened animals). Today the park extends over three regions, with more than half of it covered in thick beech forest.

Parco Nazionale del Gran Sasso e Monti della Laga

About 20km northeast of L'Aquila, the Gran Sasso massif is the centrepiece of the Parco Nazionale del Gran Sasso e Monti della Laga, one of Italy's largest national parks. The park's predominant feature is its jagged rocky landscape, through which one of Europe's southernmost glaciers, the Calderone, cuts its (increasingly narrow) course. It's also a haven for wildlife, home to an estimated 120 wolves, 1000 chamois and 11 pairs of golden eagles.

Parco Nazionale della Majella

History, geology and ecology collide in 750-sq-km Parco Nazionale della Majella, Abruzzo's most diverse park, where wolves roam in giant beech woods, ancient hermitages speckle ominous mountains, and 500km of criss-crossing paths and a handful of ski areas cater to the hyperactive. Monte Amaro, the Apennines' second-highest peak, surveys all around it from a lofty 2793m vantage point.

TRANSPORT

Buses and trains link the hub cities of Sulmona and L'Aquila with Rome and Pescara. Buses also provide links to the smaller villages in the national parks including Pacentro, Pescasseroli and Fonte Cerreto. TUA (*tuabruzzo.it*) runs the most extensive bus services.

 WHAT'S ON

Giostra Cavalleresca di Sulmona

On the last weekend in July, gaily caparisoned horse riders gallop around Sulmona's Piazza Garibaldi (*giostrasulmona.it*).

Sentiero della Libertà

Every year in early May, hundreds of people partake in a three-day mass communal hike along the 60km 'Freedom Trail' between Sulmona and Casoli.

Resources

The following three maps cover all the hikes in this region and will help immensely with navigation. All are 1:25,000.

Gran Sasso D'Italia – Carta dei Sentieri (Club Alpino Italiano)

Parco D'Abruzzo – Carta Escursionistica (Iter Edizioni)

Majella – Carta Escursionistica e Scialpinistica (Il Lupo)

 WHERE TO STAY

All of these hikes can be done from bases in the cities of L'Aquila and Sulmona. L'Aquila has recovered from the debilitating 2009 earthquake and is adding new accommodation options all the time. Sulmona excels in charismatic *locande* (inns) and *alberghi diffusi* (diffused accommodation; generally with one central reception).

14

Santo Stefano di Sessanio to Rocca Calascio

DURATION	DIFFICULTY	DISTANCE	START/END
2hrs	Moderate	7km	Santo Stefano di Sessanio/ Calascio

TERRAIN	Firm country paths, short grassy ascents

For a relatively benign introduction to the rugged ridges and peaks of the Gran Sasso mountains, look no further than this short but very attractive romp between the two historical bookends of Santo Stefano di Sessanio and Rocca Calascio.

Getting Here
There are four TUA buses a day running between L'Aquila bus station and Santo Stefano di Sessanio (€3, 50 minutes), but none on Sundays.

Starting Point
The walk starts on the western edge of the village of Santo Stefano di Sessanio on the road between Barisciano and Campo Imperatore.

01 From the car park on the west side of the once semi-abandoned but now rejuvenated Abruzzan village of Santo Stefano di Sessanio, take the road down towards a small **lake**. At a road junction by a small chapel, turn left and then veer immediately right, following the road around a bend.

02 A trail (signposted Rocca Calascio Ruta Panoramica) leads off to the right just before the 'Arrivederci Santo Stefano' sign. Follow the single-track path as it winds around a small grassy hill with **fine views** back over Santo Stefano di Sessanio and its emblematic **Medici tower**, damaged in the 2009 earthquake but recently returned to its former glory thanks to a 12-year restoration project.

66   BEST DAY WALKS : ITALY

Best for

QUAINT VILLAGES

A Village Revived

Known as Sextantio in Roman times, the somnolent but haunting village of Santo Stefano di Sessanio has a commanding position overlooking two valleys. The settlement flourished in the 16th century under the rule of the Medici family, whose coat of arms can still be seen on the entrance portal to the main piazza. Subsequently left behind by history, Santo Stefano lost most of its people to emigration and was falling into oblivion when it was 'rediscovered' by Swedish eco-restorer Daniele Kihlgren in 1999. Since then, Kihlgren and others have purchased many of the town's old buildings and turned them into lodgings and restaurants that maintain their attractiveness of yore.

Santo Stefano di Sessanio

03 The path subsequently widens and descends to a quiet road. Cross the road and make the steep ascent up the grassy slope on the other side.

04 At the top of the ascent, the path flattens out and starts to traverse beneath the southern crest of the smooth-topped **Monte delle Croci**. At this point, the silhouettes of the castle and chapel of Rocca Calascio come dramatically into view.

05 Contouring around the hill slopes, the path reaches the **Chiesa di Santa Maria della Pietà**, an octagonal late-16th-century church with a baroque portal built to give thanks for victories over local brigands.

06 From here, it's a short climb up to the **ruined castle**, which at 1460m is the highest fortress in the Apennines. The movie *The Name of the Rose* was filmed here.

07 After visiting the castle, descend back to the chapel and take the path behind down to the small hillside *borgo* of **Rocca Calascio**, with its narrow alleys and half-restored buildings.

08 From **Piazza della Chiesa** at the bottom of the *borgo*, a signposted path starts to descend, short-cutting the bends of the road. It will ultimately deliver you to the Piazza della Vittoria in **Calascio**. Descend to the main road, where you can catch a bus back to Santo Stefano di Sessanio.

Take a Break

Santo Stefano is noted for its lentils, grown by only 12 farmers on the slopes around the town. To sample them, step into the arched, 16th-century dining room of **Locanda Sotto gli Archi** (sextantio.it/en/santostefano/abruzzo-traditional-cuisine/). Furniture and crockery here are designed to re-create the austere quality of bygone times and the excellent food is made using time-honoured ingredients and techniques native to the region.

BEST DAY WALKS : ITALY 67

15

Above Pescasseroli

DURATION	DIFFICULTY	DISTANCE	START/END
2.5hrs	Moderate	6km	Pescasseroli

TERRAIN	Village streets, forest paths, one steep descent

This short circuit above the national-park hub of Pescasseroli visits a ruined castle and provides excellent views over the town and the uncluttered countryside.

From the main square in Pescasseroli, follow Via della Chiesa north. Just before you reach the impressive **Chiesa Parrocchiale** turn sharp left up a narrow alley with steps labelled 'Salita Dott. Ciolli'. The alley almost immediately joins a paved road; turn left here and then right into Via Castello. Follow the paved road to a walled cemetery and cut diagonally down a steep bank beyond it to join a track next to a cattle trough.

Follow this track away from the town. Within five minutes, bear right off the main track on a fainter path marked by a fence on the right. When the fence runs out, cut diagonally across a **sloping pasture** and pick the clear path on the opposite side. Parallel the edge of the meadow before turning right at a junction just before a river gully. The path now steepens and plunges into the forest, zigzagging up the slope. At the first fork, veer left. At the second by a signpost, turn right and start to traverse the slope.

Before long you'll reach the splayed 11th-century ruins of **Castel Mancino**, built during the Longobard era in an almost impregnable position on the crags above town. Pines that had grown up around the castle were cut down in the 1920s, resulting in some weather-inflicted damage, but the spooky remains are still strangely evocative. A fairly clear path zigzags down steeply through the ruins back to the town visible below.

Castel Mancino

16

Campo Imperatore Ridge

DURATION	DIFFICULTY	DISTANCE	START/END
2.5hrs	Moderate	6km	Upper cable-car station, Campo Imperatore

TERRAIN	Single-track mountain paths, some narrow but not overly exposed ridge walks

To enjoy a spine-chilling 'top of the world' feeling without having to scramble on all fours up precipitous rock walls, come to Italy's aptly named 'Little Tibet' and partake in this peak-punctuated ridge walk above Campo Imperatore.

Getting Here

There are several daily buses from L'Aquila's main bus station to the cable-car base station at Fonte Cerreto. From here, the Gran Sasso Funivia (June to early October) will zip you up to Campo Imperatore.

Starting Point

Nexus for numerous high plateau hikes, the 2128m-high upper station of the *funivia* (cable car) at Campo Imperatore is where this walk starts and finishes.

 From the top of the *funivia* station next to the Hotel Campo Imperatore (currently closed), walk towards the **domed astronomical observatory**. Built in 1965, the venerable space-gazing establishment specialises in the research and detection of 'near-Earth' asteroids and comets. Behind it, a clear, well-used path zigzags up a steep, treeless slope.

 After five minutes of climbing, turn right at a junction following signs to Corno Grande and Monte Aquila. The single-track path (101) climbs gradually in a smooth diagonal up the southeast face of the **Serra di Monte Aquila** with **fabulous views** of the vast Campo Imperatore plateau on the right.

Best for

MOUNTAIN VIEWS

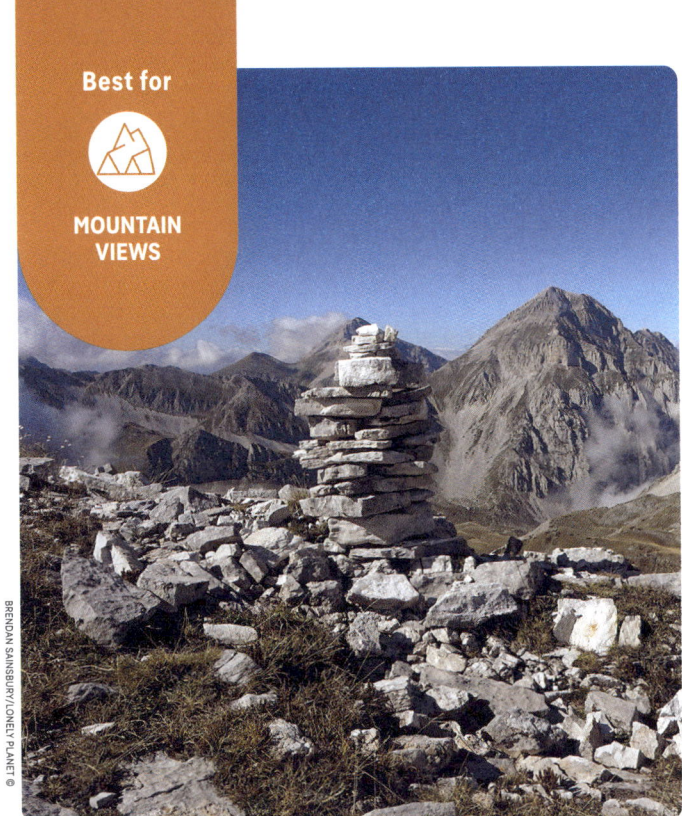

Campo Imperatore

The Gran Sasso Raid

Following his capture in 1943 during WWII, Mussolini was briefly imprisoned in the Hotel Campo Imperatore. Only weeks into his incarceration, he was rescued by the Germans in the so-called Gran Sasso Raid headed up by Otto Skorzeny, a stealthy commander in the Waffen SS. Skorzeny organised for German paratroopers to crash-land a dozen gliders into Gran Sasso Mountain on the high plateau adjacent to the hotel where Mussolini was being held. Recklessly storming the hotel with his paratroopers, the commander subsequently disabled the radio operator and the radio, and within 10 minutes had freed a flabbergasted Mussolini without a shot being fired.

03 After scrambling across a couple of rocky sections, the path delivers you to a saddle, the **Sella di Monte Aquila** (2335m), where the Corno Grande trail heads north. Turn sharp left here and follow path 161 as it traverses beneath the north side of the ridge before swapping back to the south side and descending to the ridge-top **Rifugio Duca degli Abruzzi** (open June to September), with its spectacularly sited sundeck.

04 Continue along the narrow but not overly exposed ridge (now on path 100) to the top of **Monte Portella** (2835m) and a smaller subpeak around 800m further on. The views to the north reveal the rocky majesty of the Campo Pericoli and its deceptively gentle slopes recently repopulated with chamois, a goat-antelope native to Europe.

05 From the subpeak, descend to a saddle where a signposted trail junction will direct you along path 102, doubling back around the lower southwest skirts of Monte Portella. The path contours the grassy mountain slopes with little change in elevation.

06 Ignore a right-hand turn at Paso del Lupo (which leads down to the *funivia* base station) and continue along the well-defined **mountain path** back to Campo Imperatore and the start point.

☕ Take a Break

The venerable **Ostello Campo Imperatore** (*ostellocampoimperatore.com*) hostel at the top of the *funivia* has a small bar offering coffee and cakes as well as a casual sit-down restaurant cooking up pasta, soups and sizeable mains, or – if you're in a hurry – doorstep-sized cheese-and-ham sandwiches.

17

Rocca Ridge

A bear, Parco Nazionale D'Abruzzo

DURATION	DIFFICULTY	DISTANCE	START/END
6–7hrs	Hard	19km	Pescasseroli

TERRAIN	Forest tracks, mountain-ridge paths, some paved roads

Limestone ridges, rustling beech woods, flowery meadows full of grazing sheep and perhaps even a distant bear sighting; the Rocca Ridge dominates the skyline as you look west from Pescasseroli, and is the 1924m highpoint of the Parco Nazionale D'Abruzzo, Lazio e Molise.

Getting Here

TUA buses serve Pescasseroli from either Avezzano (linked to L'Aquila and Rome by train) or Castel di Sangro (linked to Sulmona by bus).

Starting Point

Initiate proceedings in the main square in the small national-park town of Pescasseroli, which has several cafes, a water fountain and a shop selling local maps.

01 From the town hall in the centre of Pescasseroli, walk south along the Viale S Lucia and continue over a crossroads onto the Via Fontana della Difesa. This leads to a fork in the road by the Hotel Iris – follow the road to the right. The pavement soon ends and the road becomes a gravel track, passing some farm buildings before delving into open country. You'll likely see or hear large white Maremma sheepdogs around here. They may bark at you, but fear not, they'll generally leave you alone as long as you don't encroach on their territory (stay on the path!). The track soon delivers you to

National Park Visitor Centre

Centro di Visita di Pescasseroli (*parcoabruzzo.it*) has an Apennine garden and a clinic for rescued animals who can no longer live in the wild on their own. Accommodated on site are two Marsican bears and a wolf (the only ones you're likely to see, unless you're extremely lucky). It also acts as an information portal and small museum with exhibits covering archaeology, flora, caves and a short video on bear conservation.

a **spring** below the park-owned **Rifugio della Difesa**. This is the official start of the route, around 3km from the town centre.

02 A painted sign indicates the start of path C3, which leads left off the track at the spring and climbs past the *rifugio*. Relatively well marked with red-and-white paint, it winds up through a mixture of forest and more open areas. After approximately 45 minutes, the path mounts a steep, rocky section and meets the gravel track again. Cross the track, passing a roofed plaque in a clearing, before plunging back into the trees. The gravel track is crossed several more times before steeper terrain forces the path into a series of tight switchbacks which snake up to the isolated **Santuario di Monte Tranquillo** (1600m), a dowdy chapel built on a bluff. This is the end of the gravel road.

03 A faint farm track continues up open hillside ahead. Follow this and climb beneath the northern slopes of **Monte Tranquillo**. Pass **Rifugio di Monte Tranquillo**, a privately owned hut in a hollow, and continue up the rocky slope to join the ridge itself.

04 The **ridge** marks a junction of paths; turn right (northeast) to follow path C5 along the ridgeline. The route drops down briefly to the east, skirting around a small copse before returning to the ridge at a saddle. The ridge line is now followed for 5km. If you lose the path among the limestone outcrops, return to the ridge and continue uphill, and you will soon pick it up. The crest you are following marks the boundary between the two Italian regions of Abruzzo (east) and Lazio (west). Despite the national park's tri-region name, 80% of it lies within Abruzzo.

05 The first cairn, around 1km onto the ridge, marks the summit of **Monte Pietroso** (1876m). Beyond the peak, the path continues to climb to the large pile of stones at the top of **La Rocca** (1924m), where the park views are panoramic – craggy ridges and forested valleys fall steeply on either side, with Pescasseroli visible far below to the east. From here you'll be looking down on the extensive beech forests that cover 60% of the park's total area and inhabit the mountainsides up to 1800m.

06 The ridge narrows to the north of La Rocca but the path is better defined, and the terrain is largely level as the trail either follows the ridgetop or contours just below it. Snow can linger here into late June, by which time an extensive array of **wild flora** will be beginning to bloom. Look out for gentians, lilies, orchids and wild herbs.

07 The **Rifugio di Lorio** soon becomes visible on the ridge to the north. Forget late-night shots of grappa and spirited sing-songs around the hearth. The Lorio is a tiny mountain hut and usually locked. Continue along the ridge past the rifugio for around 150m, before dropping down to the right (east) on a stone path that zigzags down the **Valico Valcallano** pass. Turn right here and pick up path R5, which plunges downhill into thick beech forest.

08 Around 1km later the forest path joins a vehicle track (B1); turn right and descend past two ski tows. On the slopes opposite is **Pescasseroli ski area**, one of Abruzzo's (and Italy's) smallest, with 8km of trails and a 585m vertical drop. Beyond the ski lifts, the track ultimately joins a paved road just north of **Camping La Panoramica**.

09 Turn right along the road and follow it to a roundabout, taking the second left along the Viale Colli dell'Oro. This will lead back to the Viale S Lucia and the centre of **Pescasseroli**. It's worth exploring the town after you've imbibed a drink or two. During medieval times it was an important stop on the bi-annual sheep flock migration, or *transumanza*, that headed south to Puglia. Later on, it became popular with the European aristocracy who came here to hunt bears. These days it acts as the main headquarters for the national park and is frequented mainly by Italian tourists.

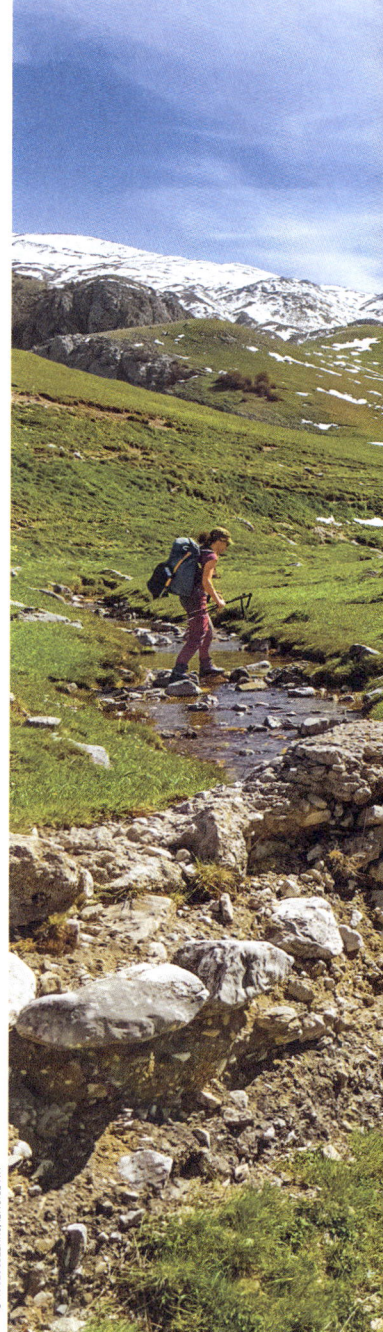

Parco Nazionale D'Abruzzo

☕ Take a Break

The handsome **Il Duca degli Abruzzi** located on a quiet square in Pescasseroli's historic centre is a little more gourmet than your average salt-of-the-earth village trattoria, but doesn't shirk on the rustic charm either. Everything is homemade and utterly delicious: try the truffle pasta, follow up with grilled pork and wash it down with Montepulciano d'Abruzzo.

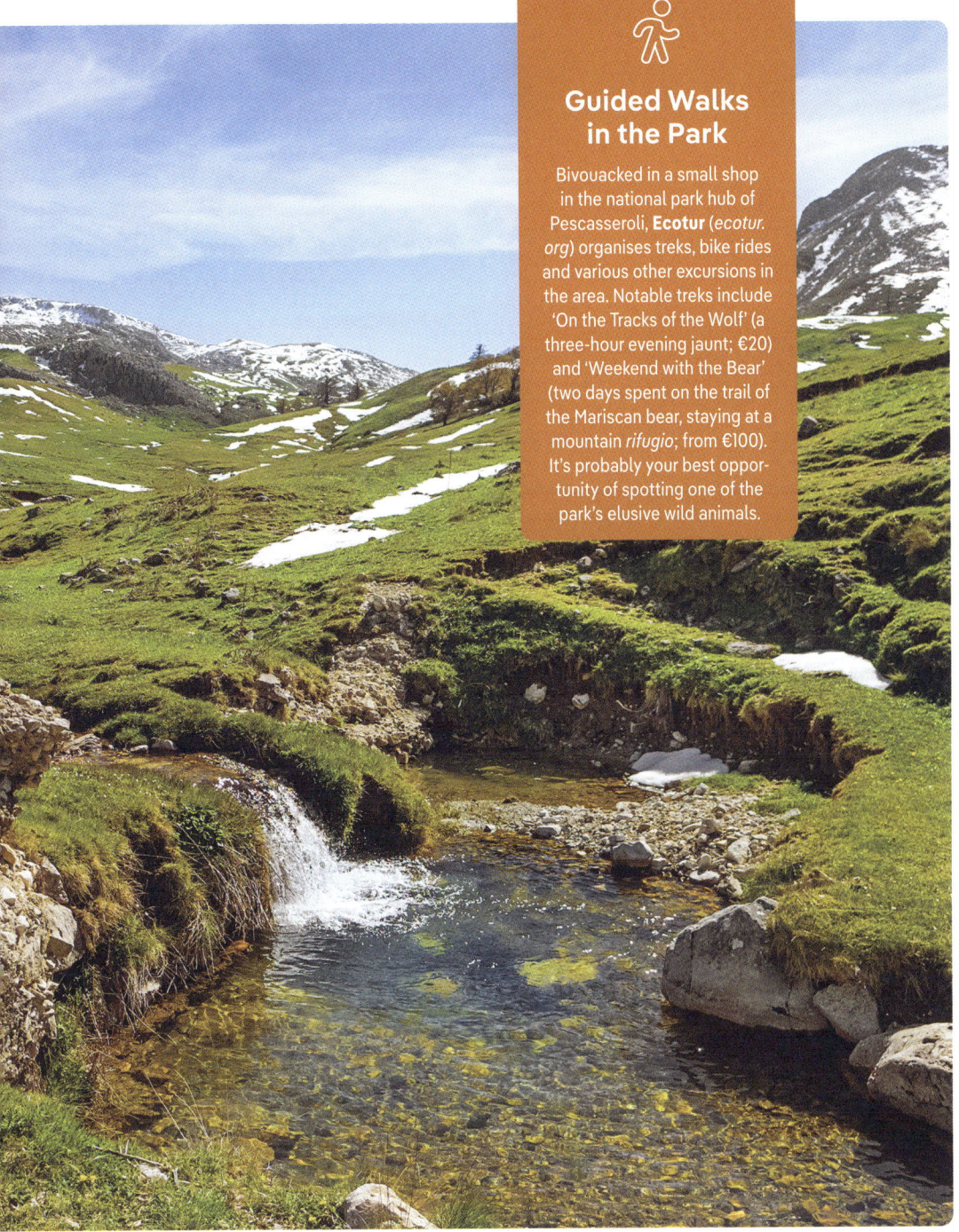

Guided Walks in the Park

Bivouacked in a small shop in the national park hub of Pescasseroli, **Ecotur** (*ecotur.org*) organises treks, bike rides and various other excursions in the area. Notable treks include 'On the Tracks of the Wolf' (a three-hour evening jaunt; €20) and 'Weekend with the Bear' (two days spent on the trail of the Mariscan bear, staying at a mountain *rifugio*; from €100). It's probably your best opportunity of spotting one of the park's elusive wild animals.

18

Best for

AVOIDING THE CROWDS

Monte Mileto

DURATION	DIFFICULTY	DISTANCE	START/END
7hrs	Hard	19km	Pacentro

TERRAIN	Steep but firm mountain paths, stony 4WD tracks

Pacentro

A steep but safe ascent to the domed summit of Monte Mileto through ancient beech woods and the spiritually soaked slopes of the Monte Morrone. The walk starts and finishes in beguiling Pacentro, situated just inside the boundary of Majella National Park, a historic village still recovering after years of abandonment following WWII.

Getting Here

Regular buses operated by TUA run the 10km between Sulmona and Pacentro.

Starting Point

Orientate yourself in the main square (Piazza del Popolo) in the spectacularly sited national park village of Pacentro. From here climb up behind the triple-towered castle and head out of town on the road (SR487) to Caramanico Terme.

01 Around 300m after joining the road, leave it on a signposted path that cuts up behind a restaurant next to a **spring**. The path climbs a slope, passes under the launch site for Pacentro's valley-spanning **zipline** (p79) and quickly rejoins the road. Follow the road for 20m before veering left on a continuation of the path as it climbs up past a farmhouse to meet the road a second time. On this occasion, turn left and follow the road uphill, past a picnic area and around two hairpin bends. On the third hairpin, path Q5 branches off to the left.

Corsa degli Zingari

Undertaken on rugged paths immediately surrounding the village of Pacentro, the Corsa degli Zingari is a barefoot running race that has been going on for more than 550 years. Its origins are the subject of conjecture. Some claim it evolved from an old hunting rite practised by Italic tribes; others suggest it was part of a medieval military initiation.

Held on the first Sunday in September, the race starts atop a stony escarpment on the hillside opposite Pacentro. Runners hurtle down a steep path and athletically ford a river before climbing another slope into the village. The finish line is the diminutive baroque Chiesa della Madonna di Loreto, where participants – their feet by now a bloody mess – collapse in front of the altar.

02 After just 50m, at the end of a wall, Q5 turns sharply and steeply uphill. Climb through fire-damaged pines alongside a gully on your left. After around 30 minutes, the tough climb eases slightly and the sometimes indistinct path veers left and enters a mix of meadow and sporadic pine and beech glades. Eagle-eye **views** of Pacentro's rooftops and towers unfold below. As the forest thickens, the path steepens again and zigzags beneath thick mature beech trees with crunchy dead leaves underfoot. After some effort, you'll finally emerge into **beautiful high mountain meadows** as the ascent gradually peters out.

03 Soon after, a track merges with the path from the right. Follow the track as it veers left through ever lusher meadows into a grassy hollow called **Valle Dentro**, guarded by a **ruined shepherd's hut**. The ridge to your left (west) reaches its apex at **Morrone di Pacentro** (1800m) and you can hike up to it from the hollow, if you have the time and inclination, for superb views of Sulmona and the Valle Peligna (there's no clear path; just aim for the ridgeline). Otherwise, from the hollow, take the clear path straight ahead (northwest) and push on up to a saddle on the opposite side where you'll encounter a signposted path junction.

04 Take Q6 (right) and within minutes you'll be on the grassy ridge behind Morrone di Pacentro, punctuated with dwarf mountain pine trees. The meadows and high pastures here abound with **seasonal orchids**, **wild roses**, **junipers** and **peonies**. The Morrone mountains acquired a special spiritual significance in the 13th century as a place of refuge and prayer for hermits and ascetics. The most notable figure was the monk Pietro da Morrone, who founded a religious order called the Morronites (aka Celestines)

BEST DAY WALKS : ITALY   77

in 1244. Pietro and his fellow hermits built several hermitages in the mountains, utilising them for extended periods of prayer, fasting and meditation. The saintly monk later briefly went on to become Pope Celestine V before resigning after just five months in office in 1294. His legacy has left a heavy mark in Sulmona and the Morrone Mountains, which are still dotted with a handful of medieval hermitages.

05 Continue along the rounded ridge to a second junction, which appears just as the **Valle d'Orta** on the eastern side of the Morrone massif comes into view. Take Q4 (right) and descend to a saddle and then track up grassy slopes to the rounded summit of **Monte Mileto** (1920m). From this vantage point, the views are sweeping, particularly those to the east dominated by the barren rocky summit of **Monte Amaro**, the second-highest mountain in the Apennines at 2793m.

06 From the summit, head SE to a sub-peak and then make a steep descent to a 4WD track visible below. Continue descending on the track, taking a shortcut on the first hairpin that rejoins the track in a beech wood further down. Passo San Leonardo and its peculiarly shaped restaurant are now clearly visible below.

07 The track continues descending and eventually reaches a junction with path Q3; turn right and head through the lower beech forest to the bottom of a ski lift. From here, descend through meadows to **Passo San Leonardo** and its restaurant, luring you like a dislodged lighthouse. The pass marks the border between Majella National Park's two main mountain ranges: the smooth-topped Morrone and the more rugged Majella. The restaurant, known locally as **Rifugio Celidonio**, is usually open for drinks and light meals.

08 Turning right outside the restaurant, follow path Q1 across a field to the bottom of a ski lift. From here the path meanders through fields, past an old stone building and along an even older rock-strewn lane. Within 40 minutes it hits the main Pacentro road. Turn left, walk for 50m on the tarmac and take a path that plunges downhill to the right. You'll cross the road three more times as you wander back to Pacentro and the start. If you have time, it's worth checking out the town's 14th-century **Caldora Castle** with its three famous towers, the mannerist-meets-baroque **Chiesa Santa Maria della Misericordia**, and a slew of **grand nobles' houses** that beautify the lanes between Piazza del Popolo and Piazza Umberto I.

☕ Take a Break

You could easily walk right past Pacentro's **Ristorante-Pizzeria Majella**: it doesn't brag about its existence. Instead, its reputation is carried by word of mouth – which in small-town Pacentro travels fast. The menu apogee is the *arrosticini*, an old Abruzzo classic comprising lamb skewers wrapped in foil and served in a sloping ceramic pot.

Pacentro

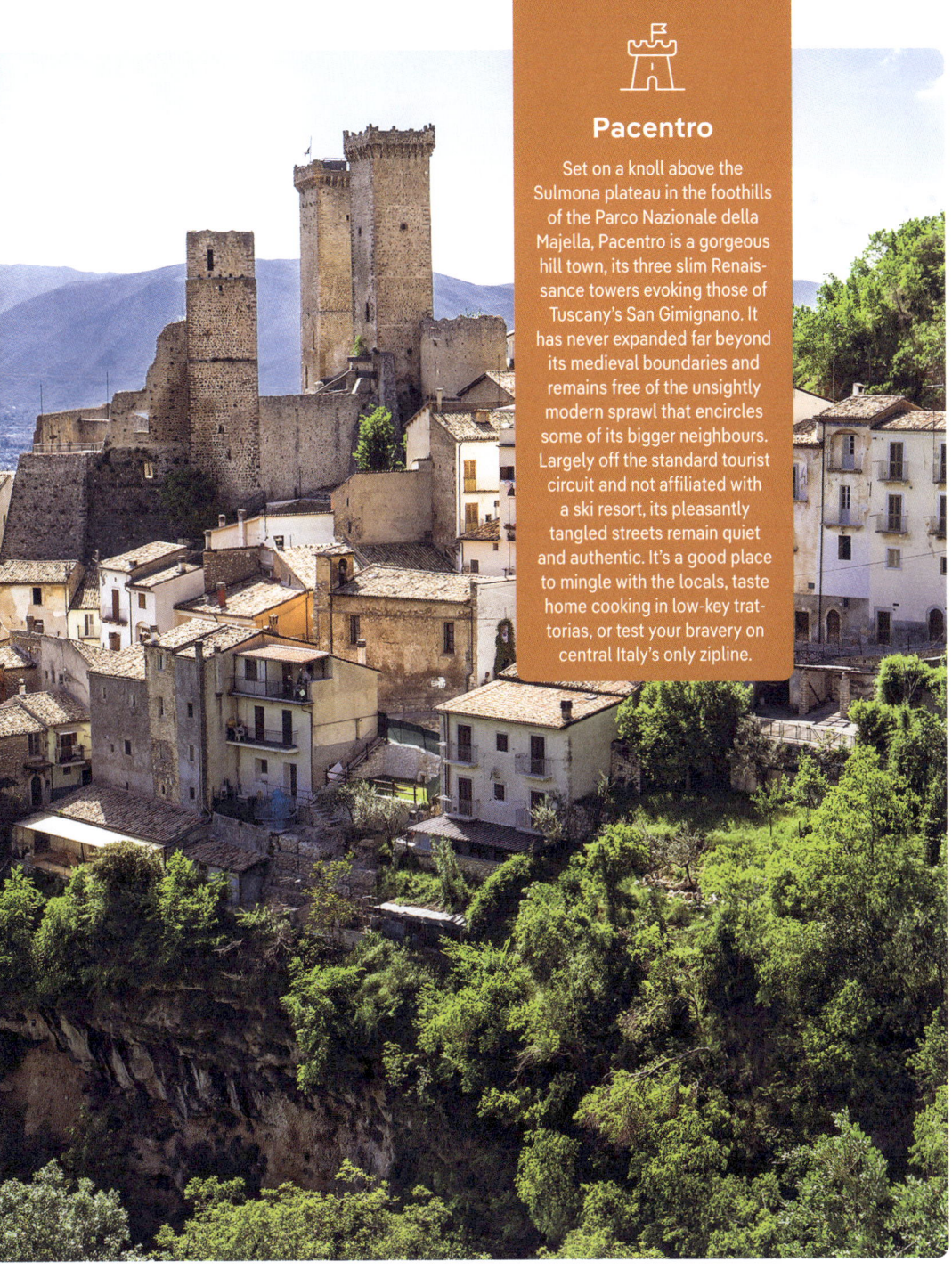

Pacentro

Set on a knoll above the Sulmona plateau in the foothills of the Parco Nazionale della Majella, Pacentro is a gorgeous hill town, its three slim Renaissance towers evoking those of Tuscany's San Gimignano. It has never expanded far beyond its medieval boundaries and remains free of the unsightly modern sprawl that encircles some of its bigger neighbours. Largely off the standard tourist circuit and not affiliated with a ski resort, its pleasantly tangled streets remain quiet and authentic. It's a good place to mingle with the locals, taste home cooking in low-key trattorias, or test your bravery on central Italy's only zipline.

19

Sentiero della Libertà

Best for

HISTORY & CULTURE

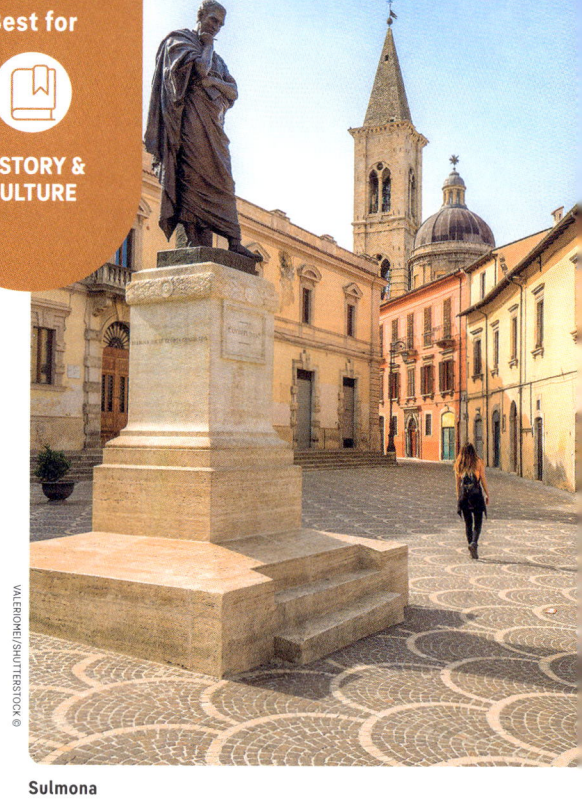

Sulmona

DURATION	DIFFICULTY	DISTANCE	START/END
10hrs	Hard	31km	Sulmona/Palena

TERRAIN	Dirt roads, mountain paths and several short paved sections

Mixing the call of the wild with the call of freedom, the Sentiero della Libertà (Freedom Trail) follows in the footsteps of escaping Allied prisoners as they forged a path across the Apennines in the winter of 1943–44, fleeing German-occupied Sulmona to liberated Palena and beyond. The full trail runs for 60km. This walk tackles the more scenic first half, crossing Majella National Park from west to east.

Getting Here

Sulmona is easily accessible by train or bus from Rome's Tiburtina station. Sulmona's train station is 2km from the city centre.

Starting Point

The walk starts 2km southeast of central Sulmona in a car park beside a cemetery on the road to Pacentro. A large signboard maps out the route and describes its highlights in Italian and English.

01 Take the paved path (marked with an 'L' for Libertà) that zigzags up the slope behind the **cemetery**. It quickly turns into a dirt vehicle track before becoming a single-track path. At a junction, fork right (ignoring signs to Grascio). Pass a **wooden bench** (from where you can look admiringly back over Sulmona and the Valle Peligna) and gradually enter scrubby mountain terrain punctuated with thorny bushes.

Long Walk to Freedom

With the help of sympathetic local partisans, many ex-prisoners from Campo 78 fled east across the Apennine Mountains to Casoli in the winter of 1943–44, forging a rough trail as they went. Casoli had been liberated by Allied soldiers a few months previously and, throughout that long winter as the Allied advance was temporarily halted by German troops along the 'Gustav Line', it became the hallowed end point of the so-called Sentiero della Libertà, an escape route that led east from German-occupied Sulmona to freedom. The Sentiero's most celebrated escapee was future Italian president Carlo Azeglio Ciampi, who was in a group of 60 soldiers who walked for 25 hours through a blizzard in March 1944.

02 Contour around the western slopes of **Colle Savente** and traverse the plateau that stretches across to **Colle Mitra**, whose summit is marked by a tall cross. Ignore all turnoffs as you pitch southeast around the skirts of Colle Mitra until you come to Fonte Pacile (spring) nestled in a small glade.

03 Look carefully for red-and-white markers here as you climb briefly up to a junction on a **grassy saddle**. At the saddle, turn left and start to descend on the other side of the Mitra plateau, following a vehicle-wide track down through mixed forest.

04 As the descent flattens out, a sign announces a sharp right turn, just before a second spring, the **Fonte Sulmonita** (if you pass the spring, you've gone too far). Follow an overgrown track under gnarly trees until it comes out in a **gorgeous meadow** where a signpost points sharply to the left. After about 200m, the trail forks again, this time heading sharply to the right on the edge of a field. This turning is unsignposted so look carefully for the red-and-white markers in the bushes.

05 The now indistinct path meanders alongside an old stone wall and through overgrown pasture to an **arched railway bridge**. Go under the bridge and descend to a paved lane where a right turn will deliver you to the busier SR55 opposite a cemetery on the edge of the village of **Cansano**.

06 Turn left, go down the road for around 300m and take the lane on the right (signposted). Bear right, follow the lane to a T-junction and turn right again. The road turns into a vehicle track, goes past a farm and meanders along sedately to another railway arch (pass underneath) and the **Fonte**

☕ Take a Break

You'll be starving by the time you reach Campo di Giove and in dire need of rustic **La Scarpetta di Venere** (*lascarpettadivenere.net*), with its classic Abruzzo cuisine cooked 'Slow Food' style. Go local by opting for the lamb *arrosticini* (skewers) and the saffron and ricotta-infused *chitarra* pasta.

Ramarozzo, where you can top up on water.

07 Continue along the flat track for another 20 minutes through verdant farmland until a sign directs you to turn sharp left across an open field.

08 After around 600m, just before reaching an **equestrian school**, go right (this crucial turn is bizarrely unsignposted) where a grassy path curves into trees and starts heading diagonally uphill. As it narrows, the path crests the modest **Serra Carpineto** ridge, where you'll encounter a set of **farm buildings** nestled in a hollow.

09 Go right here, then immediately left, and take a path down though pine trees to a set of railway arches that mark the edge of the small town of **Campo di Giove**. Turn right when you hit a paved road and left at the first junction to arrive in the town centre. Here you have two choices. You can finish the hike with 22km already under your belt and catch a bus back to Sulmona, or you can carry on for another 9km to Palena. A third option would be to bed down in Campo di Giove and tackle the next section on day two.

10 Exit Campo di Giove on Via Brigata Majella. Several hundred metres after passing the **town cemetery,** a path marked by a **large stone monument** branches off to the left.

11 This is the start of stage two of the Sentiero della Libertà. Head uphill, cross a road and follow the path as it continues southeast, ascending diagonally across the mountainside. Pretty soon you'll enter thick beech forest with occasional peek-a-boo **views** back over Campo di Giove.

12 At a Y-junction, fork left onto the higher path (the lower path leads to a small **chapel** and soon dead-ends). Within 15 minutes you'll join a wider track at the top end of a ski chairlift. Here the trees fall away and the path ascends a grassy slope to a small **ski station** and **rifugio** at the **Guado di Coccia** (1674m). This typically small Abruzzo ski area has 10km of runs but is deathly quiet in the summer.

13 This pass marked the rough border between the German and Allied occupied zones in WWII, the so-called Gustav Line, held stubbornly by the Germans until June 1944. Escapees who made it this far could practically sniff freedom. Not all were lucky. On the windswept pass, a **stone monument** stands in memoriam to Ettore De Corti, an Italian partisan captured and executed by the Germans in September 1943 – an enduring symbol of the underground resistance. Keeping the dark mass of **Monte Porrara** to your right, follow the path straight over the pass and down the other side.

14 A good dirt track progresses downhill through open grassy terrain with clusters of beech trees on either side. After about 15 minutes, the main track swings right and crosses a small river in a gully. Follow it as it zigzags down with the river on your left. The track briefly joins a paved road by a hut at the bottom of a ski lift; 200m further on, you leave the road via another track on the left and head downhill towards the village of Palena below.

15 The track joins and immediately leaves another road before finally linking up with it again by the outlying houses of the small village of **Palena** (population around 1500). Technically, you're still only halfway along the Sentiero della Libertà, which officially finishes in Casoli, over 26km to the northeast, but many walkers call it a day here. Bus services out of Palena are poor and usually involve changing in Lanciano for Pescara or Sulmona. Check ahead with *tuabruzzo.it*.

Majella National Park

Campo 78

Campo 78 is a still-intact prisoner-of-war camp, located 5km east of Sulmona in the village of Fonte d'Amore. Around 3000 Allied soldiers were imprisoned here in September 1943 when their Italian guards deserted their posts in the face of an approaching Anglo-American army. In the six days before the Germans arrived to take over the camp and thwart the Allied advance, many of the former detainees escaped into the surrounding mountains. The Germans subsequently closed down Campo 78 and its remaining inmates were marched north to prison camps in Germany.

Also Try...

Corno Grande

Sant'Onofrio Hermitage & Ercole Curino Ruins

DURATION	DIFFICULTY	DISTANCE
1.5hrs	Easy	4.5km

The Morrone mountains that guard Sulmona were once a haven for hermits and spiritualists inspired, in part, by the so-called hermit pope Celestine V.

Start the walk outside the Celestine Abbey in the village of Badia, taking the road (Via Badia) that leads toward the foot of the mountains. The road bends to the right and diagonally ascends the lower slopes to a small car park. From here a 300m-long path heads to Ercole Curino, a Roman-era sanctuary whose foundations cover a couple of mountainside terraces and include a preserved mosaic floor in a wooden hut. You'll need to return to the car park to access the cliff-clinging Sant'Onofrio hermitage, former refuge of Pietro da Morrone (aka Pope Celestine V). The arched porticoes cower under a massive rock face in the Morrone mountains.

Corno Grande

DURATION	DIFFICULTY	DISTANCE
5-6hrs	Hard	9km

As the highest peak in the Apennines, Corno Grande (2912m) receives a lot of attention from walkers, especially since it is so readily accessible from high-altitude Starting Points at either Campo Imperatore or Prati di Tivo.

The impressive rock peak has steep faces and from most viewpoints looks like the preserve of climbers. However, if you're sure-footed and not afraid of heights, the summit is hikeable in good conditions. The *via normale* (normal route) from the top of the cable-car station in Campo Imperatore is a well-marked, out-and-back route. It is relatively straightforward for most of the way, but taxing for the final steep climb to the top, where scrambling (using hands) and route-finding skills will come in handy. The mountain is generally climbable between late June and early October. Choose a clear windless day.

Sant'Onofrio Hermitage

Assergi to San Pietro della Ienca

DURATION	DIFFICULTY	DISTANCE
4hrs	Easy	11km

From the medieval lanes of Assergi, 15km northeast of L'Aquila, this hike explores the Valle del Vasto in the shadow of the Gran Sasso mountains.

Exit the village on Via delle Ville and head northwest toward San Pietro, passing the Grotta a Male, an impressive cave complex, en route. The sanctuary of San Pietro della Ienca in a tiny hamlet is dedicated to Pope John Paul II, who was a regular visitor in the 1980s and '90s. Loop back to Assergi on a vehicle track that parallels your outgoing path slightly to the north.

Orfento Gorge

DURATION	DIFFICULTY	DISTANCE
2hrs	Moderate	4km

From the salubrious spa town of Caramanico Terme in the heart of the Majella National Park, this short walk delves into a deep verdant river gorge bisected by wooden bridges that feels eerily distant from the nearby town.

From the town visitor-centre-cum-museum, take the descending path with steps down to the river where a sharp left will direct you through the narrowest and most dramatic sections of the gorge with its overhanging cliffs. On reaching a road bridge, take the zigzagging path up and head back into town along the road.

Vineyard, Tuscany

Tuscany

20 Panzano to Radda
A gentle introduction to the wine country between Florence and Siena. **p90**

21 Castellina to Radda
Undulating rural roads linking two classic Chianti towns. **p92**

22 Certaldo to San Gimignano
Easy walk that merges with the medieval Via Francigena pilgrim's route. **p94**

23 Chianti Classico
Vineyards, villas, rural churches and broad bucolic views. **p96**

24 Tuscan Hill Crests
Quintessential romp through rolling Tuscan landscapes framed by slender cypresses. **p100**

25 Medieval Towns & Villages
Beautiful *borghi* nestled between the urban bookends of San Gimignano and Volterra. **p104**

Explore

Tuscany

Low rolling hills, fields full of barley, elegant cypresses and silvery green olives, vines ripening in the late summer sun, an old ruined monastery, a priest careering downhill in a rusty Fiat 500, potted geraniums, cyclists in multicoloured jerseys and a rustic farmhouse reborn as an *agriturismo*. Welcome to Tuscany, fount of Florentine fashion and Sienese art, land that spawned the Renaissance, Leonardo da Vinci, Humanism, the Uffizi, Chianti and a hundred different trails – most of them refreshingly undemanding.

Agriturismi

With a landscape dotted with small traditional farmhouses, and a culinary tradition rooted in simple, home-grown food, Tuscany was surely invented with the concept of *agriturismi* in mind. In the circumstances, it's little wonder that these rural farm stays have become almost as popular as deluxe hotels in Florence. For virgin agri-tourists, the idea is a simple one: ditch your pricey city hotel, learn a few words of passable Italian, and decamp to an idyllic rural farm where the cheese on your breakfast platter probably came from the sheep whose baa-ing just woke you up. Beyond that, no two *agriturismi* are the same. Some produce olive oil, others raise cattle, and a growing contingent offer surprisingly deluxe digs with additional extras such as swimming pools and cookery classes. Notwithstanding, prices are usually very reasonable. For hikers, there's an additional bonus: many *agriturismi* in Tuscany are situated on, or close to, major trails. However, due to their burgeoning popularity, it's advisable to book in advance. For more information and/or reservations see *agriturismo.net* or *agriturismo.it*.

Chianti

The vineyards in this instantly seductive part of Tuscany sandwiched between Florence and Siena produce the grapes used in namesake Chianti and Chianti Classico: world-famous reds sold under the Gallo Nero (Black Cockerel/Rooster) trademark. Vines aside, this is a glorious historical landscape where you'll encounter honey-coloured stone farmhouses and imposing stone castles built in the Middle Ages by Florentine and Sienese warlords. Though now part of the province of Siena, the southern section of Chianti (Chianti Senese) was once the stronghold of the Lega del Chianti, a military and administrative alliance within the city-state of Florence. Chianti's northern part sits in

WHEN TO GO

In spring and autumn, central Tuscany's climate is sunny and mild, and the palettes of seasonal colours are wonderful. At the beginning of October there is the *vendemmia* (grape harvest). In January and February Chianti virtually closes down; summer is the least suitable time for walking due to the sultry heat.

the province of Florence (Chianti Fiorentino) and is a popular day trip from that city.

Radda in Chianti

Set like a medieval crow's nest on a hill crest with sweeping views of vineyard-striped fields, shapely trees and scattered ancient *borghi* (tiny villages), Radda is the Chianti region's most expressive lure. If you're pondering over which 'in Chianti' town to stay in, vacillate no longer. Despite its diminutive size, Radda has a varied stash of accommodation and is a crossroads for copious trails.

San Gimignano

Originally an Etruscan village, San Gimignano had morphed into a wealthy fiefdom by the beginning of the 11th century. Flaunting their wealth, the city's powerful families built 72 towers before the plague passed through in 1348, decimating the town's population and leaving all but 14 of the towers in ruins. But the historic legacy was not lost. Today San Gimignano is one of the best-preserved medieval cities in Europe and the clustered towers have earned it the moniker of the 'Manhattan of the Middle Ages'. In summer it is crowded with tourists, but most visitors are day-trippers who rarely venture outside the town walls. After dark, San Gimi maintains a deliciously tranquil allure and the surrounding trails that fan out like a giant spider's web from the hilltop town are only lightly trodden.

TRANSPORT

Italy's fast *freccia.trenitalia.com/en/frecce.html*)rains serve Florence, where you can change onto regional trains calling at Siena or Poggibonsi. To reach the smaller towns of San Gimignano and Radda in Chianti, you'll need to undertake the last leg of the journey by bus from Poggibonsi and Siena respectively.

WHAT'S ON

Expo del Chianti Classico
During its annual wine expo in September, Greve's central piazza is transformed into a huge wine-tasting area, attracting oenophiles from around the world. All of the major producers are represented, and ancillary events include musical performances (*expochianticlassico.com*).

Ferie delle Messi
San Gimignano's medieval past is evoked in the third weekend in June through re-enacted battles, archery contests and plays (*cavalieridisantafina.it*).

Resources

sangimignano.com Tourist website of San Gimignano and its surroundings.

chianti.com For information on the Chianti region, including festivals and special events.

viefrancigene.org Official website of the Via Francigena long-distance trail which has 13 Tuscan stages and a free downloadable app.

WHERE TO STAY

There's no shortage of quality accommodation in Central Tuscany, with San Gimignano and Radda in Chianti providing the best walking bases. Both towns have some fine *locande* (inns) and country-style hotels. It's also worth considering the innumerable villas and *agriturismi* that dot the countryside hereabouts. Most rural accommodation only opens April to mid-October.

20

Panzano to Radda

DURATION	DIFFICULTY	DISTANCE	START/END
4hrs	Easy	14.5km	Panzano/Radda

TERRAIN	Undulating gravel roads with the last third on paved roads

Mostly on gravel or paved roads, this foray through gently rolling hills between the two 'in Chianti' towns of Panzano and Radda comes with an abundance of vantage points from which to appreciate the wine-producing beauty of central Tuscany.

Take Via XX Luglio southeast out of Panzano. The road quickly turns to gravel as the houses fall away and a wide **vineyard-striped panorama** opens up to the south.

Keep on this road for the next 4km, parading through a **mixture of hill crests**, **woods** and **meadows**, ignoring all turnoffs until you reach a signposted T-junction.

Turn right, following signs to Radda, and begin a descent into mixed woodland on a good gravel road marked 'SP114 Traversa del Chianti'. After 300m, keep right at a second fork and stay left at a third. In 2.5km the wood is interrupted by craning cypresses and then thins out into some **beautiful meadows and cultivated fields**, arriving at the romantic *borgo* of **Castelvecchi** with its onsite winery.

From here a paved road twists down among **olive groves and vineyards** to the charming Pieve di Santa Maria Novella, which retains its original Romanesque structure of three apses.

The descent gets steeper here and reaches a fork in the road. Veer right, cross a bridge and head uphill to the main road, turning left towards Radda in Chianti. You'll need to walk 1.7km on this road until you come to a **red-brick** bridge which you pass under and then cross to get you on the final 1km climb into Radda.

Pieve di Santa Maria Novella

21

Castellina to Radda

DURATION	DIFFICULTY	DISTANCE	START/END
4hrs	Easy	14km	Castellina/Radda

TERRAIN	Undulating dirt and paved roads

Enjoy this relatively modest meander between two historic wine towns that stand like time-warped sentinels at either end of this placid hike.

Established by the Etruscans and fortified by the Florentines in the 15th century, **Castellina** is now a major centre for the wine industry. From the bus stop in Piazza Roma, head southeast along Via Trento e Trieste.

At the renovated **Romanesque church** veer right along Via Rocca, passing an **archaeological museum** and Trattoria La Torre. Take the ramp down into Viale IV Novembre and continue south as it merges with the main SR222. Pass the **emblematic town** silos and soon after turn left into Via dei Castagni. Follow the dirt road as it swings right and uphill, wheeling right at a fork just before a vineyard. The trail winds down to the villa of **Casalecchi**, where a left turn puts you on a good dirt road, the Strada del Mandorlo, your friend for the next 6km to 7km.

The meandering, undulating road passes various villas like Capoven-to and wineries such as Brancaia before descending to a farm at **Pornanino**. Turn left here at a large shed, cross a river and take the next right up through woods and vineyards to the **Petrene farm**. From here you can cut along the house's driveway to join another dirt road heading north.

At a T-junction with a paved road, turn left and proceed for 300m before taking a path on the right alongside a river and up a slope to the outskirts of Radda. You'll be delivered next to the **Casa Chianti Classico**, a wine museum and tasting room that, by now, you've clocked enough kilometres to indulge in.

Castellina

22

Certaldo to San Gimignano

DURATION	DIFFICULTY	DISTANCE	START/END
4hrs	Easy	14km	Certaldo/San Gimignano

TERRAIN	Mostly quiet paved backroads; the last 2km on a busier provincial road

Like a medieval sandwich with two handsome historic towns at either end and a typical Tuscan filling of mossy churches, hump-backed hills and voluptuous villas, this walk is easy on the eyes and legs.

Getting Here

Certaldo is on the main train line between Florence and Siena. It is also accessible by direct bus from San Gimignano.

Starting Point

The walk starts in the main square of Certaldo, which is guarded by an impressive statue of native son and scribe Giovanni Boccaccio. Standing facing the Municipio building, take the road on the left: Via XX Settembre.

 Turn left at the T-junction onto Via Giacomo Matteotti and then right into Via Trieste, following signs for San Gimignano. Cross a railway track, a bridge, a roundabout and a second bridge before turning left onto **Viale dei Platani**.

02 After less than 400m, you'll see the hotel-restaurant Latini and a road leading to the right with a blue sign indicating Pancole and Fattoria del Monte. The walk follows this road, rising southeast among houses, then **vineyards and olive groves**, and affords **beautiful views** of Certaldo to the northeast and (later) San Gimignano to the south.

03 After 3km of climbing on the road, you reach the little church of Canonica, where a double row of cypress trees lines the road up to the

San Gimignano

Boccaccio

The great Italian author, poet and humanist, Giovanni Boccaccio, is popularly regarded as one of Tuscany's most famous literary sons. He was most likely born in Certaldo in 1313 and certainly died in the town in 1375 after an influential career capped by the publication in the early 1350s of the seminal *The Decameron*, a collection of 100 bawdy fables about love in all its incarnations. For literary scholars, *The Decameron* came to define vernacular Italian in the same way that Chaucer's *The Canterbury Tales* would ultimately define Old English. Indeed, today Boccaccio, along with Petrarch and Dante, is considered to be one of the three founding fathers of the modern Italian language.

majestic **Villa del Monte**. The road continues for another 2.5km to the *borgo* of **La Piazzetta**.

04 Veer left at a fork following the Via Francigena sign and enter the *borgo* of **Pancole**. The **17th-century sanctuary** on the far side of Pancole was originally built in 1670, but was destroyed by the Germans in WWII. The existing road-spanning arch was rebuilt in 1949.

05 About 1km past the sanctuary, turn right on a hill onto a track signposted **Collemucioli**. The track bends left and past a farmhouse and through an **olive grove and garden**.

06 At a T-junction, turn left and then right at a small Via Francigena sign. Forging uphill, you'll pass through a recently restored *borgo* with a lovely tower. Continue along this road, passing under an archway, and you'll come to a wide clearing aside the splendid **Pieve di Cellole**, a working monastery with an adjoining church and small shop run by monks.

Take a Break

Hold off your hunger pangs, if you can, until you reach San Gimignano. **Gelateria Dondoli** (*gelateriadondoli.com*), the town's most famous eatery, is not a trattoria or pizzeria, but a legendary ice cream shop, decorated by multiple 'best ice cream in the world' awards and so popular its queues sometimes stretch right across the main square.

07 Descend south on a paved road that, after 300m, meets up with provincial SP63, where you turn left. This road can be busy; there are some blind bends, so proceed with caution. At a roundabout, follow signs for San Gimignano and make use of the pavement for the last couple of kilometres. Just before reaching town, veer right onto Via Niccolò Cannicci, which takes you up to the **San Matteo gate**.

23

Chianti Classico

Villa Vistarenni

DURATION	DIFFICULTY	DISTANCE	START/END
5.5hrs	Moderate	18km	Radda/Vagliagli

TERRAIN	Undulating dirt roads with some easy single-track footpaths

A Tuscan classic during which you can practically taste the fermenting grapes. This pastoral jaunt snakes along rutted farm roads, sloping vineyards and gnarly woodland on its way past medieval *pievi* (rural churches), farms reconfigured as *agriturismi* and deluxe villas. It's vintage in more ways than one.

Getting Here
Radda in Chianti is connected by several daily buses to both Siena and Florence.

Starting Point
Head out from the eastern side of the small circular urban hub of Radda in Chianti.

01 Descend east on the busy paved road to Villa Radda, 1km east of Radda in Chianti. Cross a bridge, descend to a roundabout and take the first exit (east).

02 In 300m turn right off the main road just past **Villa Miranda**. A pleasant little country road heads south into a small, cultivated valley. You'll pass the **ancient tower of Canvalle** on the right as you head up the other side of the valley.

96 BEST DAY WALKS : ITALY

Return Walk

If 18km of rolling Tuscan countryside have left you suitably inspired, you can skip the bus ride back to Radda in Chianti (via Siena) and walk instead. A shorter 10km route along the part-paved but refreshingly quiet SP102 links Vagliagli with Radda, passing several wineries and *agriturismi* en route. The road is mainly downhill or flat, with a short uphill stretch at the end. Follow the Radda sign just off Vagliagli's main square and keep walking.

03 Soon after, as the paved road descends to the right at a junction, continue straight on along a stony track heading up into the forest. In a few minutes you'll join another track: follow it straight ahead along a hill crest, ignoring any deviations. Pass a wooden cross encircled by cypresses and enjoy views over the territory of Radda to the right and the **towers of Vertine and the 16th-century Villa Vistarenni** to the left.

04 Continue to a wide, grassy clearing with a four-way crossroads. Go straight ahead here, following the main dirt road downhill (it curves slightly to the right) until you reach a T-junction where you turn right downhill in the direction of San Giusto in Salcio.

05 The road now descends in a couple of steep curves past fields and farm buildings, veering right at a Y-junction, crossing a **little bridge over a stream**, and leading to a paved road at the valley bottom, where you turn left.

06 About 100m along the road there's a turnoff for Vagliagli–San Fedele on the right. Ignore it and continue on the paved road for another 200m before turning right (signposted Poggio Antinora) onto the cypress-lined dirt road to reach **Pieve di San Giusto in Salcio**. This 11th-century, triple-apsed church is marvellously positioned among ancient farmhouses, grassy courtyards and centuries-old trees.

07 Continue past the church and walk uphill until you meet up with a dirt road, marked by a red-and-white sign on a tree, where you turn left. After 20m you'll reach a three-pronged fork with two parallel dirt roads in front of you (480m); follow the right one for Galenda-Ama. The path follows the course of an **ancient stone wall** on your right. When the wall runs out, the path swerves left downhill before crossing a shallow stream. It then proceeds uphill to **Galenda**, a delightful rural *borgo* where you can make a pleasant rest stop among the cypresses (there's a water fountain here).

Take a Break

No fuss, no pretension, family-run **Bar Dante** (*bardanteradda.com*) is a fine place to plonk down after a long day on your feet, especially if you're in the mood for bruschetta, coffee, cake or simple pastas (best enjoyed on the florid deck out front).

08 Leave the *borgo* through the vaulted passageway between the houses and, heading south, follow the narrow grassy path that traverses the side of a **vineyard**. Note the small **shrine** on your right. Walk downhill to the bottom of the small valley, cross the stream and dirt road and continue to follow the path uphill (southeast) with vines on your right and olive trees to your left. Go through one iron gate and then another, all the time keeping the vines on your right, until you reach a quiet paved road where you turn right.

09 Within five minutes you will be among the lovely houses of **Poggio San Polo**. Of interest is the ancient *parata* (a kind of vaulted garage for housing farm equipment), which has been transformed into an elegant country home.

10 Continue your descent on the asphalt road towards Castello di San Polo in Rosso, following Club Alpino Italiano (CAI) route 66. The road becomes a pleasant cypress-lined dirt track, which passes through a forest and leads to a small **cemetery**. There is a **splendid view** of San Polo in Rosso and the Sienese Chianti. Pass an elegant *casale* (farmhouse) with a portico surmounted by a rustic, double-arched window and you'll soon reach the ancient **Castello di San Polo in Rosso**. The 'castle' was founded in AD 1000 as a *pieve* (parish church), fortified in the 13th century and later embellished with a Renaissance loggia. Unfortunately, it's closed to visitors, although you can admire the grounds.

11 Take the dirt road that heads downhill beside the parking area, passing a house with a lovely staircase supported by a column. The dirt road veers to the left and then winds down into the forest, affording a view of the pieve from the south. The road continues its long descent through the forest towards Torrente Arbia. As it gets less road-like and more path-like, you'll begin to notice the rich **birdlife**. As the road-path approaches the bottom of the valley, it crosses a little grassy bridge spanning a secondary stream next to a ruined building, and continues among the poplars, maintaining a distance from the true left of the river.

12 In a few minutes you'll come to a junction marked with a **miniature shrine**. Turn right and you'll soon come to a small clearing. Just beyond here, the trail crosses the main river, veers to the left and tracks uphill; this old road, used by vehicles until 30 years ago, is now regularly consumed by rainwater. It ascends through the forest in steep, sharp curves, ultimately coming out on a dirt road beside the beautiful restored *casale* of **Bottaccio**. From here you can enjoy the panorama with the village of San Sano nestled among the vineyards.

13 Continue ascending on the dirt road to the southwest of the *casale* and, in 300m, after passing a wall on the left, turn sharp left up some steps and under a passageway to reach the courtyard and Renaissance chapel of the tiny *borgo* of Carpineto. As you continue uphill on the road, you now have a view of the remarkably beautiful **Crete Senesi**, whose dry clay hills are known for their white truffles.

14 Follow the road on the ridge, ignoring the first deviation to the left, and after a few metres you'll reach a broad semicircle of cypresses. Here you can take the dirt road to the left, descending to the noble manor house of **Villa Dievole**, today an elegant wine resort that's been around in one form or other since the 10th century. To continue to Vagliagli, follow the main cypress-lined road uphill to the asphalt road and turn right. **Vagliagli** is 2km from the entrance to Villa Dievole. Sporadic buses depart the village to Siena, where you can change for Radda.

Chianti Wines

Chianti's blockbuster wines are the ruby-red Chianti and Chianti Classico DOCGs, both of which have a minimum Sangiovese component (75% for Chianti and 80% for Chianti Classico). The biggest wine-producing estates have *cantine* (cellars) where you can taste and buy wine, but few vineyards – big or small – can be visited without reservations. For a comprehensive list and map of wine estates, buy a copy of *Le strade del Gallo Nero* (€2.50) at the tourist office in Radda in Chianti. A high-profile consortium of local producers, the Consorzio Vino Chianti Classico (*chianti classico.com*) operates Casa Chianti Classico in Radda in Chianti, which is home to a small wine museum, *enoteca* and bistro. The *consorzio*'s website has plenty of information on the wines and wine-related events.

Bruschetta and Chianti wine

24

Best for

AVOIDING THE CROWDS

Tuscan Hill Crests

San Gimignano

DURATION	DIFFICULTY	DISTANCE	START/END
6hrs	Moderate	20km	San Gimignano

TERRAIN	Mostly dirt roads, several paved sections, grassy paths through olive groves

Starting one small step outside the walls of San Gimignano, but one giant leap from the gelato-consuming tour groups for which the town is famous, this elongated pastoral circuit traverses the little-frequented hill crests of the province's bucolic hinterland. Journeying mainly through farmland, it syncs briefly with the Via Francigena, the ancient pilgrim's route that links Canterbury with Rome.

Getting Here

San Gimignano is connected by regular buses (every 30 minutes) to the town of Poggibonsi and its train station.

Starting Point

Starting at San Gimignano's Porta San Giovanni, head south around the Piazziale dei Martiri di Montemaggio to where a flight of steps cuts down to the road below (signposted 'Checkpoint Bus Turistici').

01 Turn right into Via Baccanella following the Via Francigena sign. At the roundabout, take the Volterra exit (straight ahead) and, within 50m, turn left onto a road signposted 'Santa Lucia 2.3 km'. This pleasant lane has a pedestrian pavement for the first kilometre or so and takes you past the **Agriturismo Monte Oliveto**, followed by the imposing **Monte Oliveto Convent** on the right. The convent was founded in 1340 and guards a fresco of the Crucifixion by Renaissance painter Benozzo Gozzoli from the 1460s.

Collegiata

Take time to admire San Gimignano's Romanesque **cathedral** (*duomosangimignano.it*) before or after this walk. Parts of it were built in the second half of the 11th century, but its remarkably vivid frescoes, depicting episodes from the Old and New Testaments, date from the 14th century. Look out, too, for the Cappella di Santa Fina near the main altar – a Renaissance chapel adorned with naïve and touching frescoes by Domenico Ghirlandaio depicting the life of one of the town's patron saints.

02 Fork right on the edge of Santa Lucia, bypassing the main part of the village. Where the paved road bends right on the other side, stay straight, entering an **olive grove**. The narrow lane leads sharply downhill, passes some handsome country abodes, and veers left at a junction by a **fountain**. Continue downhill and turn right at a T-junction with a dirt road at the bottom of the slope, following signs to Molino di Foci.

03 At the **Molino di Foci** B&B, veer right and push uphill through several switchbacks to a junction on the crest where you fork left (signposted 'Torraccia di Chiusi.') You're now on a magnificent hill crest with quintessential **Tuscan views** towards San Gimignano and its towers to the north. The town looks deliciously tranquil from this vantage, the gelaterie, tour groups and selfie sticks a distant memory.

04 At the **Torraccia di Chiusi** – a tempting *agriturismo* – ignore the Via Francigena sign to the left and continue straight, looping around the building. Veer left behind the house by a pylon and take a grassy track through an olive grove. Enter a wood briefly and then skirt alongside another olive grove to reach a dirt track leading to the **Fattoria Il Piano** (a farm). Cross this track and the next one and merge with another dirt track leading to the small semi-abandoned *borgo* of **Ciuciano** with its engaging chapel.

05 At a T-junction of dirt roads at the bottom of a short downhill section, go right and head towards **Ranza**, visible in the distance. Ostensibly a typically quaint Tuscan *borgo*, Ranza is also the site of San Gimignano's main prison, the **Casa di Reclusione**, a modern facility located just south of the settlement.

06 Veer right at a fork and pass through the hamlet to arrive at the main road to San Gimignano. Turn right and follow the road for around 100m before ascending on a narrow overgrown path that branches off on the opposite side. This path crests a rise and soon descends to rejoin the main road. Veer left and within a few minutes you'll reach the turnoff for the village of **San Donato** on the right. This is a great place for an elongated rest. The settlement sports a small **chapel-sized church** and a farm-winery called the **Fattoria San Donato** that offers daily tastings. It is also one of several farms in the area that produces saffron. San Gimignano's saffron is famous for its high quality. The violet crocuses have been grown in the area since the 12th century and fortunes were once made in its trade. Changing circumstances meant cultivation died out in the mid-17th century, but the product was enthusiastically reintroduced in the 1990s and has since been designated a PDO (protected designation of origin).

07 From San Donato, turn right at the far end of the village on a dirt road signposted 'Voltrona'. The road with fine **views of San Gimignano** bends left and right before passing the **Fattoria Voltrona**, near a small lake, and ending by a lone house and a wooden 'San Gimignano' sign. Follow the sign along a dried-up riverbed before emerging on the edge of a vineyard. Pitch straight up the vine-striped slope on a tractor track towards a cluster of houses visible on the crest.

08 Veer right on a dirt road here and you will soon arrive on the edge of the *borgo* of **Montauto**, where the road becomes paved.

09 Turn left before entering the *borgo* onto another paved lane that weaves pleasantly back towards San Gimignano, visible in the distance. After approximately 2km it joins the main Volterra road. Turn right and within 1km you will be delivered back to the main roundabout, from where you can retrace your steps back to the Porta San Giovanni. This **Sienese-style gate** is the most important of the three main entrances to the town and was built, along with the famous 2176m-long walls, in the 1260s. The Via Francigena pilgrim's route passes through the gate and bisects the town before passing under the San Matteo gate and pitching north towards Lucca. From the Porta San Giovanni, the Via Francigena heads south to Siena and Rome.

☕ Take a Break

Osteria delle Catene (*osteriadellecatene.it*), 'The Prison', is as popular with San Gimignano locals as it is with visitors, something that can't be said of many places in this tourist-driven town. The menu is full of delightful surprises – dishes are seasonally focussed and many utilise local saffron and Vernaccia wine.

Montauto

Borghi

Cuciano, Ranza, San Donato and Montauto – this hike, like many in Tuscany, is scattered with small rural hamlets that show up as little more than tiny specks on large-scale local maps. Sometimes the settlements are embellished with a church or a monastery; at others, you'll find little more than a villa, or an *agriturismo*. The Italians call these small clusters of buildings *borghi* (plural of *borgo*, which translates roughly as 'burg' or 'town') and you'll encounter many bucolic examples on rural walks. Connected by rough dirt roads or thin, winding ribbons of asphalt, the settlements retain the soporific air of quiet medieval villages and make excellent stops for picnics, wine-quaffing, or quiet contemplation of nature.

25

Best for

HISTORY & CULTURE

Medieval Towns & Villages

Museo Etrusco Guarnacci

DURATION	DIFFICULTY	DISTANCE	START/END
7hrs	Moderate	26km	San Gimignano/ Volterra

TERRAIN	Mostly dirt roads, some paved sections, a short stony path in the middle

Taking in the full sweep of Tuscan history, this long but easy to negotiate walk links the two walled towns of San Gimignano and Volterra and visits the ruins of an early medieval citadel en route. Landscapes sway between gnarly woodland and graceful cypress-filled lanes. Villas, farm stays and bucolic *borghi* dot the countryside.

Getting Here

San Gimignano is connected by regular buses (every 30 minutes) to the town of Poggibonsi, from where trains run to Florence and Siena.

Starting Point

Sally forth from the southern San Giovanni gate of San Gimignano.

01 Turn right outside San Gimignano's Porta San Giovanni and take the lane to the left of the car park just off the main plaza, signposted 'Santa Margherita'. After about 600m, pass under a **low bridge** and follow a gravel track on the left. The track loops around the back of a farmhouse, heads uphill and joins a paved road lined with houses.

02 At a T-junction at the top of a rise, turn left and enjoy some **magnificent views** back over San Gimignano. Keep left at a fork and

Volterra's Etruscan Museum

The vast collection of artefacts exhibited at Volterra's **Museo Etrusco Guarnacci** (volterratur.it/en/poi/guarnacci-etruscan-museum) makes this one of Italy's most impressive Etruscan collections. Found locally, they include some 600 funerary urns carved mainly from alabaster and tufa – the *Urna degli sposi* (Urn of the Spouses) is a strikingly realistic terracotta rendering of an elderly couple. The finds are displayed according to subject and era; the best examples (those dating from later periods) are on the 2nd and 3rd floors.

pass through the tiny *borgo* of **Raccicano**. The minor road joins the main road (SP47) on a bend. Turn right and follow the SP47 – which has some wide verges – for 1.5km before turning left into the village of **San Donato**, a tiny, medieval *borgo* with its own *fattoria* (farm) producing wine, olives and saffron. The farm shop offers **wine tasting**.

03 From San Donato's **Romanesque church**, head southwest to rejoin SP47. Turn right onto the road and, after about 30m, turn left and ascend a steep dirt road signposted 'Riserva Naturale di Castelvecchio'. A few steps down the road, an informative map-board marks out the details of this **nature reserve**.

04 As the dirt road emerges onto a rocky crest, you'll be able to see the ruins of Castelvecchio dotting the narrow, wooded valley below. Shortly after, the dirt road descends steeply and then goes uphill to a clearing in the woods in front of **La Tenuta di Castelvecchio**, an *agriturismo*.

05 From here descend southeast on a steep and sharply curving trail to reach a ford over the **Botro di Castelvecchio stream**. Once on the other side, continue west along the trail.

06 After a fairly brief climb, you come to a clearing where there is a dirt road closed with a chain. If you want to visit the interesting ruins of **Castelvecchio**, turn left (east) and hop over the chain. You'll probably need about 30 minutes for a decent exploration. If you don't want to visit the ruins, turn right at the clearing and ascend on the dirt road. Cross through woods, ignoring all turnoffs, until you reach an open plain. The road then passes under some high-tension wires, veers left and gradually descends until it

BEST DAY WALKS : ITALY 105

☕ Take a Break

The rear *salone* of Volterra cafe **L'Incontro** is a top spot to grab a quick antipasto plate or *panino* for lunch, and its front bar area is always crowded, with locals enjoying coffee or *aperitivi*. The house-baked biscuits are noteworthy – try the chewy and nutty *brutti ma buoni*.

reaches the intersection for the **Casa Campore farm** on your right. Follow the main dirt road to the left (west) and after a little more than 1.5km, you'll reach SP53, locally known as di Poggio Cornocchio.

07 Turn left (south) and walk along the road (which has some light traffic) on a panoramic crest for just over 1km. Here you'll find a dirt road on the right (west), marked with two **stone wayside posts**. Descend among the trees for 300m to a T-junction with another dirt road, where you head right again. Follow this cypress-lined walk up to the *borgo* of **Pignano**, a rambling country estate reborn as a luxury eco-resort.

08 From Pignano, follow the main dirt road, which descends sharply southwest, to a small **bridge**, offering a panorama over the wooded territory south of Volterra. The route continues ascending west and then descends slightly along the ridge to the buildings of Grignano. Continuing southwest, in 1.3km, you arrive at **Palazzina**, with its abandoned **12th-century San Lorenzo chapel**. A little more than 2km further on you reach **Villa Palagione**. Built in 1598 under the rocky hump of **Monte Voltraio** (458m), it functions today as a cultural and study centre. If you have the energy, climb the termite mound–shaped *monte*. There is a path just across the road from the entrance to Villa Palagione (50 minutes return).

09 From Villa Palagione, continue on the dirt road, which descends in steep, sharp curves southward. Cross a bridge over the **Fiume Era Morta**, continuing northwest until you reach SR439dir, a paved road with signs for Pontedera to the right and Saline di Volterra to the left.

10 Turn left onto the winding state road and, after just 20m, look for trail markers on the guard rail and on a tree, indicating trail 21 to the right. Ascend on a cobbled mossy trail for about 400m until you see the terraced gardens and sandy facade of **Agriturismo Podere San Lorenzo**.

11 To continue to Volterra, go straight up the San Lorenzo's approach road, ascending among the fields until you reach an **intersection** with another narrow, paved road. Turn left and, in a few metres, you'll be on the SR68 at Strada.

12 Turn right on the state road and continue along the moderately busy road. In about 2km you'll reach **Volterra**. Turn right onto a path just past an Esso garage, ascend the steps and emerge beside an arch that takes you underneath the old **Medici fortress** and into the historic town. It was founded by the Etruscans, probably in the 8th century BC, and parts of its walls date from the 3rd century BC. A wander through the winding cobbled streets dotted with **Roman**, **Etruscan** and **medieval structures** is a rare pleasure. Look out for **alabaster carving**, part of the town's wealthy artisanal heritage. Volterra's bus station is in Piazza Martiri della Libertà, atop a bluff in the centre of town. Regular buses go to Colle di Val d'Elsa, where you can catch a connecting service back to San Gimignano.

Castelvecchio Nature Reserve

The section of this walk between San Donato and Pignano is protected in a small nature reserve that harbours beech forest, a wintertime population of peregrine falcons and the medieval ruins of the fortified settlement of Castelvecchio. A citadel first grew up here in the 7th century and, by the 1200s, it had became a fortified garrison in the century-long conflict between San Gimignano and Volterra. Its demise came with the arrival of the plague in the late 1400s, after which it was largely abandoned. The site was restored by a local historical group in the late 1970s. Today the evocative ruins, including a tower, a chapel and cistern, huddle enigmatically in the fecund forest.

Also Try...

Monte Forato

Procinto, Forato & Pania della Croce

DURATION	DIFFICULTY	DISTANCE
2 days	Hard	26km

Despite the three peaks in the title, this hike is more of a ridge walk than a summit strike. The sawtoothed crest between Procinto and Pania della Croce in the Apuan Alps is a stunner that requires some steep ascents and rocky scrambles.

A highlight is the 'Mountain with a Hole', the local name given to surreally shaped Monte Forato. The high point is 1858m Pania della Croce, whose summit is reached via a short side trip. Although the first few kilometres are relatively gentle, the hike has its arduous moments – hand chains over exposed sections – while the wildness of the terrain enables you to feel a degree of poetic isolation. But, surrounded on all sides by marble quarries, clustered Apuan villages and cosy *rifugi*, civilisation is never far away.

San Fabiano to Greve in Chianti

DURATION	DIFFICULTY	DISTANCE
5hrs	Easy	16km

On the northern (Florence) side of Chianti, this largely rural walk incorporates mainly paved roads and passes a number of Tuscan *pievi* (rural churches) and abbeys. It starts in San Fabiano, a tiny *borgo* featuring a Romanesque facade that's an hour by bus from Florence.

Follow the Via Fornace Casavecchia past the Castello il Palagio, a small, medieval castle, to the Romanesque Pieve di Santo Stefano a Campo. The grassy churchyard, surrounded by stands of cypresses, provides a pleasant setting to kick back and contemplate this ancient country church, built in the 10th century. From here, Vias Campoli and Vigondoli wind south past several *agriturismi* as far as the majestic abbey of Badia a Passignano, before pitching east to the important wine-producing town and regional hub of Greve in Chianti.

Via Francigena

Via Francigena

DURATION	DIFFICULTY	DISTANCE
4hrs	Moderate	13.5km

The Via Francigena is an old pilgrims' route that has recently been gaining in popularity thanks, in part, to the renaissance of Spain's Camino de Santiago.

Several sections pass through central Tuscany. The easiest chunk for a day walk is stage 31 between the spa town of Gambassi Terme and San Gimignano, which shares part of its route with our Certaldo to San Gimignano walk. The path is marked with brown signposts and/or red-and-white-backed pilgrim symbols. See *viefrancigene.org* for more information and downloadable maps.

Castelpoggio to Campocecina

DURATION	DIFFICULTY	DISTANCE
2½hrs	Moderate	5km

For a mild introduction to Tuscany's Apuan Alps, take this wooded jaunt from the village of Castelpoggio up to the Rifugio Carrara in Campocecina.

This is the first part of the eight-stage 'Alta Via delle Alpi Apuane' and follows track 185 on a gently ascending path to the Gabellaccia Pass at 895m, where it crosses a paved road. The path continues in a mainly easterly direction, passing rock walls, caves and an unusual natural arch before it hits the road again at the former shepherd's settlement of Acquasparta.

Cefalù (p113)

Sicily

26 **Stromboli**
Watch eruptions illuminate the sky from atop this island volcano. **p114**

27 **Necropoli di Pantalica**
Follow the Anapo River between limestone walls riddled with ancient tombs. **p116**

28 **La Rocca di Cefalù**
Climb to a ruined castle overlooking Cefalù's stunning Arab-Norman cathedral. **p118**

29 **Riserva Naturale dello Zingaro**
Zigzag among coves in Sicily's oldest nature reserve. **p120**

30 **Oasi Faunistica di Vendicari**
Wander past flamingo-dotted lagoons and photogenic ruins to a pretty beach. **p124**

31 **Fossa di Vulcano**
Hold your nose and conquer the rim of this sulphur-belching volcanic crater. **p126**

32 **Punta Troia**
Walk to the far tip of an idyllic offshore island. **p128**

Explore

Sicily

For lovers of volcanoes, islands and rugged coastlines, few walking destinations compare with Sicily. The arc of fire that starts at Naples' Mt Vesuvius resurfaces in Sicily's seven volcanic sisters – the Aeolian Islands – and reaches its pinnacle at Mt Etna, Europe's loftiest active volcano. Sicily's Mediterranean, Tyrrhenian and Ionian shorelines abound in idyllic coastal strolls. Offshore, another half-dozen islands offer scenic ambles on traffic-free roads and trails, while inland the Madonie and Nebrodi mountains are home to some superb off-the-beaten-track walking. Adding icing to the cake are Sicily's exceptional home-grown cuisine and seemingly countless layers of history.

Catania

Perfectly placed for climbs up Mt Etna, vibrant Catania (Sicily's second-largest city) sits smack at the foot of the volcano, many of its grey-hued buildings built directly from the debris hurled down during the disastrous eruption of 1669. For all its noise, chaos and scruffiness, Catania compensates with cool and gritty bars, an earthy spirit and a Unesco-listed historic core where *palazzi* tower over sweeping baroque piazzas. Food is another local forte. This is the home of Sicily's iconic *pasta alla Norma* and the extraordinary La Pescheria fish market.

Noto

A lovely base for hikers planning excursions to nearby Vendicari and Pantalica, the honey-coloured hill town of Noto is home to one of Sicily's most beautiful historic centres, rebuilt in the early 18th century after a devastating 1693 earthquake. Claiming centre stage is Corso Vittorio Emanuele, an elegant walkway flanked by baroque *palazzi* and churches. Dashing at any time of the day, it's especially hypnotic in the early evening, when the red-gold buildings seem to glow with a soft inner light.

Lipari

The Aeolian Islands' main transport hub, Lipari retains a charming, laid-back island vibe while offering a full range of tourist services. The clifftop citadel and archaeological museum make a nice half-day diversion, and there are excellent day hikes along the island's north and west coasts – but it's also lovely to simply stroll Lipari's labyrinthine alleyways or sip drinks at sunset down by the Marina Corta docks. Lipari's many boat operators offer daily hiking

WHEN TO GO

Spring and autumn are delightful seasons for hiking along the coast, especially May, September and October when prices are lower, beach crowds thinner and temperatures pleasant. March and October are good for flamingo sightings in Vendicari. High-altitude destinations such as Mt Etna and the Monti Madonie and Nebrodi are suitable any time between May and October.

excursions to Stromboli, while hydrofoils make frequent connections to Vulcano and other islands in the archipelago.

Cefalù

Huddled beneath the imposing cliffs of La Rocca, Cefalù is one of Sicily's most photogenic seaside towns. The big draws here are Cefalù's gorgeous beaches, side-by-side with one of Sicily's greatest Arab-Norman cathedrals – and a compact medieval centre packed with squares and alleys perfect for slow, pedestrianised meandering. Cefalù makes a convenient base for hiking in the nearby Monti Madonie, and its location on Sicily's main north-coast train line makes it an easy stopover between Palermo and the Aeolian Islands ferry docks at Milazzo.

Scopello

The seaside hamlet of Scopello couldn't be more charming if it tried. Built around an 18th-century *baglio* (fortified manor house), the village centre is graced by white houses and smooth-stone streets, with a historic *tonnara* (tuna fishery) on the shoreline below. Scopello's handful of hotels, *pensioni* and restaurants make it a tranquil base for exploring the adjacent Zingaro nature reserve and nearby treasures such as Segesta and Erice. When it's time to move on, you're only a 45-minute drive from Palermo airport or the docks at Trapani, where hydrofoils sail for the Egadi Islands.

TRANSPORT

There's frequent hydrofoil service to the Aeolian and Egadi Islands from Milazzo and Trapani, respectively. Reliable train service in Sicily is largely limited to the Tyrrhenian and Ionian coasts, from Palermo to Messina and from Messina to Syracuse. Buses serve many interior towns, but you'll generally need your own wheels to reach the more remote trailheads.

WHAT'S ON

Pasqua (Easter)
Solemn processions and passion plays mark Holy Week in March or April.

Festival del Teatro Greco
World-class actors celebrating Greek theatre stage dramas in Syracuse's 5th-century-BC amphitheatre in May and June (*indafondazione.org*).

Cous Cous Fest
International musicians and chefs gather for 10 days in the last week of September to celebrate western Sicily's famous fish couscous (*couscousfest.it*).

Resources

Gruppo Guide Alpine Etna Sud (*etnaguide.eu*) Guided hiking excursions on Mt Etna.

Assessorato Turismo Sport e Spettacolo (*visitsicily.info*) Sicily's official regional tourist authority.

Vai col Trekking Sicilia (*vaicoltrekkingsicilia.com*) Guided hiking tours of the Nebrodi Mountains.

WHERE TO STAY

Accommodation in Sicily runs the gamut from resort hotels to reasonably priced B&Bs. Some of the most attractive options for walkers are the *pensioni* (smaller family-run hotels) and *agriturismi* (farm stays, often serving food grown onsite) that abound in smaller towns and rural areas.

26

Stromboli

DURATION	DIFFICULTY	DISTANCE	START/END
5hrs	Moderate	14km	Piazza San Vincenzo

TERRAIN	Steep volcanic slopes

No destination in Italy tantalises like Stromboli. This charismatic little island at the Aeolian archipelago's eastern edge has been spewing red-hot rock since the age of Odysseus. Gazing down from its summit at sunset, with daylight's last glow shimmering on the Tyrrhenian Sea and the crater's fireworks exploding into a darkening sky overhead, is a volcano-lover's dream come true.

Getting Here
Ferries and hydrofoils serve Stromboli from Milazzo and Naples. Piazza San Vincenzo, where most tours start, is a 10-minute walk from the docks.

Starting Point
Surrounded by restaurants, bars and shops, Piazza San Vincenzo is the hub of Stromboli village.

 01 Hikers begin assembling every afternoon about three hours before sunset in **Piazza San Vincenzo**. From here, the walk's first stage leads gently uphill along a sidewalk at the edge of town, but you soon veer right and begin climbing a well-trodden trail through a landscape of yellow broom and wild capers. As you climb, the village of Stromboli assumes dollhouse-like proportions below, with the town's **walled cemetery** and the **San Vincenzo church tower** providing convenient landmarks.

 02 An hour or so of climbing brings you to the tree line, where the trail opens onto bare slopes of black volcanic rock, revealing distant

Stromboli

Stromboli Climbing Tips

- You're required to hire a guide if climbing above 400m.
- Many agencies lead tours, but it's still best to reserve. Group size is limited to 20, and kids under seven aren't allowed.
- The standard fee for guided group tours is €28 per person.
- You'll need hiking boots, a torch and a pack large enough to hold warm clothes for the summit. All these items can be rented from Totem Trekking (*totemtrekkingstromboli.com*) in Piazza San Vincenzo.

vistas of Stromboli town, the sparkling sea and the tiny volcanic islet of **Strombolicchio**. Silhouetted against the late afternoon sky, a zigzag line of fellow hikers slogs steadily across the slopes above towards the summit.

03 Crest the summit after what may seem like an eternity (it's actually closer to two or 2½ hours), and emerge into a surreal landscape of **smouldering craters** framed by the setting sun. The weather up top is often quite a bit colder than at the base, and guides generally give their groups time to rest and add layers under a pair of concrete mountaintop shelters. For the next 45 minutes you're treated to full-on **views of Stromboli's pyrotechnics** from a perfect vantage point above the craters. The periodic eruptions grow ever brighter against the darkening sky, changing with the waning light from awe-inspiring puffs of grey smoke to fountains of brilliant orange-red, evoking oohs and aahs that mix with the sound of sizzling hot rocks rolling down the mountainside.

 Take a Break

After descending from the summit, unwind with pizzas and beer on the panoramic terrace at **Ritrovo Ingrid**, a Stromboli institution on the main church square.

04 Ready for one last moment of magic? Don your headlamp for the descent, and join the single-file line of hikers plunging across the talus-strewn wasteland of **Stromboli's precipitous eastern slope**, with the moonlit sea at your feet stretching clear to the twinkling lights of Italy's mainland. The trail down is steeper and dustier that the path you came up on, so you'll need high-top hiking boots and a bandana to keep the fine volcanic sand out of your socks and lungs. About halfway down, groups enjoy a rest stop to shed layers and shake out shoes before continuing back to Stromboli town.

27

Necropoli di Pantalica

DURATION	DIFFICULTY	DISTANCE	START/END
4hrs	Moderate	12km	Anàktoron parking area

TERRAIN	Rocky trails, converted railway bed

With its thousands of ancient tombs honeycombed into the limestone cliffs west of Syracuse, Pantalica is Sicily's most important Iron and Bronze Age necropolis. This loop weaves past stone-carved burial chambers and into the lush Anapo and Calcincara river gorges.

Begin at a dirt parking area 11km east of Ferla, next to the scant foundations of the **Anàktoron**, a ruined prince's palace. Follow signs initially for Valle dell'Anapo, then Villaggio Bizantino Filiporto. The latter (reached after 1.5km) is one of Pantalica's best-preserved necropolises, with an eerie series of stone openings peering like eyes from the cliff face.

Enjoy **stunning views** of the cliff-framed Anapo valley as the trail descends to meet an old riverside railway bed. An abandoned train station here serves as a **cultural museum** filled with artefacts of Sicilian rural life. Follow the tree-shaded valley floor past citrus orchards and colourful cliff faces, through a tunnel and over a couple of bridges.

After an hour in the valley, cross the Anapo on stepping stones, following signs for Saramenzana. Climb a dirt road to Pantalica's eastern entrance station and turn left, passing through a gate onto a narrower path marked 'Fiume Calcinara/Necropoli Nord'. You'll soon pass a rock face on your right pockmarked with more **stone-cut tombs**.

Ignore a left-hand turnoff pointing straight down to the Grotta dei Pipistrelli (Bat Cave), opting instead for the slightly more gradual descent to pools along the **Fiume Calcinara**. Cross the river and climb to a signposted dirt road that leads back to the Anàktoron (total walking time from the Saramenzana entrance about 1½ hours).

Pantalica's necropolises

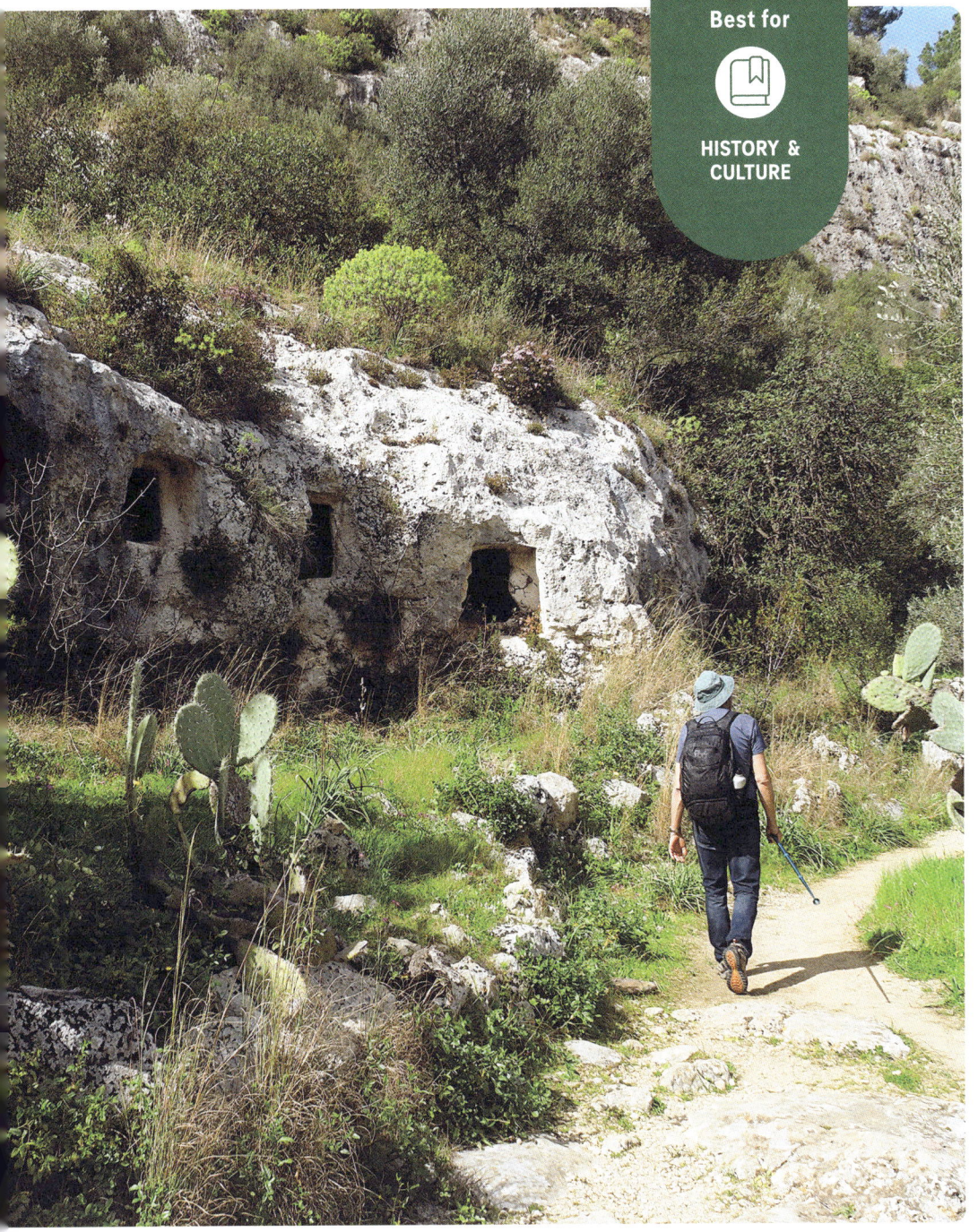

Best for

HISTORY & CULTURE

28

La Rocca di Cefalù

DURATION	DIFFICULTY	DISTANCE	START/END
1.5hrs	Moderate	3km	Piazza del Duomo, Cefalù

TERRAIN	Staircases and rocky trails

Towering high above Cefalù's sandy beach and Arab-Norman cathedral, the craggy outcrop of La Rocca makes an exhilarating half-day adventure. The 45-minute ascent traverses pine-dotted slopes and old town walls to reach the vertiginous 270m summit. Along the way, enjoy pretty views of the cathedral's honey-coloured towers juxtaposed against the deep blue sea. Crowning the hilltop are a ruined 12th-century Norman castle superimposed on a 9th-century Arab citadel, surrounded by sweeping 360-degree panoramic views.

Getting Here

Cefalù is on the main Palermo to Messina train line, served by dozens of trains daily. The Duomo is a 10-minute walk northeast of the station.

Starting Point

The Duomo is the focal point of Cefalù's pedestrianised centre, surrounded by restaurants and other facilities. Parking in downtown Cefalù is challenging, so arriving by train is recommended.

Head south from the cathedral square into Cefalù's narrow streets, walking 300m down bustling Corso Ruggero and turning left onto narrow Vicolo Saraceni. From here, the ancient stone staircase known as **Salita Saraceni** begins winding up the hillside. Pay admission (€5) at the La Rocca entrance booth and continue climbing. Within 10 minutes, cross through the first tier of Cefalù's crenellated town walls, enjoying splendid views over the Tyrrhenian, with a steep rock face in the foreground framing the long sweep of shoreline to your left.

Best for

QUAINT VILLAGES

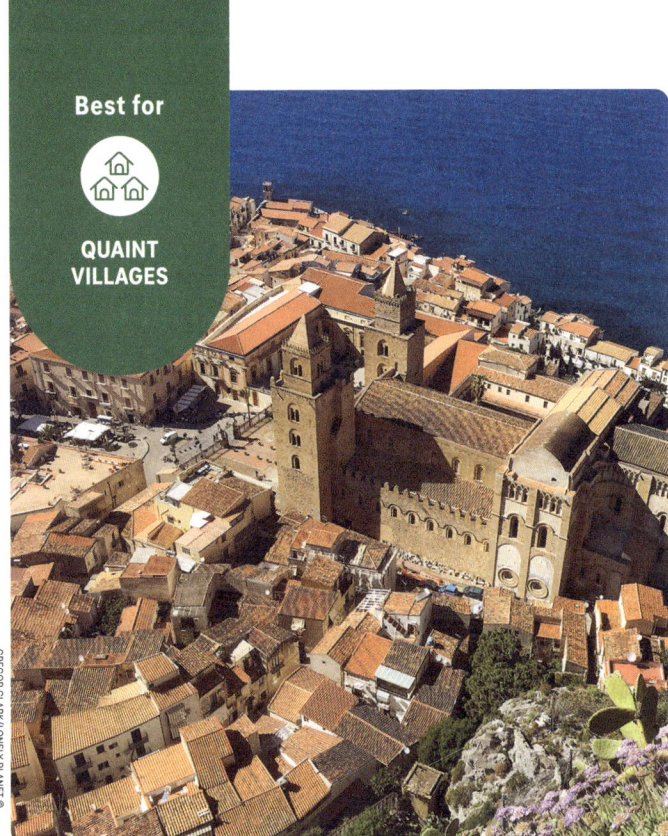

GREGOR CLARK/LONELY PLANET ©

Cefalù's Duomo

Cefalù's Magnificent Cathedral

One of the jewels in Sicily's Arab-Norman crown, Cefalù's magnificent palm-fringed 12th-century Duomo earned Unesco World Heritage status in 2015, along with Palermo's Cappella Palatina and the Cattedrale di Monreale. Filling the central apse, a towering figure of Cristo Pantocratore (Christ All Powerful) is the focal point of the elaborate Byzantine mosaics – Sicily's oldest and best preserved.

02 Turn left at a junction just up the hill, following signs for Tempio di Diana. Here the trail opens onto a high plateau. Continue straight to the cliff's edge, where guardrails allow you to peer straight down over the imposing fortress-like cathedral and the red tile rooftops of Cefalù's medieval centre, which contrast with the deep blue sea far below. Circle back from the **cathedral viewpoint** and stop in at the **Tempio di Diana**, a megalithic structure dating to the 4th or 5th century BC, built of limestone blocks quarried directly from the mountainside. On the same site are a sacred dolmen-type cistern dating to the 8th or 9th century BC, and the remains of a Byzantine church dedicated to St Venera.

03 A wooden signpost directs you uphill towards the **Castello**, which you'll reach after a steady 15- to 20-minute climb. A longtime stronghold for both the Arabs and the Normans, the remains of the castle feature a few decaying battlements commanding exceptional views east and west along the Tyrrhenian coast. A straightforward if sometimes steep trail descends from the castle through open fields bordered by eucalyptus trees to rejoin the trail you came up on. From here, simply retrace your steps to the Duomo.

 Take a Break

Picturesque setting combines with scrumptious Sicilian cuisine at Mandralisca 16 (*facebook.com/mandralisca16*), a bistro with sidewalk seating in an alley gazing up at Cefalù's cathedral towers. Start with a perfect *caponata* (eggplant, olives, capers, onions and celery in a sweet-and-sour tomato sauce), then move on to chickpea, chard and sage soup or *involtini* (roulades) of fish with citrus, bay leaves and breadcrumbs.

BEST DAY WALKS : ITALY   119

29
Riserva Naturale dello Zingaro

Best for

COASTAL SCENERY

Riserva Naturale dello Zingaro

DURATION	DIFFICULTY	DISTANCE	START/END
4–5hrs	Moderate	14km	Scopello entrance

TERRAIN	Undulating coastal hike on dirt paths

Riserva Naturale dello Zingaro shelters one of Sicily's most gorgeous and readily accessible stretches of wild coastline. A network of well-maintained and signposted trails weaves through the park – but the indisputable highlight is the 7km walk hugging the shoreline between the park's Scopello and San Vito Lo Capo entrances. From the main coastal path, side trails fan out to a series of beaches and small museums focusing on the Zingaro's cultural and natural history.

Getting Here
From the town of Scopello, take the SP63 north 2km; the road dead-ends at a parking area adjacent to the park's southern entrance.

Starting Point
The walk starts and ends at the park ticket office, where you'll find trail maps and an occasional food truck selling drinks and snacks.

01 Within paces of the park entrance, you'll pass through a **two-lane tunnel** blasted into the rock. This marks the beginning of the would-be highway through the Zingaro that was cancelled in the early 1980s due to local opposition. As you enter the tunnel, look along the side of the trail for **wooden cutouts** commemorating the 3000 people who staged a pivotal protest march along this stretch of coast in May 1980, eventually leading to the establishment of the Zingaro nature reserve.

Sicily's Original Nature Reserve

The idyllic coastal trail featured in this walk was supposed to be a highway – that is, until concerned local citizens intervened to conserve the Zingaro as Sicily's very first Riserva Naturale. In the late 1970s, planners had begun work to extend the SP63 north from Scopello to San Vito Lo Capo, which would have forever changed this pristine stretch of coast.

In spring 1980, a multi-generational mix of residents and environmentalists joined to protest the proposed road, organising a march through the Zingaro that drew 3000 people and turned the tide in favour of creating the new park.

02 After a brief initial downhill, the trail climbs gently to a right-hand turnoff for the **Museo Naturalistico**, worth a quick visit for its exhibits on the Zingaro's flora, fauna and geology. Lovingly rendered dioramas and drawings introduce you to key park inhabitants, from kestrels, owls and Bonelli's eagles to foxes, dormice and hedgehogs. Additional exhibits feature the Zingaro's wild orchids, geophytes, ferns, lichens and mushrooms, along with medicinal herbs and endemic plants such as the Sicilian snapdragon and yellow star thistle.

03 The beautiful crescent-shaped cove of **Cala Capreria** comes into view a few hundred metres north of the museum. A side path descends here to meet the pebbly beach and turquoise waters below.

04 Rejoin the main trail, climbing steadily uphill for about 1km to the spectacular **viewpoint overlooking Punta Leone**. Here you enjoy your first long views north along the rugged coast, stretching all the way to the park's northern entrance 5km ahead.

05 A few paces downhill, the **Museo della Manna** appears on the left-hand side of the trail. This converted one-room cottage traces Sicily's long history of producing manna, the natural sweetener celebrated in the Bible and derived from the sap of the manna ash tree (*Fraxinus ornus*). Manna production was once common throughout Sicily, including the Zingaro area, but is now limited to the towns of Castelbuono and Pollina in the Monti Madonie.

06 Enjoy more fine views north along the coast as you descend along a wooden fence to a right-hand turnoff for two small beaches tucked into rocky coves. **Cala della Disa**, popular with families, is a shady fine-shingle beach with shallow water, while **Cala Berretta**, just to the north, has big rocks perfect for sunbathing. Along the way, you'll pass a sign on the right for *frutta fresca* – fresh fruit sold by the Zingaro's lone remaining resident, Massimo Amodeo; it's worth popping in to see if he's home!

07 You're now roughly at the trail's midpoint, where a relatively flat stretch leads past a pair of pretty houses on the left painted yellow and salmon pink, shaded by trees and backed by the Zingaro's steep slopes. Nearby, you'll pass another turnoff on the right for **Cala Marinella**. There's no beach as such, but snorkellers love the piercing emerald green waters here, accessed directly from the rocks.

08 A few hundred metres further on, watch for a right-hand turnoff for the wonderful **Museo dell'Intreccio** (Weaving Museum). Housed in an attractive two-room stone building with a red tile roof, the museum is flanked by a few fine examples of the Palma nana (European fan palm tree), whose fronds were traditionally woven by Zingaro residents to create functional and aesthetically pleasing household objects. Inside the main room you'll find a full spectrum of locally woven pieces, including baskets, mats, hats, chair seats and an impressive cylindrical grain storage silo. Upstairs, a second room houses more contemporary woven pieces designed by students from the University of Palermo; the surrounding walls are decorated with frescoes left behind by a German hermit named Hans, who lived here with his dogs in the 1970s.

09 Next stop is the **Grotta dell'Uzzo**, a massive cave reached by a short descent about 15 minutes north of the Museo dell'Intreccio. (En route, ignore a sign on the left for the spur trail to Sughero and Borgo Cosenza, and continue straight on the main trail.) During the Mesolithic period, the cave offered shelter to hunter-gatherers who left behind one of the Mediterranean's most impressive necropolises. These days its most striking feature is its size, with sheer walls of orange and grey rock towering dozens of metres overhead.

10 Turn right towards the coast, following signs to **Cala dell'Uzzo**, the Zingaro's largest and most popular beach. A five-minute walk brings you to this attractive stretch of pebble-strewn sand backed by cacti and palms, where swimmers and sunbathers congregate.

11 Beyond the beach, the trail continues north along the shoreline, passing a **terraced picnic area** with tables and benches where you can break for a snack. Two minutes north of the picnic area you'll come to the Zingaro's former tuna-processing plant, Tonnarella dell'Uzzo, now converted into a museum, the **Museo delle Attività Marinare**. The collection here includes framed portraits of local fish and fishers and a map of Sicily's tuna fisheries – but perhaps most interesting is the series of newspaper articles and photos documenting the protest marches that helped create the Zingaro nature reserve back in 1980.

12 Just below the museum, a side path descends to **Cala Tonnarella dell'Uzzo**, a semicircular beach picturesquely framed by low cliffs and Mediterranean *macchia*. From here, a 10-minute uphill walk brings you to the park's **northern (San Vito Lo Capo) entrance**, where you'll begin the two-hour hike back south to Scopello.

13 About 15 minutes into your return journey, detour briefly inland to visit the last of the park's five museums, the **Museo della Cultura Contadina**. The collection here showcases the Zingaro's rural traditions, with displays of traditional farm equipment and cooking utensils, and bilingual photo exhibits documenting the Zingaro's annual agricultural cycle of ploughing, sowing, reaping, threshing and storage. Retrace your steps back to the Scopello entrance, another 1¾ hours south along the main coastal trail.

Take a Break

It's worth lingering overnight in Scopello, just to enjoy a multicourse dinner at **Pensione Tranchina** (*pensionetranchina.com*) in the heart of the village. This long-standing family-run *pensione*, 2km south of the nature reserve, serves stellar meals featuring home-grown olive oil and abundant local seafood and produce. To be sure of a spot for dinner, book a room with half-board; alternatively, day-trippers can inquire to see if it has a table free.

Segesta

Scopello, the ancient temple and amphitheatre at Segesta, constitutes one of Sicily's most evocative and enduring archaeological highlights. Set on the edge of a deep canyon amid desolate mountains, these 5th-century BC ruins are all that remains of the principal city of the Elymians, an ancient civilisation claiming descent from the Trojans who settled in Sicily in the Bronze Age. Segesta's centrepiece is its remarkably well-preserved temple, with a full set of Doric columns topped by a perfectly intact entablature and pediment, standing in splendid isolation amid fields of wildflowers and grasses. Occasional music concerts held beneath the stars in the amphitheatre just up the hill are nothing short of magical.

Segesta

30

Oasi Faunistica di Vendicari

DURATION	DIFFICULTY	DISTANCE	START/END
2hrs	Easy	8km	Vendicari parking area

TERRAIN	Flat dirt roads and sandy paths

One of Sicily's easiest and most rewarding coastal walks runs through this birdwatcher's paradise just south of Syracuse, where marshes rich in migratory waterfowl share the stage with pretty beaches and the photogenic remains of a historic tuna-processing plant.

Getting Here

You'll need your own wheels. The reserve entrance is down a signposted dirt road off the SP19 between Noto and Pachino.

Starting Point

A dusty car park and a restaurant sit just outside the reserve. Staff at the nearby entrance kiosk hand out free maps.

01 From the car park, follow a stone wall bordered by olive trees to the **park entrance station**. The broad, flat dirt path soon comes to a left-hand turnoff for a bird hide overlooking **Pantano Grande**, Vendicari's largest lagoon. Bear right towards the coast, following a stone-paved walkway onto a wooden boardwalk. You'll soon reach the junction of three broad sand-strewn paths. Straight ahead lies a long beach; right is a bird hide overlooking the Pantano Roveto. Take the left fork, following signs for Tonnara and Calmosche. Within minutes, another left-hand detour leads to the edge of Pantano Grande, where flamingoes often throng the shoreline, while the main trail curves right to Vendicari's abandoned *tonnara* (tuna factory).

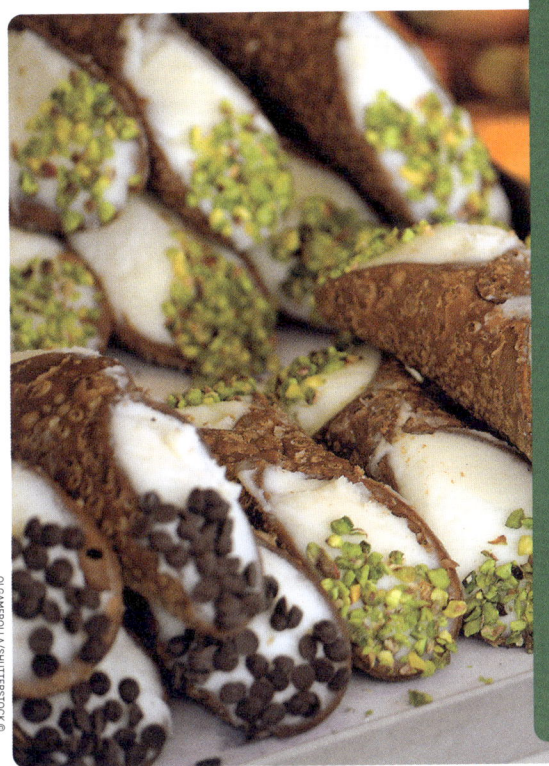

Sicilian Cuisine

Sicily boasts one of Italy's finest cuisines. Feed your post-hike cravings with these specialities:

Arancine Savoury, fried rice balls.

Caponata Sweet-and-sour mix of aubergines, capers and olives.

Pasta alla Norma Pasta with tomatoes, aubergines and salted ricotta.

Pasta con le sarde Pasta with sardines, pine nuts, raisins and wild fennel.

Couscous alla trapanese Fish couscous, typical of Western Sicily.

Cannoli Pastry tubes filled with sweetened ricotta, often finished off with crumbled hazelnuts or pistachios.

Cannoli, Sicily

02 The impressive ruins ahead of you testify to Vendicari's multi-layered history. The ancient Romans processed garum here – a highly prized condiment of salty fermented fish; tuna production also thrived under the Greeks and Arabs, and remained a mainstay of the local economy until WWII. The **tonnara** – now reduced to a maze of processing pools, stone columns and a tall brick chimney – stands lonely sentinel over the waterfront, side by side with the **Torre Sveva**, an imposing stone defensive tower commissioned by the Duke of Noto in 1424 and modified by 16th-century Spanish military engineers.

03 Dwarf palms, wild thyme and prickly pear cactus border the broad path, which soon becomes rockier, threading its way north between the **Pantano Piccolo** and the Ionian Sea. Lizards scurry underfoot as you curve left around a crumbling stucco building and come to another bird hide on the shores of Pantano Piccolo. Just beyond a sign for Cozzo Balsamo, the trail splits, with the right fork contouring the shoreline and the left fork charting a more direct course inland. Within 45 minutes of leaving the tuna factory, a flight of steps on your right drops down to lovely **Calamosche beach**, wedged between low headlands. Linger as long as you like, then retrace your steps to the parking lot.

Take a Break

The baroque hill town of Noto, 13km north of Vendicari, claims two of Italy's finest *gelaterie*: **Dolceria Costanzo** wins the prize for best ice cream – try a lick of pistachio or *amaro* (dark liqueur) – but **Caffè Sicilia** steals the show when it comes to granite (flavoured crushed ice); try classic flavours such as *caffè* (coffee) and *mandorla* (almond), or indulge in seasonal specials like *fragolini* (tiny wild strawberries) and *gelsi* (mulberries). Don't know which to choose? Try them both. (Your secret is safe with us.)

31

Fossa di Vulcano

DURATION	DIFFICULTY	DISTANCE	START/END
2hrs	Moderate	7km	Vulcano hydrofoil dock

TERRAIN	Paved road and broad dirt track

Smoky gateway to Sicily's Aeolian archipelago, the island of Vulcano was celebrated in Roman times as the site of Vulcan's forge. Today it's the first stop on the hydrofoil north from Milazzo. For walkers, Vulcano's star attraction is the straightforward trek up to Fossa di Vulcano (391m), a massive crater whose sulphurous plumes are visible (and sniffable) long before you reach the dock.

Getting Here

Liberty Lines (*libertylines. it*) runs hydrofoils to Vulcano several times daily from neighbouring Lipari (10 minutes) and from Milazzo on the Sicilian 'mainland' (45 minutes).

Starting Point

The hydrofoil dock sits just north of the crater in Vulcano Porto, the island's commercial hub, where you'll find restaurants, cafes, shops and other tourist amenities.

01 Brace yourself for the stench of rotten eggs as you walk 150m west from Vulcano's main dock to the **Pozza dei Fanghi**. Long the island's favourite beauty spot, this pool of thick, coffee-coloured mud is usually filled with curious swimsuit-clad tourists dousing their bodies with sulphurous gloop, then running out to the adjacent seawater pool to rinse off and dip their toes in the natural hot springs bubbling up from under the sea.

02 Return towards the hydrofoil dock and turn right (south) along Vulcano's eastern waterfront. Continue 15 minutes down Vulcano's main street, passing the port and a mix of ferry ticket

Vulcano island

offices, hotels, restaurants and rental agencies to reach the trailhead, on the left side of the road at the base of the volcano. Along the way you'll enjoy insanely cool perspectives of the **mineral-rich slopes** – streaked grey, yellow and pink – above you.

 Splendid **views of the island** unfold as you begin climbing the wide zigzag path gently up the volcano's ruddy, sulphur-streaked flanks. A climb of less than 300m brings you to the rim, where you can peer down into the crater, a spot long mythologised by the Romans as Vulcan's forge. There's no lava here, just hot steam and hissing smoke emanating from the crater's otherworldly depths.

 For truly all-encompassing **views**, continue climbing anti-clockwise around the crater. From the heights along the southern rim, the panorama is breathtaking, with the other six Aeolian islands lined up on the northern horizon and the gaping crater smoking in the foreground. To return to Vulcano's port, simply retrace your steps.

 Take a Break

For a post-volcano feast, stop in at **La Forgia Maurizio**, smack on the path from the volcano to the hydrofoil dock. Maurizio, owner of this devilishly good restaurant, spent 20 winters in Goa, India. Eastern influences sneak into his menu of Sicilian specialities, and several items are vegan- or vegetarian-friendly. Check out the multicourse tasting menu, finished off with homemade kumquat-cardamom liqueur.

32

Punta Troia

DURATION	DIFFICULTY	DISTANCE	START/END
3hrs	Moderate	8km	Marettimo hydrofoil dock

TERRAIN	Packed dirt trails

The wildest, westernmost and least developed of the Egadi Islands off Sicily's west coast, Marettimo is a collection of green mountain peaks and whitewashed houses surrounding a harbour lapped by iridescent turquoise waters. Fanning out from the port, a beautifully maintained, well-marked trail network leads quickly into the unspoilt nature of Marettimo's hinterland: fragrant pine forests, dramatic coastal lookouts and remote beaches.

Getting Here
Liberty Lines (*libertylines. it*) runs hydrofoils to Marettimo several times daily from Trapani on Sicily's west coast. Travel time is 1¼ to 1½ hours.

Starting Point
The hydrofoil dock sits at the centre of Marettimo village, with restaurants, bar-cafes and other services all within easy walking distance.

01 Follow the shoreline north from Marettimo's **hydrofoil dock**, passing Il Veliero restaurant on your left and continuing onto a dirt trail that transitions into a broad flagstoned path. A signboard announces your entry into the **Area Marina Protetta degli Egadi**, a conservation zone protecting the three Egadi islands.

02 Ten minutes from the dock, turn left onto a narrower trail, following signs for Punta Troia. Stone steps help navigate the steeper sections as you climb steadily up the hillside. Soon

Best for

AVOIDING THE CROWDS

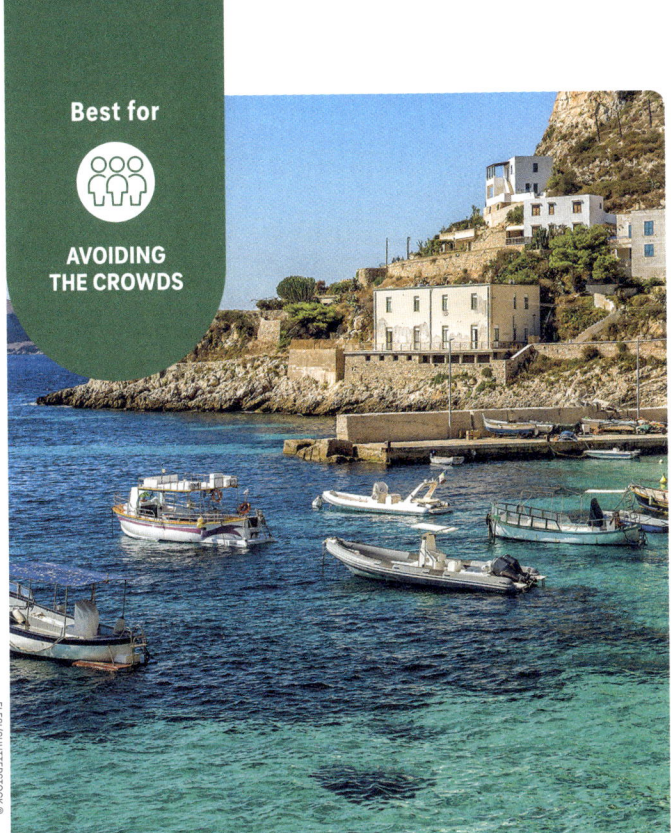

Levanzo

The Prehistoric Cave Art of Levanzo

En route to Marettimo, jump ship on the tiny island of Levanzo to see the prehistoric cave art at **Grotta del Genovese**. Between 6000 and 10,000 years old, the Upper Palaeolithic wall paintings and Neolithic incised drawings at this seaside cave feature bulls, horses, men and tuna. Visits are by guided tour only, and reservations are required (*grottadelgenovese.it*). The all-inclusive tour takes two hours; transport is by boat if weather conditions are favourable – otherwise, it's a 10-minute drive by 4WD, then a steep but scenic 700m descent on foot from the end of the rough gravel road to the cave.

you're enjoying unimpeded **views of the shoreline**, with the craggy headland of Punta Troia looming in the distance. Continue contouring Marettimo's eastern bluffs for the next 45 minutes on a narrow trail high above the deep blue sea. Clusters of flowering **wild rosemary** appear along the trailside, as amazing **views** unfurl back to the village of Marettimo splashed upon the rocks far to the south.

03 Signs warn you to watch your step and stay close to the rock wall on the left as you round the edge of a **picturesque gorge** cutting inland from the sea. Within minutes, you're enjoying tantalising full-on views of **Punta Troia** juxtaposed against the vast, deep-blue sweep of the Mediterranean. Concrete walls and steps facilitate your descent along a steep stretch of trail, as a long downhill leads to the flat isthmus that separates Punta Troia from the rest of the island.

04 It's now just a short climb to the **old fortress** up top, built on the ruins of an earlier Saracen watchtower, on this strategically important pinnacle of land at Marettimo's northeastern tip. Not far from here, in 241 BC, the Romans and Carthaginians once fought the decisive battle of the First Punic War; these days it's about as peaceful a spot as you could wish for. When you're ready to retrace your steps, the walk back to Marettimo's port takes about 1½ hours.

Take a Break

On the waterfront just north of Marettimo's hydrofoil dock, family-run **Trattoria Il Veliero** is a seafood-lover's fantasy. Chef-owner Peppe Bevilacqua goes to the market daily, picking out the freshest catches. Superbly prepared Sicilian classics like *pasta con le sarde* (pasta with sardines) and *fritto misto* (fried shrimp and calamari) share the menu with octopus salad, tuna carpaccio, perfectly grilled fish and countless other delights.

Also Try...

Lago di Biviere

Alicudi

DURATION	DIFFICULTY	DISTANCE
3.5hrs	Hard	5km

Ever dream of getting away from it all? The remote island of Alicudi off Sicily's north coast is as isolated a place as you'll find in the entire Mediterranean. Last stop on the Aeolian Islands' hydrofoil line, Alicudi has less than 100 residents and no roads, with boats, mules and hiking providing the only transport.

To reach Alicudi's central peak (675m), follow the blue arrows up from the port. The two-hour trek scales a steep series of stone staircases (nearly 1400 steps in all) past pastel-coloured houses, citrus trees, cactus and wildflowers, with the church of San Bartolo marking the hike's midpoint. At the T-intersection up top, turn left along a stone wall to circle the extinct volcanic crater, or right across a grassy plateau to the vertigo-inducing cliffs at Alicudi's western edge. The end-of-the-world feeling here is intoxicating.

Lago di Biviere

DURATION	DIFFICULTY	DISTANCE
5hrs	Moderate	16km

Sicily's sun-dappled beech forests are the setting for this walk through the wilds of the Nebrodi Mountains.

From Portella Calacudera, 1.5km off the SS289, follow signs for Lago di Biviere downhill along an unpaved track. You're walking along the Dorsale dei Nebrodi, a 70km segment of the Sentiero Italia, Italy's long-distance hiking trail. Passing the Lago Maulazzo reservoir after 2.5km, the road descends another 5.3km, opening onto views of the Aeolian Islands framed by the Rocche di Crasto as you approach Lago di Biviere. On a clear day, Mt Etna is reflected in the lake's waters, while wild horses and pigs scurry about the fields and forest. Afterwards, stop in at nearby Relais Villa Miraglia (*relaisvillamiraglia.it/restaurant*), a converted hunting lodge serving Nebrodi specialities such as roast lamb, pork and wild mushrooms.

Mt Etna

Mt Etna

DURATION	DIFFICULTY	DISTANCE
1.5hrs	Moderate	5km

Europe's largest active volcano, Mt Etna (3350m) is an irresistible magnet for walkers.

From Rifugio Sapienza (1920m) on Etna's southern slopes, the **Funivia dell'Etna** (*funiviaetna.com*) whisks you up to 2500m, where a wide gravel road ascends through an otherworldly landscape of grey ash to the Torre del Filosofo (2920m), a favourite vantage point over Etna's craters. How close you can get depends on the level of volcanic activity. Return downhill in time to catch the last cable car.

Capo di Milazzo

DURATION	DIFFICULTY	DISTANCE
1hr	Easy	2km

On Sicily's north coast, the one-hour loop around sickle-shaped Capo di Milazzo makes for an easy, scenic day hike.

Park near the lighthouse at the end of the isthmus and walk through a landscape of olive groves, cactus and stone walls to reach the Piscina di Venere, an idyllic natural pool at the cape's western tip. Next, follow the shoreline south past the atmospheric ruins of the 13th-century Santuario Rupestre di Sant'Antonio, where St Anthony of Padua famously sought refuge after a shipwreck. From here, the trail climbs back to the parking lot.

Pragser Wildsee (Lago di Braies, p150)

The Dolomites & Stelvio

33 Hans & Paula Steger Weg
Wander the wide-open expanses of Europe's largest alpine meadow. **p136**

34 Passo Gardena to Vallunga
Descend from sublime rocky high country to a steep-walled green valley. **p138**

35 Sassolungo Circuit
Circuit Watch hang-gliders soaring above Val Gardena. **p142**

36 Tre Cime di Lavaredo
Circumnavigate this iconic three-toothed massif near Cortina d'Ampezzo. **p144**

37 Alpe di Fanes
Follow the legendary Alta Via 1 to an alpine hut and over a steep pass. **p146**

38 Pragser Wildsee
Enjoy a family-friendly stroll around this mountain-fringed lake. **p150**

39 Percorso delle Segherie
Tour historic water-driven mills in a verdant valley at Stelvio National Park. **p154**

40 Adolf Munkel Weg
Gaze up at the soul-stirring spires of the Odle (Geisler) group. **p156**

Explore

The Dolomites & Stelvio

Among the planet's most bewitching mountains, the Dolomites thrust their jagged spires up from the emerald pastures of northeastern Italy. Until WWI, much of this region belonged to Austria, a fact reflected in the continued prevalence of German and in the ubiquitous apple strudel and dumplings served at the region's trailside huts. The walking tradition here goes back centuries, and the wealth of trails – impeccably signposted and easily accessible by summer gondolas and chairlifts – is astounding. To the west, the alpine heights of Parco Nazionale dello Stelvio offer similar enticement for hikers, with a comparable network of trails and mountain *rifugi*.

Bolzano

Straddling the confluence of the Adige and Isarco rivers and well-placed on the busy train line between Verona, Innsbruck and Munich, South Tyrol's capital makes a delightful gateway to the Dolomites. A long-time conduit between Italy and the Alps, Bolzano (Bozen in German) buzzes with multicultural energy and a high quality of life. The city's backdrop of verdant foothills and rocky pinnacles sets off rows of pastel-painted townhouses, while bicycles ply riverside paths and wooden market stalls heave with alpine cheeses, speck (cured ham) and dark, seeded loaves.

Selva di Val Gardena

Cradled between the mountain walls of Sassolungo, the Sella massif, and Parco Naturale Puez-Odle, tiny Selva sits at the far end of Ladin-speaking Val Gardena, equipped with gondolas that can whisk you in minutes to the surrounding high-country trails.

Corvara in Badia

Val Badia's tourist hub, chic Corvara bustles with skiers in winter and hikers in summer. Its prime position at the foot of Passo Gardena makes it a good jumping-off point for hikes in the high country of Parco Naturale Puez-Odle, but it's also a convenient base for exploring Parco Naturale Fanes-Sennes-Braies to the east.

Cortina d'Ampezzo

The Italian supermodel of ski resorts, Cortina d'Ampezzo is pricey and undeniably beautiful. The town's stone church steeples and pleasant cascading piazzas are framed by magnificent mountains, making Cortina a sought-after summertime base for hiking, biking and rock climbing.

WHEN TO GO

Summer and early autumn are prime time for exploring the Dolomites' *alte vie* (high-altitude walking trails). Note that many *rifugi*, hotels, chairlifts and gondolas wait until late May or early June to open for the summer season, and close up shop in late September or early October.

TRANSPORT

The closest airports are at Verona, Venice and Innsbruck (Austria). From Verona, Trenitalia's north–south railway line parallels the A22 motorway up through the Adige valley to Trento and Bolzano, then over Brenner Pass to Innsbruck. An admirably efficient network of smaller train and bus lines, operated by SAD (*sad.it*), fans out from Bolzano to side valleys such as Val Gardena, Val Badia, Val Venosta and Val Pusteria. Many local hotels offer a free public transport pass.

In neighbouring Trentino, **Ferrovia Trento–Malè** (*trentinotrasporti.it/en/travel-with-us/train*) runs trains through the Val di Sole at the edge of Parco Nazionale dello Stelvio, while **Dolomiti Bus** (*dolomitibus.it*) serves Cortina d'Ampezzo to the east. If you're short on time, hiring a car may still be the most efficient way to get around; roads are notoriously squiggly but well signposted and maintained.

 WHAT'S ON

Soirées at Tyrol Castle
In June and July, enjoy live concerts by international ensembles in the Great Hall of South Tyrol's ancestral 12th-century castle.

South Tyrolean Knights' Festival
The Alps' largest festival of medieval-style jousting is held against the atmospheric backdrop of castles and abbeys in Schluderns in August.

Kalterer Weinfest
The wine-growing village of Kaltern celebrates the Adige Valley's viticultural traditions in August, with free-flowing wine, traditional culinary specialities and music in the streets.

Vipiteno/Sterzing Dumpling Festival
Savoury and sweet dumplings, a mainstay of every Dolomites hiker's diet, take centre stage at this annual culinary festival in September near Brixen.

 WHERE TO STAY

The Dolomites boast some of the world's most stylish alpine resorts, small hotels and campgrounds, along with numerous comfy farm stays (see *redrooster.it*). Higher up the mountainside, a host of well-placed and impeccably maintained *rifugi* (mountain huts) offer cosy dorm-style accommodation with down duvets, hot showers and hearty home-cooked meals.

Resources

South Tyrol Tourism (*suedtirol.info*) Excellent website with abundant info about hiking trails and other tourist attractions.

Parco Nazionale dello Stelvio (*stelviopark.it*) Comprehensive info on this national park just west of the Dolomites.

Sportler (*sportler.com*) Superb source for outdoor gear and trekking maps, with shops in Bolzano, Selva di Val Gardena and several other locations around Trentino and South Tyrol.

SAD (*sad.it/it/siitimetables query*) Helpful resource for bus timetables throughout South Tyrol.

Salewa (*salewa.com*) South Tyrolean manufacturer of alpine footwear, with a huge showroom and climbing wall in Bolzano.

La Sportiva (*lasportiva.com*) Trentino-based manufacturer of hiking boots and outdoor gear, with headquarters and a retail outlet in Ziano di Fiemme.

33

Hans & Paula Steger Weg

DURATION	DIFFICULTY	DISTANCE	START/END
33hrs	Moderate	9km	Seiser Alm Bahn/Ritsch bus stop

TERRAIN	Undulating dirt roads and trails

Spreading like a soft green blanket at the foot of the Dolomites, the Seiser Alm (Alpe di Siusi) is Europe's vastest alpine meadow, threaded with some of Italy's most enchanting footpaths. This walk between the ski villages of Compatsch (Compaccio) and Saltria undulates through forests and green pastures.

Getting Here

Take the Seiser Alm cable car (seiseralm.it) from Seis (Siusi) to Compatsch. There's paid parking at Compatsch, but the road from Seis closes between 9am and 5pm to discourage driving.

Starting Point

Compatsch has abundant shops, restaurants and free restrooms at the Seiser Alm cable-car station.

01 From the cable-car station, head 250m downhill to the paved Compatsch–Saltria road. Turn left, passing the tourist office on your right, then left again at the Bergrettung Südtirol first-aid station. Trail 30 (also labelled 'Hans and Paula Steger Weg') starts as a broad dirt road heading east across the ski slopes. Within 10 minutes, cross the paved road at a bus stop and continue gently uphill. Past a junction with trail 6B for Gostner Schwaige, the unpaved track soon emerges into grassy pastures extending to the mountainous horizon on all sides. Just beyond a new junction with trail 6, you'll come to the edge of a

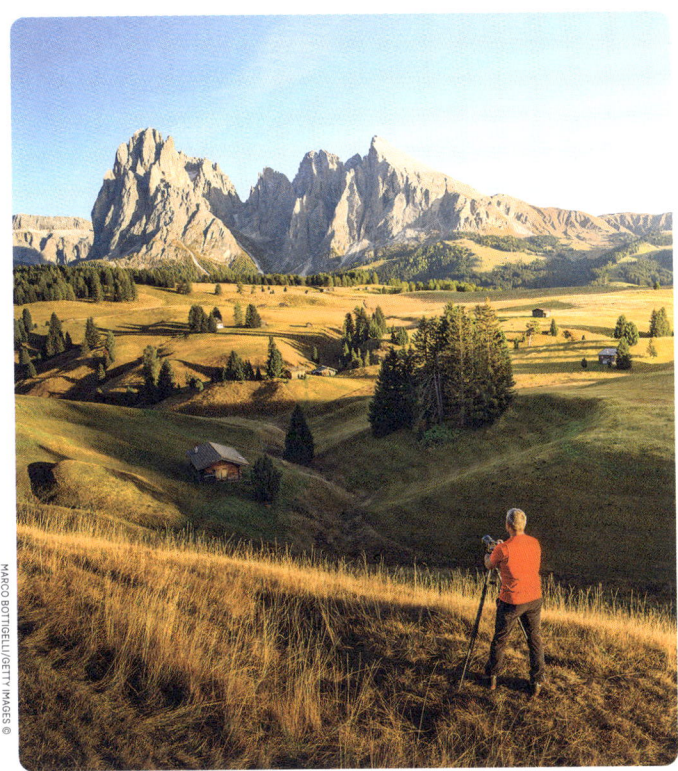

Seiser Alm (Alpe di Siusi)

meadow swooping east towards Sassolungo. **Tree-shaded benches** invite you to sit and contemplate this majestic landscape. Your path ahead is visible on the hillside far below, dotted with cows and hikers. About 45 minutes from Compatsch, trail 30 again meets the paved road. Turn right (south) here, following signs for trail 12A (still marked 'Hans and Paula Steger Weg').

02 Grazing cows and wooden huts with enormous piles of stacked firewood spread across green waves of pastureland as far as the eye can see. Starting as a broad unpaved farm track, trail 12A meanders between fields and forest, reaching **Laranzer Schwaige hut** – a pleasant spot for a snack break – in about half an hour. Trail 12A branches left here onto a narrower path (signs for Almrosen Hütte), soon crossing a creek and passing through a gate. The forest encroaches as you continue along the creek valley. After crossing another bridge, climb away from the creek, and you'll soon reach another signpost.

03 Briefly jog right, then left on trail 12 towards **Saltria**, following the fence line at the meadow's edge. Cross a boardwalk and drop into the forest, where the trail widens into a dirt road. Within 15 minutes, turn left again, descending a narrow woodsy path (signs for Saltria). Turn right at the bottom, then left onto a paved road on Saltria's outskirts. Beyond the Sporthotel Floralpina, come to a T-intersection near a bus stop. Turn left on trail 30 towards Compatsch, briefly following the pavement, then forking left onto a footpath through a mix of forest and meadows. After crossing a wooden bridge, the trail climbs high grassy slopes with delirious **views** east to Sassolungo. About 25 minutes from Saltria, reach the Ritsch bus stop on the main road, where you can catch bus 11 or 14 back to Compatsch.

Take a Break

'Locally sourced' says it all at Gostner Schwaige (*gostnerschwaige.com*). Dairy products come from the barn next door, while salads come decorated with a rainbow of wildflowers from the adjacent garden and pastures. Other specialities include hay soup, home-cured meats and refreshing herb-infused soft drinks bottled on-site.

34

Passo Gardena to Vallunga

DURATION	DIFFICULTY	DISTANCE	START/END
6hrs	Hard	17km	Passo Gardena/Dantercepies cable-car base station

TERRAIN	Steep rocky trails, flat dirt roads

Passo Gardena

It's hard to imagine a more satisfying introduction to the Dolomites than this loop through the heart of Parco Naturale Puez Odle, from the windswept mountain ridges above Passo Gardena to the cliff-fringed cow pastures of Vallunga. Yes, it's a long walk, with its fair share of climbing at the start – but the hike's overall profile is downhill, thanks to a cable car that zips you into the high country to start the day. Meanwhile, the opportunity to break for lunch at Rifugio Puez – one of the Dolomites' iconic mountain huts – makes it the more enticing.

Getting Here

Reach Passo Gardena by taking the Dantercepies cable car (*dantercepies.it*) from its base station in Selva to its upper station near the pass; alternatively, drive up to Passo Gardena and park in one of the paid car parks along the SS243.

Starting Point

Paid parking, food, drinks and restrooms are all available at Passo Gardena.

01 A quick and easy ride on the Dantercepies gondola whisks you from Selva di Val Gardena up into the glorious high country where this walk begins. Alight into the dizzying mountainscape above **Passo Gardena**, one of the Dolomites' most magnificent passes – known in German as **Grödnerjoch** and in Ladin as **Jëuf de Frea** or **Ju de Frara**. From the upper cable-car station follow trail 12A towards Jimmi Hütte and Forcella Cir. Alternatively, if you've driven up to Passo Gardena, follow signs for trail 2 uphill (northeast) from the parking lot towards Passo Crespëina and Jimmi Hütte.

BEST DAY WALKS : ITALY

Trailside Gastronomy

Perhaps the greatest joy of hiking in the Dolomites is the food. Wherever you walk you'll find mountain huts serving home-cooked alpine treats that reflect the region's multicultural roots. Austrian-style *knödel* (dumplings) share the menu with Italian and Ladin pasta specialities such as *mezzelune* (spinach-ricotta ravioli) and *casunziei* (beet-filled pasta with poppy seeds), accompanied by excellent draft beer, refreshing Radler (beer mixed with lemonade) and regional wines such as sparkling Trentino DOC or ruby-red Lagrein. Afterwards, save room for the ever-tempting *Apfelstrudel* (apple strudel) and *Kaiserschmarren* (fluffy pancakes with lingonberries)!

02 From **Jimmi Hütte** (Rifugio Jimmy; 2222m), begin a steady 45-minute climb along the legendary Alta Via 2 towards the impressive sawtooth ridge to your north, enjoying increasingly expansive **views** south back over the Sella group as you go. Here you're in the northern reaches of one of Europe's most iconic long-distance hikes, stretching 185km from Brixen (Bressanone) near the Austrian border all the way to Feltre, in the Piave valley above Venice. Trekking enthusiasts devote two weeks to hiking the Alta Via 2 in its entirety; you'll be getting a taste of one of its most spectacular sections over the next two hours. As you near Forcella Cir, the trail weaves through a landscape of massive rocky spires thrusting skyward.

03 From atop **Forcella Cir** (2462m), enjoy sweeping new perspectives into the **Val de Chedul**, a long narrow valley to your north. Trail 2 drops abruptly over the edge, wasting no time in pointing you east towards your next goal, the 2528m Forcella de Crespëina. Climb east up the broad valley at the base of rock-strewn slopes, ignoring signs for trail 12 to Vallunga and Val de Chedul.

04 A spiky two-pronged stick marks the summit of **Forcella de Crespëina**, where glances west back down the long, distinctively U-shaped glacial Chedul valley compete for your attention with views over the rocky wasteland that lies ahead. After catching your breath, descend into the barren bowl to your northeast, following signs for Rifugio Puez en route to another saddle 30 minutes away; around the halfway point you'll pass **Lech de Crespëina**, a lonely alpine lake to the left of the trail.

05 Your next major landmark is the **Forcella de Ciampei** (2366m), a low pass with **astounding views** east down a steep-walled valley towards Val Badia and west over the deep verdant Vallunga (which will be your return route to Selva at the end of this walk). For now, the Alta Via lives up to its name, staying high above both valleys as it forges on towards Rifugio Puez.

06 Alta Via 2 continues along the high ridgeline, yielding ever more impressive views down over Vallunga, with an occasional flock of sheep posing picturesquely beside the trail. Within 40 minutes, a set of tattered flags (representing Italy, South Tyrol and the European Union) flapping in the wind announces your arrival at **Rifugio Puez** (2475m), a perfect spot to break for lunch.

07 Leave Rifugio Puez via trail 2, peering steeply down into the deep green pastures of Vallunga 700m below. Within about 20 minutes, trail 16 branches left at a signposted junction for Vallunga (Langental), and almost immediately begins steeply descending across a meadow towards a sheer rock wall to the south. The route soon bears left, charting a zigzag course at the foot of the wall, then dropping down a series of log steps as it continues descending through rocky meadows with fantastic **views** of Vallunga ahead, slowly getting closer.

08 As it nears the valley floor, trail 16 re-enters the forest, then makes a final rocky descent along a river gorge as the full verdant sweep of **Vallunga** comes into view. Upon reaching the valley, turn right onto a wide, unpaved track, descending gradually for the next 40 minutes through broad grassy meadows filled with cows, dotted with occasional patches of evergreen forest and backed by sheer rock walls. About 25 minutes into the descent, you can refill your water bottles at a freshwater spring pouring into a hollow log on the right.

09 Standing astride a grassy field on the right, the sweet little chapel of **San Silvestro** (Silvesterkapelle Wolkenstein) marks the far end of the valley, on the outskirts of Selva. Soon thereafter, you'll pass the Jausenstation La Ciajota, a great place to break for a beer and a bite before walking the remaining 20 minutes back to the Dantercepies cable car in the heart of the village.

☕ Take a Break

On a high craggy ridgeline with bird's-eye views down to Vallunga's green meadows, **Rifugio Puez** (*rifugiopuez.it*) is the kind of mountain oasis that old-school hikers dream of: totally no frills, with a menu that's all about loading you up with calories and sending you back out on the trail. Grab a bowl of dumplings in broth or a plate of eggs, speck and potatoes, finish it off with a quick apple strudel, and you're good to go!

Val de Chedul (p1390)

Circling the Sella Massif

The Sella Ronda, a 40km circumnavigation of the Gruppo di Sella range – linked by various cable cars and chairlifts – is one of the Alps' iconic ski routes. The tour takes in four passes and the four surrounding valleys – Val Gardena, Val Badia, Arabba and Val di Fassa – all deeply steeped in the region's unique Ladin heritage. In summer, the same trails are utilised by mountain bikers and there's a hop-on, hop-off bus for walkers. The paved roads surrounding the Sella massif also figure prominently in the annual Giro d'Italia bike race, and one or two days each summer, the whole driving loop around the mountain is closed to motorised traffic during Sella Ronda Bike Day (sellarondabikeday.com).

35

Sassolungo Circuit

DURATION	DIFFICULTY	DISTANCE	START/END
5hrs	Moderate	14km	Passo Sella Resort

TERRAIN		Dirt roads and trails

There's no Dolomites landmark more captivating than Sassolungo (Langkofel; 3181m) or its kid brother Sassopiatto (Plattkofel; 2969m). Beloved by hikers, climbers and hang-gliders, these twin monoliths dominate the landscape south of Val Gardena. This long but leisurely high-country loop takes you around the base of both peaks.

Getting Here

From Selva, take SAD bus 471 to Passo Sella Resort (30 minutes), or drive 12km up the tortuous SS242.

Starting Point

At the trailhead, Passo Sella Resort has a restaurant, with ample parking nearby. Food, drinks and restrooms are available at several *rifugi* along the trail.

 Set off southwest on trail 557 towards Col Rodela. The undulating track passes **Rifugio Salei** and **Chalet Margherita** on its half-hour climb to **Forcella Rodella** (2318m), where a signboard marks the start of the Friedrich August Weg. You're now on one of the Dolomites' oldest trails, named for the mountain-loving Saxon King Frederick Augustus (1750–1827) and inaugurated in 1911. **Sassopiatto** rears above meadows on the northern horizon, complemented by views south towards Canazei. A five-minute stroll brings you to **Rifugio Friedrich August** with its yak-themed decor and killer **views**.

 For the next 90 minutes, the narrow Friedrich August Weg meanders through meadows beneath Sassopiatto's rocky spires. Beyond

142   BEST DAY WALKS : ITALY

Best for

MOUNTAIN VIEWS

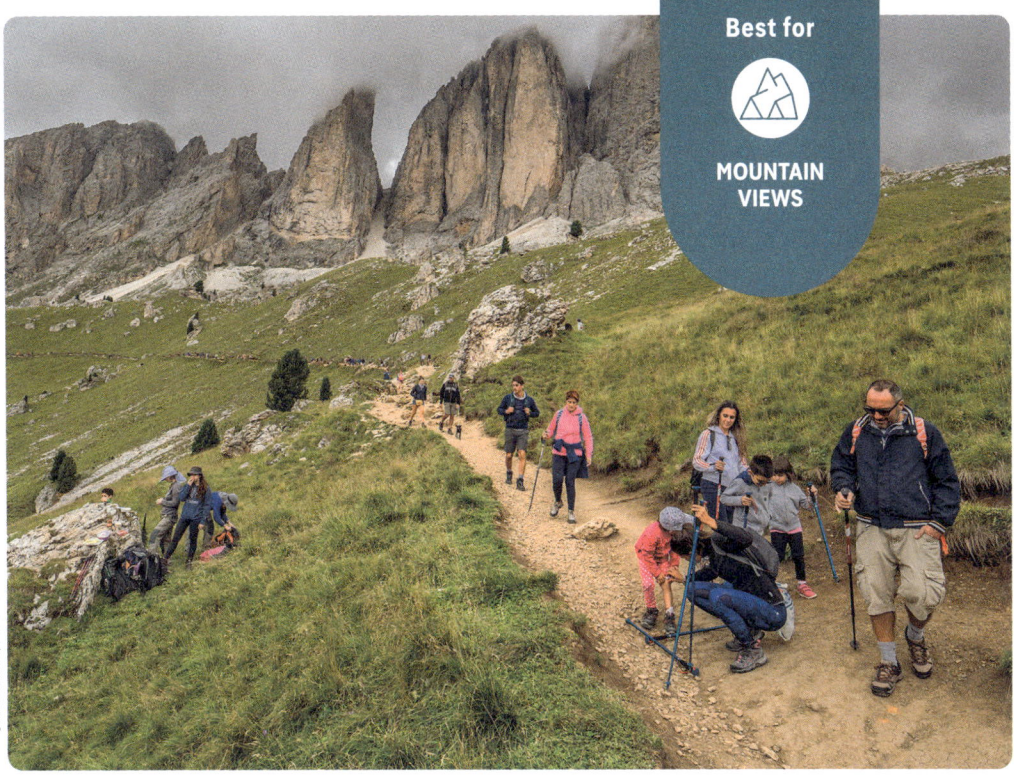

Sassolungo

Rifugio Sandro Pertini, the trail gets rockier and the meadows steepen, affording near-vertical views up Sassopiatto's south face. Near **Plattkofelhütte** – the Friedrich August Weg's official endpoint – the ridgeline of **Sciliar** (Schlern) appears on the western horizon as you pass a turnoff for trail 553A to **Malga Sassopiatto**, a farm selling homemade cheese.

03 From Plattkofelhütte, trail 527 (signs for Langkofelhütte/Rifugio Vicenza) descends along a broad road, then narrows and weaves 30 minutes north through meadows along Sassopiatto's western flank. Near **Piz da Uridl** (2101m), emerge onto a high shelf with **sweeping views** over Saltria and the Alpe di Siusi. The trail descends through trees, then rises to cross scree-strewn slopes, revealing views northeast to Sassolungo. At a prominent crossroads, trail 527 veers southeast to the legendary climbers' hut, Langkofelhütte, while you follow trail 526 north towards Comici.

04 Trail 526 climbs to a promontory with great views north into Val Gardena. Turn east here to begin circumnavigating Sassolungo's north face, winding through scree at the base of colossal cliffs. Within 40 minutes, killer views over the Sella massif open up at **Rifugio Emilio Comici** (2154m). Complete the loop with a 45-minute jaunt through the meadows below Sassolungo's eastern face. Starting as a broad track, trail 526 eventually narrows and descends through the rugged City of Rocks to reach the Passo Sella.

Take a Break

On a high ridge near the hike's midpoint, the Kasseroler family's **Plattkofelhütte** (plattkofel.com) has been feeding hungry hikers since 1935. The alpine-Mediterranean menu features many ingredients grown at their nearby farm, Maso Örtlhof.

36

Tre Cime di Lavaredo

DURATION	DIFFICULTY	DISTANCE	START/END
3hrs	Moderate	9km	Rifugio Auronzo

TERRAIN	Dirt roads and trails

When the Dolomites attained Unesco World Heritage status in 2009, the Tre Cime emerged as the region's official symbol. Soaring to nearly 3000m, these three ravishing rock towers exert a magnetic attraction on all who venture near. This popular loop circumnavigates the massif, offering front-row views from multiple angles.

Getting Here

Dolomitibus (*dolomitibus.it*) runs buses from Cortina d'Ampezzo (one hour, 22km). Drivers must pay a toll on the SP49 from Misurina.

Starting Point

At the foot of the Tre Cime, Rifugio Auronzo offers parking, restrooms, food and lodging.

 01 The Tre Cime tower is to your left as you leave Rifugio Auronzo on trail 101, a flat path signposted for Rifugio Lavaredo. Within 15 minutes, pass a **chapel** dedicated to the Italian soldiers who died here in WWI. Continue another 10 minutes around the mountain's base to **Rifugio Lavaredo** (2344m), a cute two-storey structure whose red shutters contrast with the stark, treeless rockscape. Hikers crowd the front terrace, sipping coffee and beers.

 02 The views keep getting better as trail 101 narrows and winds closer to Tre Cime's crags. A steady 10-minute ascent brings you to **Forcella Lavaredo** (Paternsattel), a high saddle marking the border between Belluno and South Tyrol. Spectacular **Dolomites vistas** unfold in all directions, and a

Best for MOUNTAIN VIEWS

Tre Cime di Lavaredo

plaque commemorates Pope John Paul II's visit to this spot in 1996. The northern horizon is dominated by **Toblinger Knoten**, a blocky tower of rock jutting above the red roof of the precariously perched Dreizinnenhütte (Rifugio Locatelli). Trail 101, now an unpaved track, snakes downhill for 20 minutes to a junction below the *rifugio*.

03 A signpost announces that you've joined the Alta Via 4. Turn right, following signs uphill towards **Dreizinnenhütte**. In 10 minutes, you're on top of the world, with the *rifugio*'s terrace offering a **panoramic lunch stop**. Pause to admire the **Laghi dei Piani**, a pair of lakes adjoining the *rifugio*, then return to the junction below. This time head south on trail 105 towards Lange Alm, with the north face of the Tre Cime looming ahead. A long descent, partly on log steps, leads into a bowl before climbing back up the opposite side.

04 Arrive at **Langalmhütte** (2283m), a massive stone hut with outdoor seating on rustic wood benches and a menu featuring organic yogurt, homemade cakes, cold cuts, wood-oven bread and local draft beer. Time for another break? Sure, why not! You're now only 40 minutes from Rifugio Auronzo. Follow trail 105 past a small lake and over **Forcella Col de Mezo** summit (2315m), completing the loop with a final descent past a whimsical collection of cairns.

 Take a Break

A hikers' beacon of hope amidst Tre Cime's rocky wastes, **Dreizinnenhütte** (*dreizinnenhuette.com*) sits at the foot of evocatively named Sausage Mountain (Frankfurter Würstl in German, Monolite della Salsiccia in Italian). Feast on regional specialities such as *casunziei con finferli* (Cortina-style half-moon pasta with chanterelles) in the wood-panelled dining room or on the panoramic outdoor terrace.

37

Alpe di Fanes

Rifugio Scotoni, Dolomites

DURATION	DIFFICULTY	DISTANCE	START/END
7hrs	Hard	20km	Capanna Alpina

TERRAIN	Dirt roads and trails, some very steep

Forming the heart of Parco Naturale Fanes-Sennes-Braies, the Alpe di Fanes is renowned as one of the most evocative settings in the Dolomites. Centuries of potent Ladin legends have their roots in this mystical landscape, and JRR Tolkien is said to have drawn inspiration for *The Hobbit* and *The Lord of the Rings* from this half-ethereal, half-forbidding high country. This epic loop takes you first across the high Fanes plateau, then gives you a taste of the challenging Alta Via 1, one of Italy's most exhilarating long-distance hiking trails.

Getting Here
From Corvara, take SAD bus 465 to Sciaré (25 minutes) and walk the 15-minute dirt road to Capanna Alpina, or drive 11km to Armentarola and follow signs 1.5km off the SP37 to the parking lot.

Starting Point
Food, drinks, picnic tables, restrooms and paid parking are all available at Capanna Alpina.

01 Fronting a green meadow at the threshold of **Parco Naturale Fanes-Sennes-Braies**, the trailside snack shack of **Capanna Alpina** makes an inspiring spot to launch into your journey. Embark on a broad dirt track, with the rocky sentinels of Piz dl Lech (2654m) and Piz dles Cunturines (3064m) standing watch over the verdant valley before you. Within a couple of minutes, your outbound route (signposted as trail 11) branches left towards Col de Locia, while trail 20 (your eventual return route) branches right to Rifugio Scotoni.

Linguistic Diversity

If you're a first-time visitor to the Dolomites, you may be surprised to find that Italian is not always the predominant language. Especially in South Tyrol, which belonged to the Austro-Hungarian Empire until 1918, German is still the mother tongue of most residents. And a handful of valleys in the Dolomites, including Val Badia, Val Gardena and Val di Fassa, are still strongholds of ancient Ladin, a Latin-derived cousin of the Romansch language spoken in southeastern Switzerland. You'll often see addresses and other signage written in two or even three languages, so be prepared!

02 **Views back down the valley** get better and better as the trail passes first through grassy meadows, then begins steadily climbing towards **Col de Locia**. About 45 minutes into the walk, a **natural spring** on the right lets you know you're nearing the summit (a climb of nearly 350m from the parking lot). From here, a series of log steps brings you up top, where **amazing views** open up south towards Marmolada from a wood bench and railing at the precipice's edge.

03 Following signs for Gran Fanes, the trail now descends towards a **rocky creek** at the edge of the high Fanes plateau. Within 10 minutes the trail crosses the creek and widens, climbing gently as it parallels the creek bed, then descends again to cross a narrow log bridge, with the Fanes high country opening up in the distance.

04 Just over an hour into the walk, reach a **key junction with Alta Via 1**, one of the Dolomites' fabled high routes (signposted on the right here as trail 20B to Lago Lagazuoi). You'll be taking this trail later in the day, but for now continue straight on trail 11 to Gran Fanes. For the next 40 minutes, wide-open **vistas** abound as the broad, nearly flat trail traverses the high plateau, with larger mountains looming on either side. About halfway along you'll pass a huge expanse of boulders cascading down the slopes of **Piza Nord** (2834m) on the right.

05 Enjoy long views east and downstream across rock-strewn meadows as you cross a bridge and arrive at **Malga Gran Fanes**, a hut at the junction with trail 10 coming up from Cortina d'Ampezzo. The gorgeous vistas continue as trail 11 winds gradually uphill and north towards a low pass.

BEST DAY WALKS : ITALY   147

☕ Take a Break

A welcoming oasis in the heart of the mountains, **Rifugio Fanes** (*rifugiofanes.com*) seduces passing hikers with its sunny front terrace and platters of delicious South Tyrolean fare. Go for bratwurst and sauerkraut, goulash with polenta, trout with sautéed veggies or the colourful Knödeltris – a trio of beet, spinach and alpine cheese dumplings. Whatever you do, don't leave without sampling at least one dessert (hint: the buckwheat Torte is a perennial favourite).

Continue following signs for Fanes and Pederü, and you'll soon reach an **iron cross** on your right memorialising the Tiroler Standschützen, Austrian troops who fought in these remote uplands during WWI.

 The trail levels off at **Lé de Limo**, a lake on the right, then begins descending along a wide dirt road with nice views north to a new range of mountains. Within 15 minutes from the lake, follow a crude wooden signpost pointing downhill towards **Rifugio Fanes** on the right. A narrow, steep trail brings you in short order to the front terrace of this rather luxurious mountain hut, which makes an excellent lunch stop.

 Retrace your steps south across the Fanes plateau to the junction with trail 20B (a walk of 1¼ to 1½ hours). Fork left here and begin following blazes painted on rocks beside the trail. Dramatic **rock faces** begin peeking out above the forested lowlands ahead as the trail climbs – gradually at first, then more steeply – towards the saddle at Forcella del Lago.

 Just beyond a **hand-carved wooden memorial plaque** on the left, the trail begins crossing scree slopes towards rock pinnacles. The ensuing 45-minute climb reveals astounding views west towards green valleys and slopes far below. As you near the summit, **Forcella del Lago** comes into view as a distinct notch in the barren rockscape ahead.

 Nothing you've seen on the north side prepares you for the **jaw-dropping views** south from Forcella del Lago (2486m). Directly ahead, sheer-edged slopes plummet into the valley of Lago Lagazuoi. You now begin an implausibly steep descent on the masterfully engineered Alta Via 1, which runs 150km through the Dolomites from the Pragser Wildsee to Belluno. The views down to Lago Lagazuoi far below (300m to be exact) are riveting as you pick your way down a series of switchbacks anchored by rough-and-ready log and stone steps for the next 45 minutes or so.

 The trail begins hugging the cliff face to your left as it continues its steady descent towards the lake, with the continuation of Alta Via 1 traversing raw scree slopes visible far ahead. Level off briefly as you finally reach the frigid shores of **Lago Lagazuoi**, then resume your precipitous descent towards Rifugio Scotoni, following signs for trail 20 on your right at a signposted junction.

 Set in a stunning green valley backed by craggy Dolomites peaks, **Rifugio Scotoni** is a welcoming sight indeed after your steep 20-minute jaunt down the rocky gorge below Lago Lagazuoi. After so much exertion, the fluffy duvets and well-stocked bar and restaurant here make an overnight stay mighty tempting. Even if you plan to forge on, it's worth grabbing a beer on the front terrace to relish your completion of the walk's most challenging leg.

Your return route to Capanna Alpina is steep but scenic, zigzagging down to the parking lot on a wide dirt road through inviting **green meadows**, with the familiar jagged profile of Piz dles Cunturines towering once again before you.

The High Road...

The Dolomites' most legendary hiking routes are the Alte Vie delle Dolomiti (or Dolomiten-Höhenwege) – long-distance 'high routes' that criss-cross the mountains' rarefied upper reaches, passing by dozens of mountain refuges en route and intersecting periodically with the trails described in this guide. Here are some basic specs for the four most famous Alte Vie:

Alta Via 1 From Pragser Wildsee to Belluno; 150km

Alta Via 2 From Brixen to Feltre; 185km

Alta Via 3 From Toblach to Longarone; 120km

Alta Via 4 From Innichen to Pieve di Cadore; 90km

For further info, see *altabadia.org/en/summer-holidays/trekking-hiking/dolomites-high-routes.html*.

Forcella del Lago

38

Pragser Wildsee

DURATION	DIFFICULTY	DISTANCE	START/END
1.25hrs	Easy	3.5km	Hotel Pragser Wildsee

TERRAIN	Mainly flat, with one short uphill

Traversing forests and beaches, this easygoing loop circles the shores of the gorgeous, mountain-ringed Pragser Wildsee (Lago di Braies). The first half of the walk, along the lake's western shore, readily accommodates strollers and wheelchairs, while the narrower path along the eastern shore involves one brief climb.

Getting Here

From Niederdorf (Villabassa) train station, drive or take bus 442 (20 minutes, hourly) 13km southwest through the Pragsertal to Hotel Pragser Wildsee.

Starting Point

The walk starts and ends at the Hotel Pragser Wildsee, where you'll find restaurants, toilets, a paid car park and a wall-mounted trail map.

01 Walk towards the boathouse, 100m south of the parking lot on the lake's northern shore. You're instantly rewarded with your first views of the emerald green Pragser Wildsee, backed by the imposing peaks of Seekofel (2810m), Grosser Rosskofel (2559m) and Herrstein (2447m) in Parco Naturale di Fanes-Sennes-Braies. Head counterclockwise around the lake, following signs for Seeweg (Giro del Lago), a broad flat path skirting the lake's western shore. Within five minutes, you'll reach a large stone barn, famous throughout Italy as a filming location for the TV series *Un Passo dal Cielo*. A few paces further on, stop to admire the thin-steepled **lakeside chapel**, where a plaque commemorates the 133 Allied hostages liberated here at the end of WWII.

Lakeside Hospitality

Dominating the lakeshore since 1899, the grand old Hotel Pragser Wildsee (*pragser wildsee.com*) is a longtime favourite European vacation spot. Its tradition of hospitality dates back to Austro-Hungarian imperial days, when it hosted the likes of Archduke Franz Ferdinand. In the waning days of WWII, the three-storey hotel also offered shelter to several dozen freed prisoners from 17 European countries upon their transfer from Dachau and other Nazi concentration camps.

Chapel, Parco Naturale di Fanes-Sennes-Braies

02 Continue through a shady wood, catching occasional glimpses of boaters rowing against a backdrop of peaks reflected in the lake's placid waters. At a junction with trail 19 to Grünwald Alm, keep left, continuing past signposted toilet facilities towards the broad expanse of **beach** at the lake's southern edge. The pebbly shores here offer a welcome break – and an invigorating swimming spot for those undaunted by the lake's icy waters. Traditional legends of the local Ladin people immortalised this end of the lake as 'Sass dla Porta', the gateway to the underworld.

03 The trail narrows as you continue towards the steeper eastern shore, passing a signposted junction with the Alta Via 1, one of the Dolomites' legendary 'high routes'. Long-distance backpackers turn right here to reach the high country of Parco Naturale di Fanes-Sennes-Braies – but your easier lakeside route hugs the shoreline as it curves left and re-enters the forest. Pass a lovely green cove on the left, cross through a gate with an amusing 'Beware of Cows' sign, and zigzag 100m uphill along a wooden railing to reach the **high point**. Benches allow you to pause and soak up views of the eastern slopes plunging into the waters below. A 15-minute walk brings you back to the **boathouse**, where you can extend your visit by renting a handmade 'Lancetta' rowboat.

☕ Take a Break

Bypass the trailside chalet snack shack and head 25 minutes north to Durnwald (*http://restaurantdurnwald.it*), a family-run gem in the pastoral Gsiesertal. Seasonal, locally sourced South Tyrolean specialities such as venison goulash with polenta, pork medallions with chanterelles and porcini, spinach dumplings, house-cured meats, smoked trout mousse and homemade apple fritters are all served with a smile.

39

Percorso delle Segherie

DURATION	DIFFICULTY	DISTANCE	START/END
1.5hrs	Easy	4km	Terme di Rabbi

TERRAIN	Level paved and dirt roads

Gentle terrain and outstanding scenery combine on this walk through the verdant Val di Rabbi on Parco Nazionale dello Stelvio's eastern doorstep. The trail, whose name means 'Path of the Sawmills', connects a pair of historic water-driven mills along the Torrente Rabbies.

The signposted **Percorso delle Segherie** starts from **Terme di Rabbi**, the 19th-century spa-hotel complex surrounding Val di Rabbi's natural hot springs. Steep green meadows rise towards pine and larch forest on either side as the paved road follows the valley floor west. Pass a parking lot on the right and continue gently uphill another 700m to a left-hand turnoff marked 'Segheria Bègoi'. Here, the trail becomes a wide unpaved path following the rushing **Torrente Rabbies** downstream.

Immediately on your right is the **Segheria Veneziana dei Bègoi**, a working 18th-century sawmill with an impressive **river-driven water wheel**. In summer, free guided tours offer a close-up glimpse of its ingenious hydraulic mechanisms sawing wood. Continue down the wide footpath through shady forest. About 500m downstream, turn your gaze right (uphill) to see a waterfall and a dizzyingly perched 100m.

Still paralleling the river, the trail gently rises and falls through the forest, rejoining the paved valley road 1km downstream. At the junction, a sprawling **playground** in a grassy field invites kids to get their wiggles out. Continue 500m downstream past the spa hotel and branch right onto a smaller road just beyond the orange village church. Within minutes, you'll reach the **Seghja Di Braghje**, a second historic sawmill. Cross a wooden bridge and turn left, returning along the main road to your Starting Point.

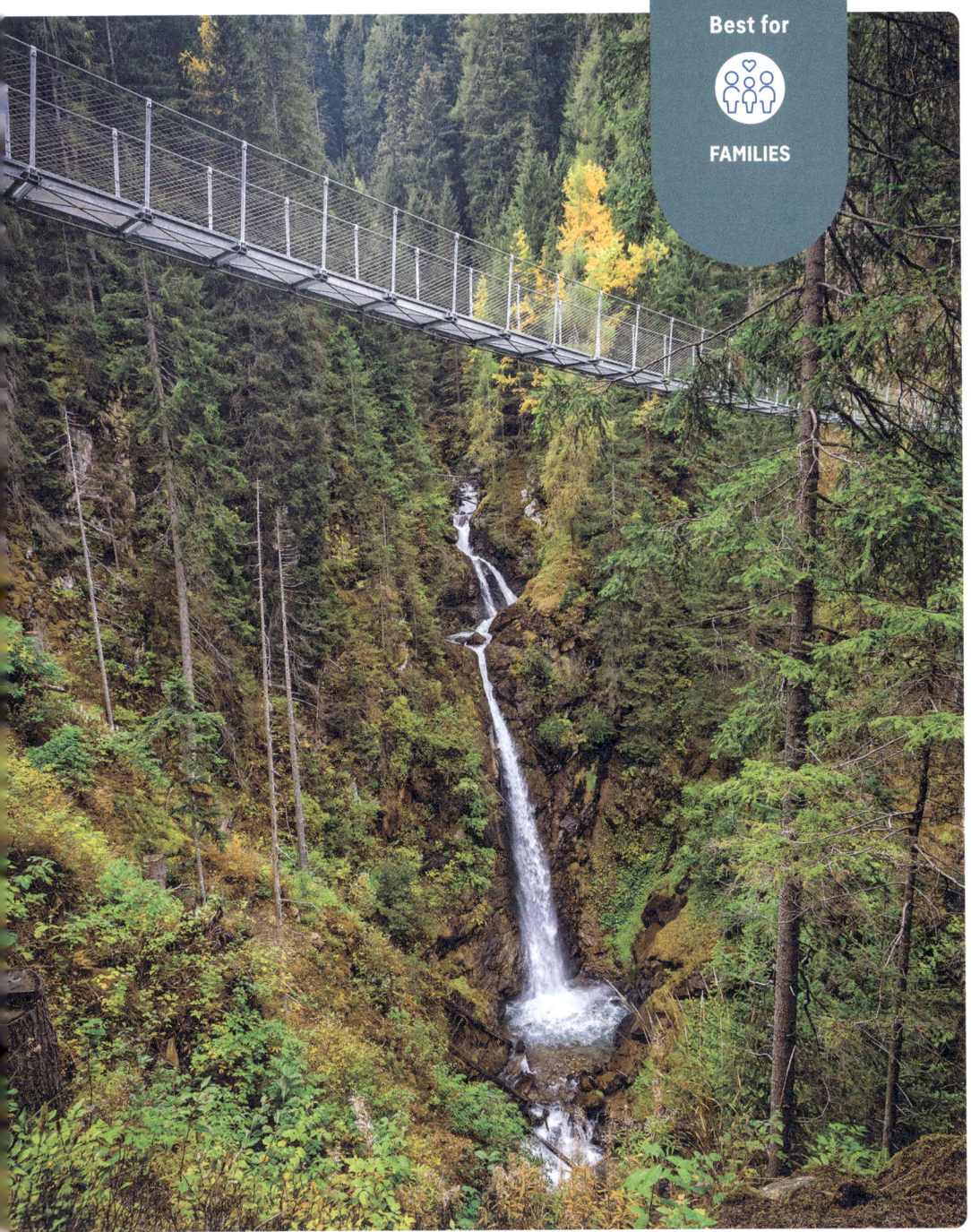
Val di Rabbi

40

Adolf Munkel Weg

DURATION	DIFFICULTY	DISTANCE	START/END
2.5hrs	Moderate	9km	Zans parking lot

TERRAIN	Dirt roads and forest trails

For mesmerising in-your-face views of the Odle group without breaking too much of a sweat, consider this family-friendly loop, which shepherds you through the high country at the base of these peaks in less than three hours.

Getting Here

Zans sits in the upper Val di Funes, 50km northeast of Bolzano. SAD buses run here from Brixen (50 minutes). Drivers can follow the squiggly, signposted road 6km uphill from St Magdalena.

Starting Point

At Zans, you'll find a parking lot and a cafe-restaurant with restroom facilities.

01 Hit the dirt road east of the Zans parking lot, following signs for trail 6 (Adolf Munkel Weg). The broad path climbs between fences into the forest, with a creek running parallel and rock spires peeking out between the trees ahead. After 20 minutes, at a clearing with a cluster of signposts, turn right to follow trail 35 (Adolf Munkel Weg) towards Brogles Alm. The trail crosses a creek, narrows and enters the woods, soon yielding **sublime views** of the rocky pinnacles of Sass Rigais (3025m) and Furchetta (3030m) towering overhead. An unnumbered trail on the left leads to the Klettergarten, a popular spot for rock climbers. Keep straight here and at two other intersections on the right for trails 36B and 36A. Throughout this stretch, the views of the Odle group to the left are stupendous, especially when rays of morning sunlight come streaming through the crags.

Fairy-Tale Mountain Chapel

If a single image can sum up the Dolomites' mix of natural beauty and human stewardship, it's the chapel of **St Johann** in Ranui, just east of St Magdalena Villnöss (Santa Maddalena di Funes), 45km northeast of Bolzano. Sitting alone in a meadow below the Odle group, this teensy baroque church is one of South Tyrol's most iconic photo-ops. The surrounding Villnösstal (Val di Funes) is a charmed land of small villages and working farmsteads. For bird's-eye perspectives on the valley, snake uphill towards Würzjoch (Passo delle Erbe, 2006m) on the insanely narrow but staggeringly scenic SP163 and SP29.

Chapel of St Johann

02 At the next junction, after an hour zigzagging along the rocky face, turn away from the mountains and join trail 36 towards Gschnagenhardt Alm. A staircase climbs into the forest on your right, affording **gorgeous views** back over the Dolomites. The trail soon levels out and passes through a gate into a vast meadow dotted with evergreens. Moments later, you arrive at **Gschnagenhardt Alm** (Malga Casnago, 2006m), a high-country farmstead with a large front terrace beckoning you in for a beer. Less than five minutes further on, you'll come to **Geisler Alm**, another high-country hut at the junction of trails 34 and 36. Take the right fork onto trail 36 and cross a boardwalk through the field, reaching a new crossroads within moments. Here you take the left fork, trail 36 to Dusler Alm and Zans.

03 Trail 36 continues down through the woods, reaching a junction with trail 36B after 15 minutes. Turn left here on a wide dirt road and shortly after enter a clearing where the **Dusler Alm** mountain hut sets a classic South Tyrolean tone with its red eagle flag, wooden shutters, geranium-filled flower boxes and gnomes peeking out from cutouts in the woodpile. Trail 36 leaves Dusler Alm as a narrow path through the meadow, soon entering the woods and reaching a junction with trail 34B. Turn right and climb through the woods on a root-ridden, rocky stretch of trail; 10 minutes later, turn left, taking trail 33 back to your Starting Point.

 Take a Break

Boasting panoramic views of the Odle group, the family-run **Gschnagenhardt Alm** (*gschnagenhardtalm.it*) sits surrounded by alpine meadows in the high country east of St Magdalena. It makes a festive place to stop for dumplings and beer on a walk through the high country, especially when the live accordion music is in full swing!

Also Try...

Roda de Pütia

Roda de Pütia

DURATION	DIFFICULTY	DISTANCE
4hrs	Moderate	13km

Encompassing everything from gentle pastures to rugged ravines, this high-altitude loop offers the added bonus of multiple mountain huts where you can recharge your batteries.

Park at Wurzjoch (1987m), one of the Dolomites' most remote passes, and take the signposted Roda de Pütia trail towards Sass de Pütia (Peitlerkofel), the hulking 2875m mountain to your south. At the Malga Fornella hut, branch right on trail 8A, then continue onto trail 4, proceeding anti-clockwise around the mountain's base and climbing 1¼ hours through a barren, rock-strewn landscape to Forcella de Putia (2361m). East of the pass, a dirt road descends through huge green meadows. Continue circumnavigating Sass de Putia on trails 35 and 8B, passing two welcoming mountain huts – Ütia Vaćiara and Ütia de Göma – to close the loop at Malga Fornella and return to Wurzjoch.

Seceda to Pieralongia

DURATION	DIFFICULTY	DISTANCE
1.75hrs	Easy	5km

For top-of-the-world views with limited exertion, nothing beats this family-friendly, gondola-assisted loop through the high pastures and ski slopes above Val Gardena.

Ride the cable car from Ortisei up to Seceda (2518m), where a vast trail network fans out below the ridge separating Val Gardena from Val di Funes. Walk east from the gondola station, following trails 1 and 2B towards the prominent rocky outcrop of Pieralongia. Here you can stop for homemade hot chocolate, buttermilk or beer at family-run Malga Pieralongia. Loop back to Seceda, serenaded by mooing cows and goat bells. First descend trail 4A toward Col Raiser, then climb trail 1, with another optional snack stop at the luxurious Trojer Hütte. For a last-minute thrill, detour up trail 6 towards Furcela de Pana, where views of the knife-edged ridge dropping into Val de Funes are spellbinding.

Val di Pejo

Giro del Bullaccia

DURATION	DIFFICULTY	DISTANCE
3hrs	Moderate	10km/miles

Europe's largest alpine meadow forms the backdrop for this panoramic loop with wraparound views of the Dolomites.

From Compatsch's cable-car station, trail 14 meanders north through meadows to Arnika Hütte, revealing views west to Schlern's spiky-toothed profile. Climb 20 minutes further to Hexenbänke (Witches' Benches), a rocky outcrop with bird's-eye perspectives over Val Gardena, then loop back to the cable car via Puflatschhütte, through pastures overlooking Sassolungo and the Seiser Alm (Alpe di Siusi).

Giro dei Laghi

DURATION	DIFFICULTY	DISTANCE
5.5hrs	Hard	12km

Val di Pejo in Parco Nazionale dello Stelvio is home to several famous peaks and glaciers, and the lake-riddled highlands that form the backdrop for this strenuous half-day loop.

From Malga Mare (2031m), climb steadily up trail 102 to Rifugio Larcher (2607m), enjoying views to Monte Cevedale (3769m) and the Careser Glacier. Trail 104 continues to Lago delle Marmotte, then joins trail 123, descending past Lago Lungo and Lago Nero to the dam at Lago Careser before dropping steeply back to Malga Mare.

Cala Luna (p170)

Sardinia

41 **Cala Goloritzé**
Descend through ancient oaks to a secluded turquoise cove. **p162**

42 **Gola di Gorropu**
Follow a river valley into one of Europe's deepest canyons. **p164**

43 **Tiscali**
Climb to a mysterious abandoned village in a collapsed cave. **p166**

44 **Cala Sisine to Cala Luna**
Explore one of Italy's most secluded and dramatic coastlines. **p170**

45 **Monte Corrasi**
Survey the rugged Supramonte from a windswept limestone summit. **p172**

Explore

Sardinia

Lapped by seductively beautiful blue-green waters and crowned by sparsely vegetated limestone highlands, Sardinia is one of Italy's most unique and eye-catching regions. The island's remote mid-Med location – roughly equidistant from Tunisia, Spain, France and Italy – has left Sardinia with a culture, cuisine and language all its own. Hikers here will find a world of intrigue, from gorgeous coastal walks to mysterious archaeological sites, isolated mountaintops and deep canyons. Of particular interest is Parco Nazionale Gennargentu, sprawling from the Golfo di Orosei across the vast limestone massif of the Supramonte to Sardinia's highest peak, Punta La Marmora.

Cala Gonone

Reached by a long descent through hairpin bends and boasting grandstand views of the dazzling blue Golfo di Orosei, the seaside resort of Cala Gonone has a low-key, family-friendly vibe. A slew of boat operators based at Cala Gonone's port run tours down the glorious coastline, granting access to the gulf's most pristine and secluded beaches. Outside of August, conditions are relatively uncrowded and rates affordable at Cala Gonone's glut of hotels and restaurants. In winter, the resort slumbers, closing from November until Easter.

Baunei

Clinging to a high ridge on the tortuous road between Arbatax and Dorgali, the old stone shepherds' village of Baunei is an agreeable mountain outpost on the Supramonte's southeastern edge. Just above town sits the Altopiano del Golgo, an otherworldly plateau where goats, pigs and donkeys graze in the *macchia* (Mediterranean scrub), and where you'll find the trailhead for the magnificent walk to Cala Goloritzé. Services in Baunei are limited to a handful of hotels and restaurants, but in this lonely corner of the island, it feels like a welcome oasis indeed.

WHEN TO GO

The best period for walking is springtime, when days are lengthening, wildflowers are in bloom and there are frequent patron saint feast days in the local villages. Autumn is also a pleasant time to walk. Winter is too cold, and summer – when the beaches get packed with tourists – is far too hot for walking.

Dorgali

Dorgali is a workaday town with a grandiose backdrop, nestled at the foot of Monte Bardia and framed by vineyards and olive groves. Limestone peaks rear above the centre's pastel-coloured houses and steep, narrow streets, luring hikers and climbers to their summits. While the town itself is not particularly prepossessing, the sparkling Golfo di Orosei and spectacular Supramonte are within easy striking distance, making it a convenient base, especially for trips to nearby Gola di Gorropu.

Nuoro

About 40km inland from the coast, Nuoro is Sardinia's sixth-largest city, home to a university and a good ethnographic museum. A hodgepodge of modern buildings sprawls down Nuoro's hillsides, backed by the granite peak of Monte Ortobene (955m). With a full range of tourist services, it makes a good base for exploring the nearby Supramonte.

TRANSPORT

Sardinia has commercial airports at Cagliari in the south, Olbia in the northeast and Alghero in the northwest. Ferries serve the island from Corsica, Toulon and Marseille (France), Sicily, Genoa, Livorno, Civitavecchia and Naples (Italy), and Barcelona (Spain). Train service on the island is slow and limited to a few main routes connecting urban centres such as Cagliari, Oristano, Sassari and Olbia. Buses operated by **Azienda Regionale Sarda Trasporti** (*arst.sardegna.it*) offer service to smaller towns around the island. However, to really explore Sardinia and reach the most interesting trailheads, you'll greatly benefit from having your own wheels.

 WHAT'S ON

Settimana Santa

Holy Week in Sardinia is a big deal, with solemn processions and Passion plays all over the island.

Sagra del Redentore (*Festa del Redentore*)

Horsemen and dancers accompany Sardinia's grandest costumed parade in August, a pilgrimage to the statue of Christ the Redeemer on Nuoro's Monte Ortobene.

Autunno in Barbagia

Rural villages in Barbagia host foodie events, craft fairs and workshops at this autumn festival, held from September to December.

Resources

Sardegna Turismo (*sardegnaturismo.it*) Sardinia's official tourism website.

Corrado Conca (*corradoconca.it*) Sardinian hiking and climbing guru, offering a variety of guided adventures.

Nurnet (*nurnet.crs4.it/nurnetgeo*) Geoportal mapping hundreds of Sardinian nuraghic sites.

 WHERE TO STAY

Sardinia offers a variety of attractive accommodation options, from beach hotels to family-run B&Bs to *agriturismi* (farm stays). Top choices include **Casa Solotti** (*casasolotti.it*) in Nuoro, where hosts Mario and Frédérique offer a wealth of walking advice, and the side-by-side *agriturismi* of **Codula Fuili** (*codulafuili.com*) and **Nuraghe Mannu** (*nuraghemannu.com*) in Cala Gonone, both picturesquely perched above the Golfo di Orosei and regaling hikers with fabulous multi-course home-cooked dinners.

41

Cala Goloritzé

DURATION	DIFFICULTY	DISTANCE	START/END
2.5hrs	Moderate	7.5km	Bar Su Porteddu

TERRAIN	Wide rocky path, moderately steep

Descending to the sea through a canyon replete with ancient oaks and sheer limestone outcrops, this trail is a Sardinian classic. The walk culminates at one of Sardinia's most dazzling coves, where limpid turquoise waters compete for your attention with a long sweep of coastal cliffs and a dagger-shaped pinnacle popular with climbers.

Getting Here

Climb from Baunei onto the Altopiano del Golgo. After 8km, turn right on a dirt track, following signs 1.2km to the trailhead.

Starting Point

The trailhead at Su Porteddu has a ticket kiosk, restrooms, parking and a bar-restaurant serving drinks and snacks.

01 Start with a gradual but steady 10-minute ascent from the **Su Porteddu ticket booth**. Scurrying pigs add a dose of atmosphere as the rocky trail climbs through scrubby vegetation, then levels out, rounding a bend along the hilltop ridge to reveal first glimpses of Aguglia, the distinctive rocky pinnacle on the shoreline far below. At an unmarked junction 15 minutes from the trailhead, a trail to Punta Salinas heads uphill on your right. The main trail bears left here – watch for a stone engraved with the word 'Goloritzé' – and begins descending a rock-strewn canyon, passing between low stone walls and under a succession of ancient oaks. Moments later, amidst a heavily eroded section of trail, another rock engraved 'Goloritzé' offers reassurance that you're on the right track.

Best for

COASTAL SCENERY

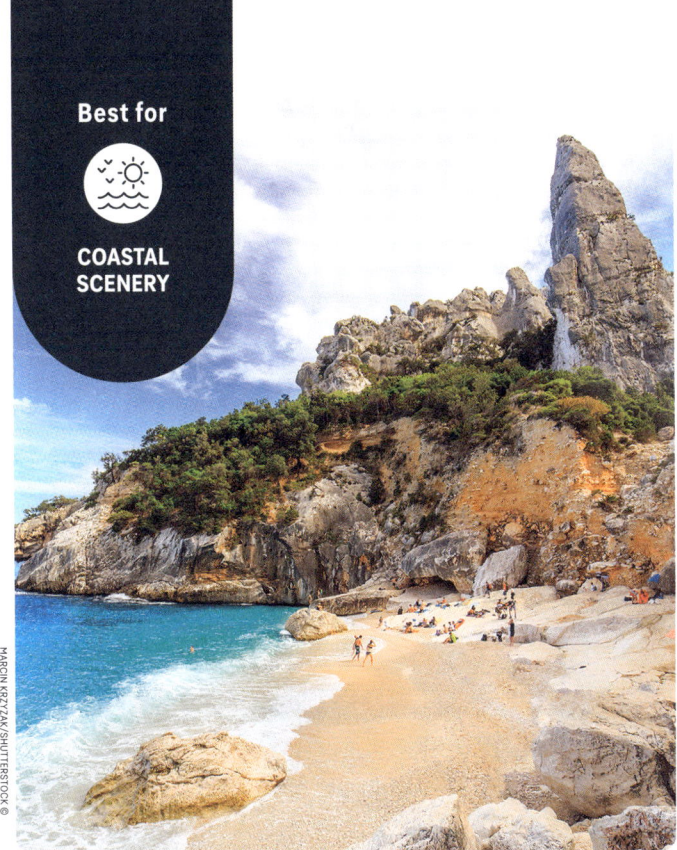

Cala Goloritzé

Google Maps Goof-Ups

In 2019, Baunei mayor Salvatore Corrias made an impassioned plea to all tourists travelling through Sardinia's sparsely populated Supramonte region: don't rely on Google Maps! The problem? Way too many hapless visitors were putting their faith in Google and getting lost in the Supramonte on remote roads unsuited even for donkey traffic; official tallies counted 144 stranded vehicles in a two-year period, including some with 4WD! Corrias's solution? Put up dozens of official signs on local roadways warning people not to follow Google's instructions. So trust your instincts when traveling Sardinia's rural byways, and if the road ahead doesn't look right, inquire locally or make a U-turn back to civilisation.

02 Chirping birds accompany your descent into the canyon, through a landscape regularly punctuated by oaks growing among boulders. Occasional shepherds' dwellings are built into the rocky outcrop, while a pronounced cliff face towers to your left. Half an hour into the descent, just beyond a section bordered by low moss-covered stone walls, arrive at a clearing with **dramatic perspectives** on the Aguglia pinnacle framed by trees.

03 Continuing downhill, pass under a giant oak below a sheer white rock wall on your right, then come to another clearing with views of cavelike depressions on the canyon wall to the north. You're now deep into the canyon, with rock walls on all sides, and a stone fence defining the edges of the rocky path. The trail passes through an archway, then re-enters shady woods. After a final flat and easy stretch through the forest, you get your first close-up **views of the coastline** ahead.

04 Moments later, reach the fence and wooden staircase that mark the end of the trail, and zigzag on down to the beach at **Cala Goloritzé**. A ravishing landscape of **white rocks and turquoise seas** greets you at this secluded cove accessible only by foot or boat. The beach is especially splendid early morning or late afternoon, when the absence of tour boats allows you to fully absorb Goloritzé's raw natural beauty. Linger as long as you like, then retrace your steps to Su Porteddu.

☕ Take a Break

Set in a huge parking lot directly opposite the Cala Goritzè trailhead, **Bar Su Porteddu** (*facebook.com/suporteddu*) is a welcome stop for morning cappuccinos, trail snacks or homemade sandwiches and drinks after your hike. There are also basic camping facilities here.

42

Gola di Gorropu

DURATION	DIFFICULTY	DISTANCE	START/END
4.5hrs	Moderate	14km	Chiosco Sa Barva

TERRAIN	Wide multi-surface road, dirt trails

Sometimes touted as Sardinia's Grand Canyon, the precipitous Gorropu gorge is flanked by limestone walls towering up to 500m. This popular approach along a scenic stretch of river offers opportunities for a swim and/or a picnic along the way.

 ### Getting Here

Turn off the SS125 3km south of Dorgali and follow the signposted dirt road 10km southwest to Chiosco Sa Barva (on your right just before a bridge).

 ### Starting Point

Selling drinks and snacks, Chiosco Sa Barva is a simple kiosk with a dirt parking area. ('Sa Barva', also spelled 'S'Abba Arva', means 'white water' in Sardinian.)

 01 Cross the Flumineddu at the bridge below the parking lot, turning left at the Ponte S'Abba Arva (200m) signpost to head upstream on a wide flat road. At the next junction (Sa Roda), pass through a wooden gate and enjoy views over a bend in the river as you climb along cobblestones and concrete pavement to **S'Arcu 'e Dispensa** (255m). A rough descent marked by sand, protruding rocks and rutted dirt leads to **Su Balladorzu** (225m), where picnic tables and a pretty beach by the riverside. The road eventually peters out completely at a rocky outcrop where only red-and-white blazes mark the route.

 02 The trail narrows and enters the woods, soon arriving at shady **Cantaru Orruos** (275m), a natural spring surrounded by stone walls. Five minutes beyond the spring, a 'Jeep Transfer' sign

Gorropu gorge

points left to a river crossing used by jeeps coming in from the SS125 (steeply uphill to your east). Over the next half-hour climb through forest, then zigzag up an embankment to a high, open **viewpoint** near the signposted Sant'Anna junction (375m). Fine views of the gorge walls loom ahead, and you soon descend steeply to the entrance booth on the valley floor.

03 Enter the boulder-choked canyon and begin exploring. The dry river bed is accessible for 1.5km here, with the Flumineddu flowing through unseen subterranean channels. Flora and fauna in the gorge includes **golden eagles**, **mouflons**, **foxes**,

and a rare endemic species of **Aquilegia** (columbine). Green arrows and paint dots mark the route for the first 500m. Cross improvised wooden bridges and climb towards a cave-like overhang on the right, where a burst of greenery contrasts with the gorge's barren landscape. The canyon walls, which towered 350m above you at the entrance, rise to 500m at the gorge's narrowest, most vertiginous point, a 5m-wide gap that you'll reach within 15 minutes. Beyond this point, yellow paint marks the 500m intermediate section, with bigger rocks and more slippery footing. The last 500m section of the gorge, marked with red blazes, is only open to experienced climbers with equipment. The most famous spot for climbing is called **Hotel Supramonte**, a 400m climb rated 8B at the foot of an 888m peak. When you've reached your limit, retrace your steps to Sa Barva.

Take a Break

Snacks are available at Chiosco Sa Barva, but hungry hikers should hold out for dinner and panoramic sunset views at **Ristorante Ispinigoli** (*hotelispinigoli.it*), in the countryside northeast of Dorgali. Linger over local delights such as black ravioli with mullet roe, herb-infused roast kid and a waistline-expanding selection of cheeses.

43

Tiscali

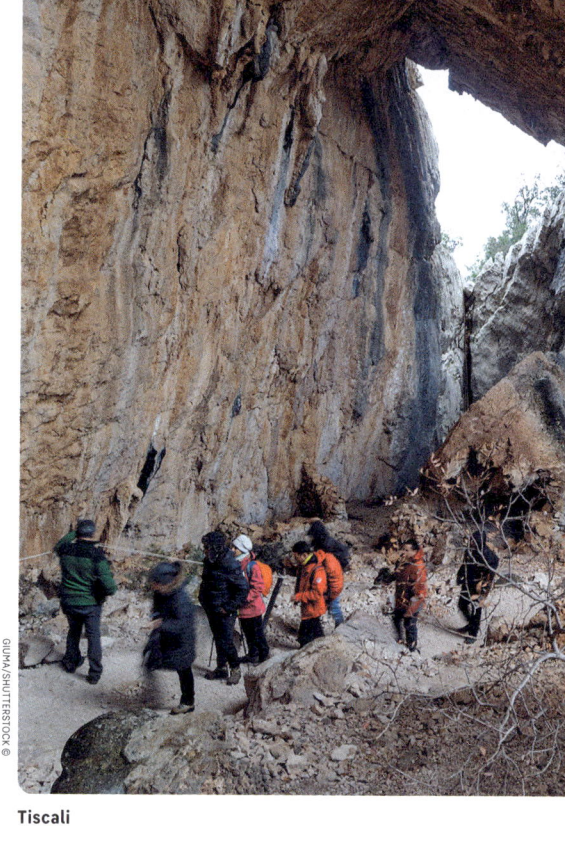
Tiscali

DURATION	DIFFICULTY	DISTANCE	START/END
3hrs	Moderate	9km	Su Ruvagliu

TERRAIN	Dirt road and rocky trails

Hidden in a mountaintop cave high above the Valle di Lanaittu, the mysterious nuraghic village of Tiscali is one of Sardinia's must-see archaeological highlights. Dating from the 6th century BC and populated until Roman times, the village was rediscovered in the late 19th century. At that time it was relatively intact, but since then grave robbers have done a pretty good job of looting the place, stripping the conical stone-and-mud huts down to the skeletal remains that you see today.

Getting Here

You'll need your own wheels. Leave the SP46 between Oliena and Dorgali, following signs to Su Gologone, then continuing 7km south through the remote Lanaitto valley on a rough dirt road.

Starting Point

Near the southeastern end of the Lanaitto valley road, Su Ruvagliu (180m) is nothing more than a dirt parking area. Services are 7km north at Su Gologone.

01 From the parking lot, follow signs for trail 410 to Tiscali, heading uphill (southeast) along a continuation of the same broad dirt road you drove in on. After a few switchbacks, just beyond a bend where the park ranger often parks a vehicle, continue ascending steadily on a stony old woodcutters' path marked by red-and-white blazes on rocks and trees. The trail passes through a **forest** of holm oak (*Quercus ilex*) and mastic (*Pistacia lentiscus*), with occasional switchbacks as you climb.

Nuraghic Culture

Sardinia's unique prehistoric culture remains mysterious, even to scholars. Starting in the second millennium BC, the island's nuraghic people evolved from Bronze Age farmers into skilled metallurgists and stonemasons. Their upland settlements featured distinctive conical towers, so sturdily built that over 7000 of them still remain. Nuraghic civilisation also fashioned human-like statuettes known as *bronzetti* from locally produced bronze, and traded them with societies in the Balearics, Greece, Crete and Sicily. Nuraghic culture mysteriously began fizzling out around 500 BC with the arrival of the Phoenicians. Its final trouncing came with the Romans' arrival in 238 BC.

02 Straight ahead, about 40 minutes into the walk, is a huge exposed white rock commanding **exceptional views over the Valle di Lanaittu** below. The sun-baked landscape that spreads before you – seas of olive groves backed by the stark limestone profile of Monte Corrasi – served as a film location for John Huston's 1966 film *The Bible: In the Beginning*. The valley is also home to some important prehistoric archaeological sites, most notably the 5-hectare **Sa Sedda 'e Sos Carros**, whose circular Temple of the Sacred Well – surrounded by stone spouts that would have fed spring water into a huge central basin – is unique in Sardinia.

03 Be careful not to continue straight (south) beyond the white rock; rather, watch on the left (east) side of the road for a pair of stones with well-defined red-and-white stripes and a faded red arrow; these mark the continuation of trail 410, which branches off the main road here and begins climbing, with roots and rocks underfoot, towards an imposing orange-and-grey outcrop clearly visible above the trees to the northeast. Wooden steps ease your progress through a forest punctuated with wind-sculpted ancient junipers. About 20 minutes after leaving the white rock, reach the signposted Curtigia 'e Tiscali junction (485m), where trail 410 meets up with trail 480. Turn left at the signpost, following trail 410 up a series of rocky steps to a **secret cleft** in the rock face. A narrow passage takes you straight through to the other side of the crevice, where the trail begins descending.

04 You now skirt a wide **rocky ledge** bordered on your right by an impressive vertical wall of wind- and water-sculpted grey-and-orange limestone. After passing a prominent gnarled juniper on your left (one of several such trees along this stretch), pay careful attention to stay on the

☕ Take a Break

Nestled at the foot of mountains, the rural retreat of **Su Gologone** (*sugologone.it*) is a delightful spot for lunch or dinner, with a terrace for sunny afternoons and balmy evenings. The local Cannonau red goes well with regional classics such as *culurgiones* (Sardinian ravioli stuffed with ricotta and mint) and *seadas al miele* (light pastries served with bitter honey).

trail and avoid a drop-off on the right. The path becomes uneven, with stones clinking underfoot as you descend, but remains well marked with frequent red-and-white blazes. Round the corner of the mountain, soon reaching Tiscali junction (420m).

05 A spur trail branches right here, climbing to the ruins of **Tiscali**. Within five minutes, cross the lip of the cave and continue down a stone staircase with wood and rope handrails to the entrance gate, where you pay a €5 fee. Despite the fragmentary condition of the ruins themselves, Tiscali is an awe-inspiring sight, with jumbled stone foundations amid holm oak and turpentine trees huddled in the eerie twilight of the limestone overhang. The inhabitants of nearby Sa Sedda 'e Sos Carros used this remote outpost as a hiding place from the Romans, and its inaccessibility ensured that the Sards were able to hold out here until well into the 2nd century BC.

06 Leave Tiscali on trail 481 towards Dolovèrre, descending steeply at first through a labyrinth of juniper forest before levelling out after about 15 minutes. You'll soon come to a junction labeled **Pala Úporo** (305m), where trail 480A branches southeast towards Su Praicarzu, S'Arcu 'e Doronè and Donanigoro. Stay on trail 481 and continue gradually downhill, north towards Dolovèrre and Ponte S'Abba Arva. The packed earth and stone trail widens and weaves gently downhill below the junction.

07 Just past a weather-beaten, hand-carved sign pointing towards Oddoene and Dorgali, reach **Dolovèrre junction** (240m), an open clearing with a more reassuring CAI sign atop a brand-new post. Take the left fork, following trail 411 west towards Budurrài and leaving trail 481, which branches east here to Ponte Sa Barva (the alternate route to Tiscali).

08 For the next half-hour stay on trail 411, ignoring a couple of new trail junctions on your right. Pass a clearing with old stone foundations on your left, followed by a pair of caves traditionally used as shelters by herders and their animals, and stay left at the next fork. You'll soon come to **Bilichinzos junction** (160m), where trail 411 branches right towards Buddurài, while trail 410A branches left towards Su Ruvagliu.

09 A 10-minute jaunt on trail 410A – a broad dirt road climbing gently at first through Mediterranean scrub forest and then into denser woods – returns you to your Starting Point.

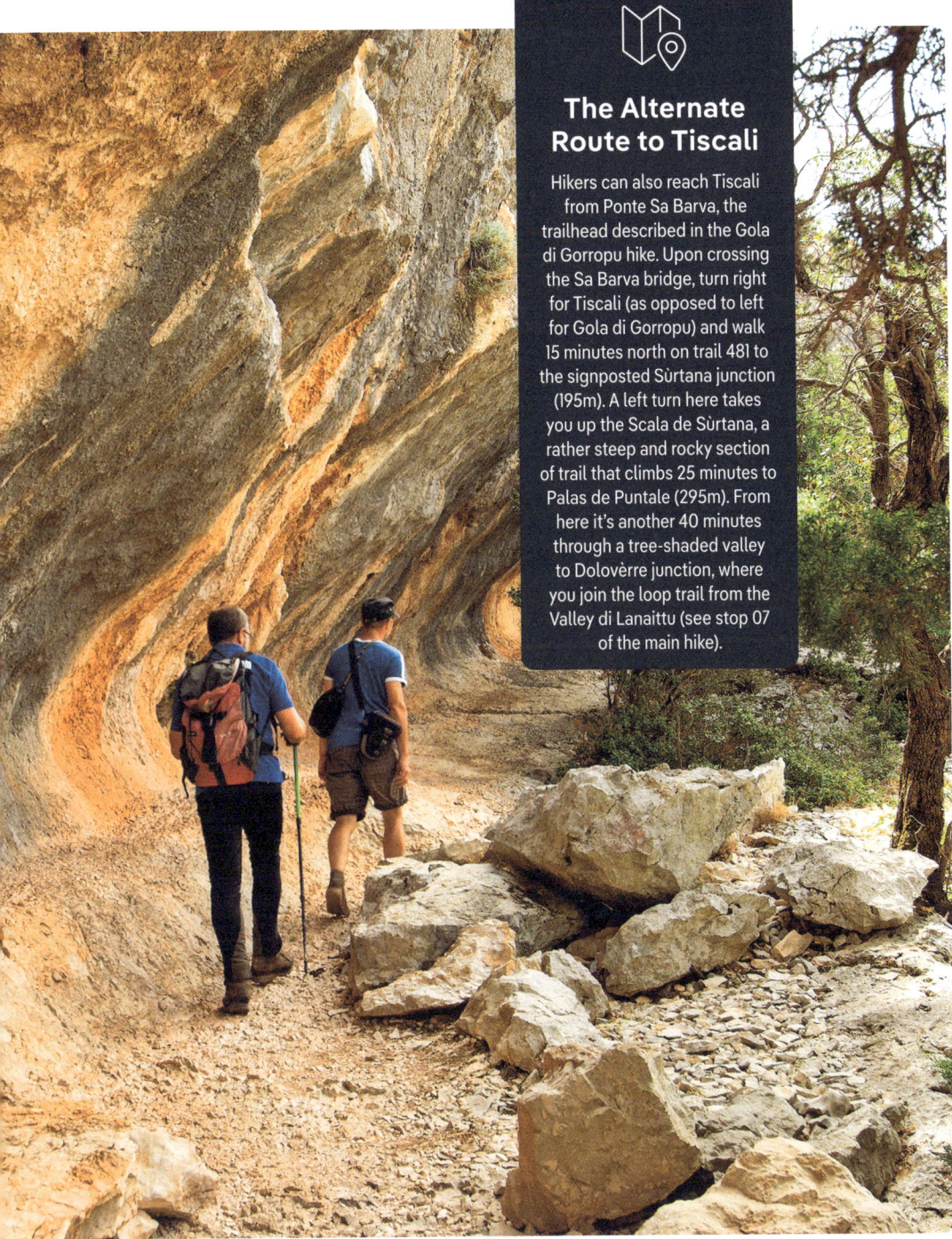

The Alternate Route to Tiscali

Hikers can also reach Tiscali from Ponte Sa Barva, the trailhead described in the Gola di Gorropu hike. Upon crossing the Sa Barva bridge, turn right for Tiscali (as opposed to left for Gola di Gorropu) and walk 15 minutes north on trail 481 to the signposted Sùrtana junction (195m). A left turn here takes you up the Scala de Sùrtana, a rather steep and rocky section of trail that climbs 25 minutes to Palas de Puntale (295m). From here it's another 40 minutes through a tree-shaded valley to Dolovèrre junction, where you join the loop trail from the Valley di Lanaittu (see stop 07 of the main hike).

Tiscali

44

Cala Sisine to Cala Luna

DURATION	DIFFICULTY	DISTANCE	START/END
4hrs	Moderate	12km	Cala Sisine/ Cala Luna

TERRAIN	Dirt trails, some steep sections

A northward extension of Sardinia's legendary Selvaggio Blu climbing route, this stunning coastal walk connects two of Golfo di Orosei's dreamiest beaches. En route, you'll cross the Supramonte's lonely, lovely limestone uplands and visit Arco di Lupiru, an extraordinary natural stone arch.

Getting Here

From Cala Gonone's port, boat operators cruise the coast between April and October (€35 one way to Cala Sisine). Arrange pickup from Cala Luna at day's end, or hike another 9km north to Cala Gonone.

Starting Point

Cala Sisine is accessible only by boat or by 4WD from the Altopiano di Baunei. In season, Bar Su Coile serves snacks just inland from the beach.

01 Follow the riverbed inland from **Cala Sisine**, turning right at a tree-shaded camping area and climbing onto the slopes north of the beach. You're soon rewarded with **stunning views** up and down the coast. Within 15 minutes, the trail, still climbing, curves hard left away from the sea, then doubles back and levels out on a rocky ledge. Lovely views continue to unfold over Cala Sisine's distinctive hat-shaped promontory and the *macchia*-clad outcrops stretching north towards Cala Gonone.

02 An hour into the journey, after a 15-minute ascent through forest, the trail enters a heavily eroded clearing, then climbs to a second clearing with an amazing pigsty made of driftwood at its centre. The sturdy stone wall here makes a pleasant

Selvaggio Blu

It's not Italy's longest hike, but Sardinia's four- to seven-day Selvaggio Blu ('Savage Blue') is a definite contender for the nation's toughest trail. Stretching 40km from Pedra Longa to Cala Sisine, the 'Blu' preserves a network of old charcoal burners' and shepherds' paths criss-crossing the high cliffs above the Golfo di Orosei. UIAA technical ratings ranging from EE to IV+ put it out of reach for all but experienced climbers or those traveling with a professional guide – but mere mortals can appreciate the same vertigo-inducing landscape from below at Cala Goloritzé and Cala Sisine, where the coastal hiking trails described in this guide intersect with the Selvaggio Blu.

Arco di Lupiru

picnic spot – provided you can keep the hungry pigs at bay. Climb another 15 minutes through rocky terrain, watching for cairns that signal your impending arrival at a T-junction with a larger north–south trail. Turn right onto the new trail, bordered by a rock wall.

03 Meander through open high country, enjoying views west over the Supramonte's limestone uplands. Towards the coast, a sea of *macchia* obscures all but a sliver of distant blue – but soon after passing a 'Cala Luna' sign engraved on a rock, you're greeted by all-encompassing **views of the shoreline**. Moments later begin a steady descent along a shrub-shaded section of trail. Half an hour down the hill, a cairn marks the short right-hand detour to **Arco di Lupiru**, a symmetrical natural stone arch already visible above the trees. The views are spellbinding once you emerge onto the open, rocky shelf below the arch, and a short scramble up the hillside reveals full-on vistas of the north coast, seen through the enormous 15m-tall hole in the rock.

Take a Break

04 Resume your descent on the main trail, entering a canyon where rock walls loom above a stony riverbed. Soon after exiting the canyon, arrive at a **viewpoint** with views over the sandy beach at Cala Luna. Zigzag downhill, passing through a tunnel of trees, to reach a restaurant. The trail turns towards the sea, paralleling a stream channel to your left, and crosses a pontoon bridge to deposit you on the **beach**.

Nestled amid silvery olive groves on a high bluff above Cala Gonone (a 10-minute drive from the port), **Agriturismo Nuraghe Mannu** (*nuraghemannu.com*) puts on a feast of home-produced pecorino, salami, olives and wine, followed by handmade pasta, succulent roast kid or lamb, and Sardinian sweets.

45

Monte Corrasi

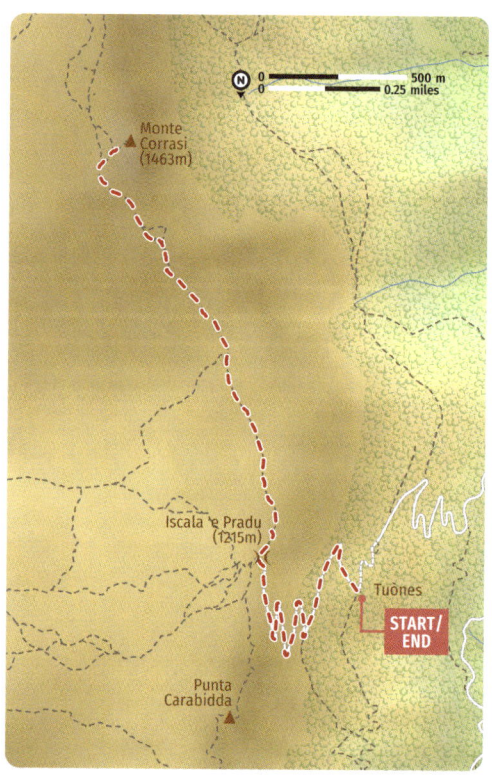

DURATION	DIFFICULTY	DISTANCE	START/END
2.5hrs	Moderate	7km	Tuònes

TERRAIN	Wide dirt road and rocky path

Standing proud at the pinnacle of Sardinia's rugged Supramonte region, the limestone peak of Monte Corrasi (1463m) commands amazing perspectives over the eastern reaches of the island. The fairly straightforward climb to its summit yields great scenic rewards.

To reach the trailhead at **Tuònes** (1025m), follow signs for Albergo Monte Maccione off the SP22 south of Oliena, then switchback up a rough dirt road, parking near a **stone circle** 4km past the hotel. Trail 401, marked with red-and-white blazes, starts as a well-graded dirt track climbing past grand old oaks, with an imposing ridge towering overhead. Over the next half hour, the trees disappear as you navigate a series of six switchbacks, dead-ending atop the high exposed saddle of **Iscala 'e Pradu** (1215m).

A forbidding landscape of **whitish-grey stone dotted with junipers** opens up as your trail branches right (south), leaving the road between an unmarked pole and a statuette of the Virgin Mary (watch for a red-and-white '401' painted on a nearby rock). Descending into a vast karst basin, the rocky trail briefly levels out opposite a circular stone-walled sheep pen and some weather-sculpted rocks, then begins climbing steadily, marked by occasional red-and-white blazes.

After 25 minutes, reach a false summit marked Corrasi (1430m). Wonderful long views unfurl northeast to the Mediterranean, while sheep jingle their bells on the surrounding crags. To reach the true summit, zigzag five more minutes uphill, following signs for **Punta Corrasi**. Atop the windswept peak, cliffs drop off to the southwest. Enjoy the magnificent **360-degree views**, then retrace your steps to Tuònes.

Monte Corrasi

Also Try...

Cala Luna

Cala Fuili to Cala Luna

DURATION	DIFFICULTY	DISTANCE
3.75hrs	Moderate	10.5km

Linking two of the Golfo di Orosei's prettiest beaches, this out-and-back coastal hike makes an easy half-day trip from Cala Gonone.

At the vehicle turnaround where the paved coastal road dead-ends, 4km south of Cala Gonone, descend a staircase to cross Codula Fuili, a long, deep gorge extending inland from the pleasant beach of Cala Fuili. Continue south, climbing the opposite side of the gorge along a route marked sporadically by green arrows. The stony path cuts through high bushes and low trees, with occasional peek-a-boo glimpses of the sea. Descend past the rocky entrance of the Oddoana cave into the gorge of Codula Oddoana, then climb back out. Beyond the hill known as Fruncu Nieddu, begin a steep switchbacking descent to the gravel riverbed of the captivating Codula di Luna. A short walk east brings you to magnificent Cala Luna beach.

Monte Entu

DURATION	DIFFICULTY	DISTANCE
4hrs	Moderate	12km

This half-day excursion climbs to the summit of Monte Entu (1024m), one of the highest peaks in western Sardinia.

You'll need a car to get to the start, which is by the Nuraghe Ruju picnic area, 9km northwest of Seneghe. Join the path a few metres down from the car park, in the wood to the left of the stone wall. Heading upwards, you'll arrive at an opening, marked by a holm oak tree, where you should go left. Carry on past the wooden gate until you reach a second metal gate. Go through it and continue to a fork in the trail. Head left for some marvellous views of the coast, as far as Alghero on a clear day. From here you can continue onwards to the foot of the volcanic cone that marks the summit of Monte Entu.

Capo Testa

Capo Testa

DURATION	DIFFICULTY	DISTANCE
3.50hrs	Easy	10km

Resembling a vast sculpture garden, the lighthouse-topped headland of Capo Testa is an appealing spot for a day hike.

Set off from the isthmus 4km west of Santa Teresa Gallura, flanked by the twin beaches of Rena di Levante and Rena di Ponente. Circle the cape clockwise, passing through boulder-strewn scrub and admiring the weird and wonderful rock formations created by centuries of wind erosion. Along the way, you can stop to swim and gaze across the Strait of Bonifacio to not-so-distant Corsica.

Punta La Marmora

DURATION	DIFFICULTY	DISTANCE
5hr	Moderate	14km

This classic ascent leads through treeless high country to Sardinia's highest summit, Punta La Marmora (1834m).

Follow signs from Rifugio S'Arena (off the SP7 south of Fonni) to Arcu Artilai (I1660m), a pass with fine views south across Parco Nazionale Gennargentu. Bear right across the slopes of Bruncu Spina (1828m), passing the ruins of Rifugio La Marmora. Beyond the summits of Arcu Gennargentu (1659m) and Genna Orisa (1782m), it's another 15 minutes to Punta La Marmora, whose top-of-the-world credentials are marked by a large cross.

Parco Nazionale dei Monti Sibillini (p179)

Umbria & Le Marche

46 Passo del Lupo
Enjoy riveting views of Le Marche's rugged Adriatic coast. **p180**

47 Gola dell'Infernaccio
Hike through a deep river gorge in Parco Nazionale dei Monti Sibillini. **p182**

48 Monte Subasio
Climb to St Francis's spiritual retreat high above Assisi. **p184**

49 Around the Pian Piccolo
Explore vast, lonely grasslands on the Umbria–Le Marche border. **p188**

50 Bosco di San Francesco
Descend through reclaimed woodland into the olive groves. **p192**

Explore

Umbria & Le Marche

Umbria bills itself as the 'Green Heart of Italy' for good reason. The rolling verdant landscape makes this a dreamy walking destination, and the region's *centralissima* location between Rome, Florence and Venice makes it an easy addition to any northern Italian itinerary. Neighbouring Le Marche gets far less press but shares a similar topography, with a long Adriatic coastline thrown in for good measure. For serious walkers, the top draw here is the Parco Nazionale dei Monti Sibillini. Straddling the Umbria–Le Marche border, this little-visited national park boasts some hauntingly lovely landscapes, with wildflower-carpeted plateaus and sheep pastures rising abruptly to craggy peaks.

Assisi

With the Umbrian plains spreading picturesquely below, and Monte Subasio rearing steeply above, the sight of Assisi in the rosy glow of dusk is enough to send pilgrims' souls spiralling to heaven. When the day trippers have left and the town is shrouded in saintly silence, the true spirit of St Francis of Assisi, born here in 1181, can be keenly felt. As befits a pilgrimage destination, accommodation options and restaurants are abundant and relatively well-priced. However, you don't have to be religious to be struck by Assisi's beauty and enjoy its pristine *centro storico* (historic centre) and Unesco-listed basilica.

Castelluccio

Severely damaged by earthquakes in 2016, the hilltop town of Castelluccio has been steadily rebuilding its tourist infrastructure and remains a mecca for hikers and hang-gliders thanks to its stunning setting at the heart of the Piano Grande, an ethereal high plateau that explodes with colourful floral displays every spring. Castelluccio is also a popular gateway for hikes through the mountains and gorges of neighbouring Parco Nazionale dei Monti Sibillini. The village has only a limited handful of accommodations (best booked well in advance), and local restaurants mostly operate out of provisional structures along the main road below

WHEN TO GO

Spring and fall are gorgeous times to experience Umbria's green rolling hills and the coastal paths of Le Marche without full-on summertime heat and crowds. Late spring is peak season for viewing wildflowers on the Piano Grande. If you plan to hike at higher elevations in the Monti Sibillini, the summer months (between June and September) are ideal.

the earthquake-shattered heart of town. Still, nothing compares to the magic of spending a night in this remote, peaceful outpost, especially when the moon is full.

Ancona

More a transport hub than a destination in its own right, Le Marche's seafront capital offers ferries across the Adriatic and train connections throughout Italy. For hikers, it's the gateway to the Conero Riviera, a scenic stretch of cliffs and beaches just south of the city that breaks the monotony of the otherwise flat Adriatic shoreline. Founded by Greek settlers from Syracuse around 387 BC, Ancona's old town is crowned by a theatrically sited cathedral, and there are enough archaeological artefacts, Roman arches, Romanesque churches and Renaissance *palazzi* to keep you busy before and after a day of hiking.

TRANSPORT

Umbria International Airport San Francesco d'Assisi (*airport.umbria.it*) outside Perugia and **Ancona International Airport** (*ancona-airport.com*) in Ancona are the main international gateways to Umbria and Le Marche respectively. Trains serve the two regions on the Rome–Ancona and Rome–Florence lines. By car, the A14 *autostrada* and slower SS16 run down Le Marche's coastline while the A1 and SS3bis connect Rome with Umbria's capital, Perugia. If driving to Perugia from Florence and the north, take the A1 and RA6 (*raccordo autostradale*). To properly explore the Parco Nazionale dei Monti Sibillini, you really need your own wheels.

 WHAT'S ON

Corsa dei Ceri
Gubbio's centuries-old race features three teams carrying massive wooden pillars bearing the statues of saints through the city's streets in May (*ceri.it*).

Umbria Jazz
Perugia's swinging 10-day festival in July has put the city firmly on the world jazz map, with international headliners and events all over town (*umbriajazz.it*).

Festa del Duca
Every August, Urbino time-travels back to the Middle Ages, with medieval fun in the form of costumed pageants, markets and the re-enactment of a horseback tournament (*urbinofestadelduca.it*).

Macerata Opera Festival
Macerata's Arena Sferisterio provides the stage for one of Italy's foremost musical events, attracting the cream of the operatic world every summer (*sferisterio.it*).

Resources
Umbria Tourism (*umbriatourism.it*) Umbria's official tourism website.

Le Marche Tourism (*letsmarche.it*) Le Marche's official tourism website.

Parco Nazionale dei Monti Sibillini (*sibillini.net*) Information on Sibillini National Park.

 WHERE TO STAY

B&Bs, hotels and *affittacamere* (simple rooms for let) make up the bulk of accommodation in most hilltop villages, but the best way to experience Umbria and Le Marche's pastoral scenery is to stay at one of the regions' many *agriturismi* (farm stays). Assisi offers a fair share of pilgrimage and/or religiously affiliated sleeps as well, and there's plenty of camping on Le Marche's coast and around Umbria's Lago Trasimeno.

46

Passo del Lupo

DURATION	DIFFICULTY	DISTANCE	START/END
1.5hrs	Easy	4.5km	Cimitero di Sirolo

TERRAIN	Mostly level dirt roads and paths

Much of Italy's Adriatic coast is flat as a pancake, so Le Marche's spectacular Conero Riviera comes as a welcome surprise. Notable for its chalky white cliffs and limpid turquoise waters, this rugged 20km stretch of shoreline rises dramatically to the summit of Monte Conero (572m). The eponymous 6011-hectare Parco Regionale del Conero shelters a network of family-friendly hiking trails, including this short jaunt to an immensely scenic coastal overlook.

Getting Here

Reni (*anconarenibus.it*) runs buses (35 minutes) from Ancona to Via Giulietti in Sirolo – a 750m walk from the trailhead. Drivers can park opposite the cemetery.

Starting Point

At the cemetery, you'll find nothing more than a parking lot. For other services, head south to Sirolo's town centre.

01 Start uphill from the parking lot, keeping the wall of the **cemetery** on your right as you follow the gently ascending dirt road. About 900m up the hill, turn right at a T-junction with another dirt road, following signs for Belvedere Sud.

02 You'll encounter two **Y-intersections** in the next 400m. At the first, just a stone's throw down the road, take the downhill (right) fork, ignoring the signposted left fork for Belvedere Sud. About 250m further along, take the uphill (left) fork onto a dirt road with a circular red 'motor vehicles prohibited' sign.

Due Sorelle

03 You're now on the trail to Passo del Lupo. The wide dirt road continues without much change in elevation, passing a villa on the left before narrowing to a packed dirt walking path. Here you'll enter a pleasant **shady forest**, with the sea below you to the right obscured by trees. Another 500m along, pass a junction with a trail descending steeply from the Belvedere Sud above. Continue straight through the forest here, and within a couple hundred metres arrive at a rocky clearing with a heart-stopping view.

04 Dazzling perspectives open up over the deep blue Adriatic and surrounding cliffs at the **Passo del Lupo viewpoint**, marked only by an interpretive signboard with Italian-language explanations of local geology. Views to the north are especially breathtaking, with the blindingly white offshore rocks known as the **Due Sorelle** (Two Sisters) adding exuberant punctuation to a steep limestone promontory.

05 A rough and very **steep trail** continues from here towards the beach below, but for safety's sake resist the temptation and retrace your steps to the parking lot.

 Take a Break

A 1km walk south from the Passo del Lupo trailhead brings you to Sirolo's main square, where you'll find **Osteria Sara**, an old-school *osteria* serving excellent seafood. The small dining room here, all white walls and ageing framed pictures, fills quickly as diners pour in to sample marinated anchovies and tuna carpaccio starters, followed by seafood risotto and mains such as grilled catch of the day.

47

Gola dell' Infernaccio

DURATION	DIFFICULTY	DISTANCE	START/END
2.5hrs	Moderate	7km	Infernaccio parking area

TERRAIN	Dirt roads and paths

On the Monti Sibillini's eastern edge, this classic trail leads through the Gola dell'Infernaccio (Hell's Gorge), a thrilling canyon wedged between vertiginous rock walls. The silence here is broken only by birdsong and the rush of the fast-flowing Fiume Tenna.

Starting from a dusty parking lot off the SP83 north of Montefortino, the trail (initially a broad dirt track) descends to meet the **River Tenne**. Enjoy a free shower as drops cascade from the cliff face above.

Cross the river and climb the steep, narrow trail to your left. For the next 20 minutes, you'll traverse the most striking part of the gorge via a series of **four bridges** spaced at five-minute intervals, with limestone walls towering overhead on both sides.

After the last river crossing, enter a shady **beech forest**, watching for a signposted right-hand turnoff for San Leonardo; this will be your return route. For now, follow the valley floor 10 minutes upstream to cross a culvert; just beyond is an **eerie lake** created by the region's 2016 earthquakes, filled with the vestiges of submerged trees.

Turn back the way you came. Two minutes after re-crossing the culvert, an un-signposted but distinct trail on your left climbs into the forest: follow this for 15 minutes to a junction with a dirt road ascending from below. Continue 10 minutes uphill on this 'new' road (it's actually the 'San Leonardo' road you passed previously) to reach the hermitage **church of San Leonardo al Volubrio**, tucked into a sunny clearing with fine mountain views. Your return route to the parking lot descends the dirt road through three switchbacks to the river, then retraces your steps through the gorge.

Gola dell'Infernaccio

48

Monte Subasio

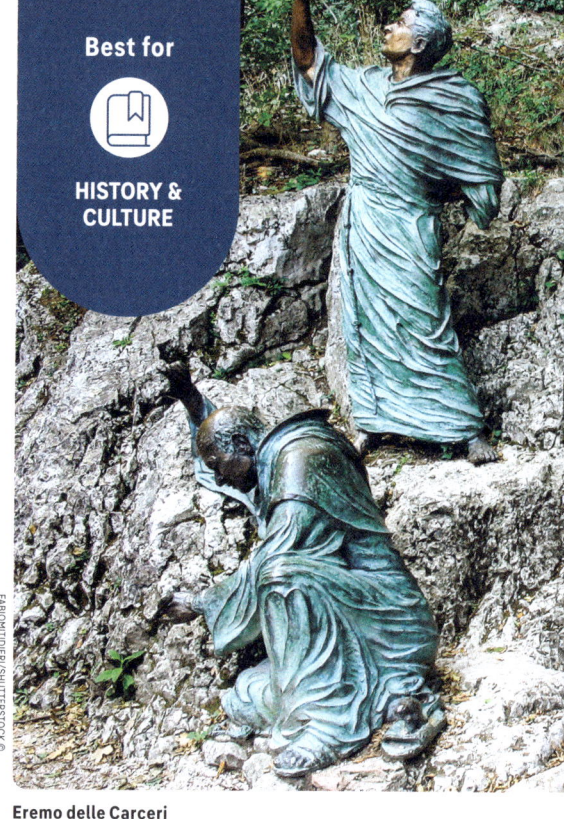

Best for

HISTORY & CULTURE

Eremo delle Carceri

DURATION	DIFFICULTY	DISTANCE	START/END
6.5hrs	Moderate	18km	Porta dei Cappuccini, Assisi

TERRAIN	Dirt road and trails

St Francis of Assisi spent much of his life walking through the Umbrian hills. Few spots held as much spiritual sway for him as Monte Subasio, the half-forested, half-meadowy mountain due east of his native village. Halfway up Subasio's slopes, the Eremo delle Carceri – a mountain hermitage built around a cluster of caves – was a place of frequent spiritual retreat for Francis, lovingly preserved to this day. This hike retraces Francis's route from Assisi to the hermitage and beyond, onto the celestial summit of Subasio itself.

Getting Here

Buses from Assisi's train station drop you at Piazza Matteotti, 400m west of the trailhead. Drivers can park in the adjacent Matteotti lot.

Starting Point

Porta dei Cappuccini is just 300m east of Assisi's medieval centre, where you'll find parking, restrooms, restaurants, bars, shops and cultural attractions.

 01 Leave Assisi through the northeastern town gate **Porta dei Cappuccini**, heading towards the olive-clad hills above town. Immediately after passing through the gate, look for a dirt road framed by rows of cypresses on your left, signposted 'Regione Umbria, Sistema dei Parchi, Parco del Monte Subasio, Sentiero dei Rifugi'.

 02 Turn left onto the dirt road and continue through the row of trees for about five minutes until you reach the 14th-century stone tower of the **Rocca Minore** on your left. From here,

Gubbio's Corsa dei Ceri

Walking Umbria's hilly landscape is sufficient exercise for most people – but some hearty souls take things a step further in Gubbio, 50km north of Assisi. The town's favourite springtime festival culminates in the Corsa dei Ceri, a centuries-old race held each 15 May to celebrate Gubbio's patron, Sant'Ubaldo. It involves three teams, each carrying *a cero* (a massive wooden pillar weighing 300kg) bearing the statue of a saint (Sant'Ubaldo, St George or St Antony). Participants race through the city's medieval streets, making a final push up the steep slopes of Monte Ingino to the hilltop Basilica di Sant' Ubaldo.

there are **excellent views** along Assisi's town walls to the Rocca Maggiore, a larger castle crowning the hills to the west.

03 Opposite the Rocca Minore, the road – now marked with yellow-and-blue signs for the Via di Roma and Via Francigena pilgrimage routes to Rome – curves right and begins climbing into the hills. Within five minutes you reach **Rocchicciola junction** (altitude 500m), where an official metallic CAI signpost indicates that you're on trail 350, one hour from the Eremo delle Carceri. Continue east, bearing right 10 minutes further along at hand-painted signs for Via di Roma and Eremo Carceri (do not turn left onto trail 51 here). The path narrows and continues east through the forest for the next 45 minutes, with pretty views over **Assisi's southern hills** occasionally opening up to your right.

04 At the next junction – signposted Montarone (797m) – turn right onto a wider dirt road, as more impressive **views** open up across a grassy clearing to the valley below. Re-enter the forest, passing trees with red-and-white blazes and a picnic area on your right.

05 After 10 or 15 minutes, emerge onto a wider paved road, where you again turn right following signs for the Eremo. Within five minutes, the tile rooftops, stone walls and arcaded galleries of the **hermitage** come into view, peeking out of the deep green forest ahead.

06 Take at least half an hour to explore the **hermitage**. After soaking up the sun on the upstairs patio with its flowerpots and photogenic views of the ancient stone building and surrounding forest, you can descend a set of narrow stairs to the claustrophobic confines of St Francis's **grotta** (cave), where he prayed and slept on a stone

☕ Take a Break

Just inside the town walls on Assisi's northeastern edge – a stone's throw from the Porta dei Cappuccini – family-run **Ristorante La Rocca** (*hotelarocca.it/en/restaurant-assisi*) serves a full lineup of Umbrian classics at bargain prices. The large interior dining room is a bit sterile and formal (and noisy when packed with fellow diners), but both the food and the atmosphere are pure bliss if you can snag a spot on the breezy upstairs terrace.

bed in his later years. The oak woods around the Eremo are criss-crossed by several additional hiking trails, dotted with **bronze statues** of St Francis (kicking back on the ground, sandals off) and two friars, Ginepro and Leone, staring at the constellations. As you exit toward the main road, a small shack serving coffee and snacks invites you to linger before resuming your journey.

07 Rejoining the main paved road outside the Eremo, turn right (uphill), following signs for SP251 San Benedetto. Yellow, blue, white and red stripes painted on the metal signpost let you know you're also still on CAI trail 350 and the Via di Roma/Via Francigena pilgrimage route. Follow the pavement through **shady forest** for 15 minutes; about halfway along you'll pass a junction labelled Fosso delle Carceri (830m) on your left – this will be your return route. For now, continue straight and gradually uphill along the paved road.

08 At a junction on your left marked Rinboschimento (868m), leave the paved road and join the rocky trail 360, signposted for Sasso Piano (45 minutes). After 20 minutes climbing steadily uphill through the forest, the trees begin to thin. As the trail emerges above the tree line 10 minutes later, look back to the north, where **views** open up to Sasso Piano, a high promontory with a large wooden cross. The trail doubles back on itself here, bringing you up to the cross in about five minutes.

09 Linger a few minutes atop **Sasso Piano** to enjoy the amazing views down over Assisi. At the base of the cross is a metal box containing a book where pilgrims are invited to write messages. From here, head 100m or so uphill to the signposted Sasso Piano trail junction (1124m), and continue uphill into the surrounding pastureland, following signs for trail 350 towards the grazing cows and horses silhouetted on the high ridgeline above.

10 The radio antennae atop **Monte Subasio** come into view as you near the crest of the hill. After passing an animal watering trough marked with red-and-white blazes on your left (15 minutes above Sasso Piano), continue climbing another 15 minutes through the fields, reaching a T-intersection with a dirt road opposite the radio towers.

11 Bear right on the dirt road, following it south past fenceposts marked with red-and-white blazes and the trail number 350. In 10 minutes, turn left off the road at a signpost marked '**Mortaro** 10 min; Fonte Bregno 50 min' and continue through open fields to reach the Mortaro, a deep *dolina* (sinkhole) on the right. With a spiral of stones at the bottom, this symmetrical cavity of sunken pastureland has a mystical feel, especially when mists are swirling through the surrounding hills.

12 The trail gets fainter for the next 10-minute stretch through high meadows; watch for stones at ground level painted red and white. When you reach a long **animal trough**, scan the ridgeline ahead for a prominent signpost and head towards it.

13 Turn right at the signposted junction – marked Prati di Pizzo (1128m) – and stay on trail 350 towards Fonte Bregno. Within a couple of minutes you'll cross a dirt road, continuing through high meadows marked with painted stones to reach an animal trough on a hill crest. The next 15 minutes are all downhill, with **fabulous long views** across pastures and the valley far below. Take care to follow the blazes, which will point you left and then right as you descend.

14 Turn right as the trail dead-ends into a dirt road (watch for a tree with waymarks near the junction). Within a minute you'll reach **Fonte Bregno**, a natural spring (sometimes dry) where trail 360 comes in from the north.

Rocca Minore (p184)

15 Head north for 45 minutes on trail 360, initially contouring the lower edge of a large meadow, with trees along the left side offering shade. After 20 minutes, break into open meadows and begin climbing, eventually turning east to parallel a river gully visible to your left. Beyond a small thicket of bushes and a metal pole painted with yellow, blue, white and red stripes, the trail turns north to cross the gully. Soon the **cross at Sasso Piano** comes into view on the promontory ahead, and the trail rises to meet it within 10 minutes.

16 Back at the signposted Sasso Piano junction, continue north, following signs for trail 350 towards Rifugio Vallonica, Eremo Carceri and Assisi. The trail descends through cow and horse pastures, passing a water trough and the abandoned **Rifugio Vallonica** on the right within 15 minutes. Turn left at the signposted junction beyond the *rifugio* to stay on trail 350, soon leaving the high pastures and beginning a sustained 20-minute descent through the woods.

17 Just beyond some picnic benches on the left, reach the familiar **Fosso delle Carceri junction** that you passed a few hours ago. Here, trail 350 dead-ends into the paved road coming up from Eremo delle Carceri. Turn right and retrace your steps for 1¼ hours or so downhill to Assisi.

49

Around the Pian Piccolo

DURATION	DIFFICULTY	DISTANCE	START/END
4.5hrs	Moderate	14km	Forca di Presta

TERRAIN		Dirt roads and trails

The high plateaus around Castelluccio take on an otherworldly beauty each spring during the annual explosion of poppies, cornflowers and other blooms. This walk leads you across one such plateau and climbs into the surrounding hills for spellbinding views of the Monti Sibillini.

Getting Here

Summer-only buses from Ascoli Piceno to Castelluccio pass by Forca di Presta – but given the region's remoteness, your own vehicle is more dependable.

Starting Point

Straddling the Umbria–Le Marche border, lonely Forca di Presta (1550m) offers only a parking lot. Head 6km west to Castelluccio for other services.

01 Descend west from Forca di Presta on the paved SP477. Just beyond a right-hand bend, turn left at a concrete culvert painted with red-and-white blazes numbered 207. Continue downhill on a faint trail paralleling a gully to your right, with a **beech-forested hillside** above to your left. At a T-junction 15 minutes along, turn left onto a wider dirt road and round the edge of the hillside to your left, emerging onto the vast grassy expanses of the **Pian Piccolo**. For the next hour, continue southwest across the plateau, slowly approaching a second ridge of hills to the west. Trail markings here are nonexistent; simply stay on the valley floor between the two ranges of hills. After half an hour, near the valley's western edge, a new dirt road merges in from the north. Branch left and continue past an animal watering trough; 15 minutes further on, branch onto a faint road along the

Best for

AVOIDING THE CROWDS

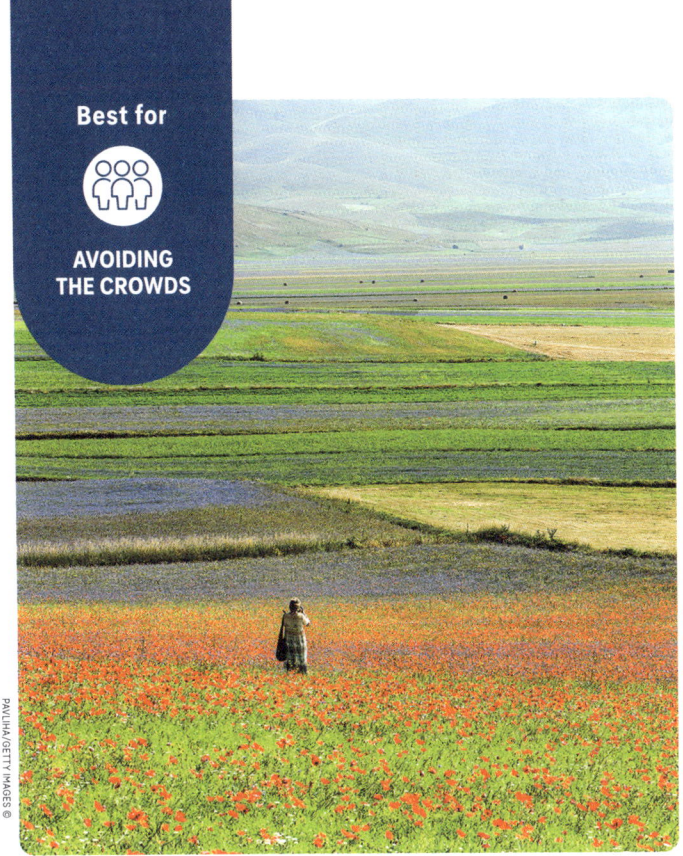

Piano Grande

Umbria's Piano Grande

Tucked into Umbria's far-eastern corner, the 1270m-high Piano Grande is a karstic plateau framed by the bare-backed peaks of the Sibillini mountains. It's an alluring sight at any time of the year but is especially enchanting between May and June when the snows have melted and wildflowers carpet the grassy plain. Poppies, cornflowers, wild tulips, daisies, crocuses and narcissi produce an extraordinary display of reds, golds, violets and whites to add to the greens and browns of the surrounding slopes. It's a florist's heaven, a hay-fever sufferer's hell and an endless source of fascination for walkers, who flock here for strolls through the meadows.

valley's eastern edge, keeping the aptly named **Laghetto** – a small lake – on your right.

02 Ten minutes beyond Il Laghetto, branch left onto a dirt road at a junction marked with a short pole, green paint and barbed wire. Begin steadily uphill, crossing in and out of beech forest. After 30 minutes of climbing, arrive at **Forca Canapine**, where the abandoned **Rifugio Colle le Cese** sits surrounded by sheep pastures. Turn left onto a broad dirt road, following signs for Forca di Presta. Red-and-white blazes mark the trail from here on. About 15 minutes along, branch left at a low post onto a smaller, ascending trail, with the main road still visible below to your right. **Views over the Sibillini** stretch clear to the southern horizon.

03 The trail dips gently, passing to the left of some beeches. Watch for an arrow painted on a stone here, and follow it left onto a new dirt road into the forest. About 10 minutes later, the road rises to enter another meadow, where you branch right at a post and begin climbing a narrower trail across the flank of a bald hill. **Ravishing views** north towards Monte Vettore soon open up. The trail levels out and within 15 minutes joins a wide dirt road curving north. Moments later, you reach a right-hand turnoff where an optional detour along a boardwalk leads to a scenic **belvedere**. From this junction, continue straight on the main dirt road to reach Forca di Presta.

☕ Take a Break

After a walk on the Piano Grande, there's no more satisfying place for a snack than **Panino allo Scarafischio**, a food truck parked at Castelluccio's main crossroads and named for the region's spicy sausage sandwich. Everything is served with a smile by the friendly proprietor, who has been feeding hikers here since before the Castelluccio earthquakes.

50

Bosco di San Francesco

DURATION	DIFFICULTY	DISTANCE	START/END
2hrs	Moderate	5km	Piazza de San Francesco Assisi
TERRAIN	Dirt roads and trails, paved paths		

In 2008, Fondo Ambiente Italiano (FAI) – the Italian counterpart to Britain's National Trust – began recuperating 64 hectares of long-neglected, donated woodland on the slopes below Assisi's world-famous Basilica di San Francesco. The result is a lovingly maintained nature preserve threaded with peaceful walking trails, ideal for a meditative half-day stroll.

Getting Here
Buses from Assisi's train station drop you 500m from the basilica and the FAI ticket booth.

Starting Point
Assisi's medieval centre, directly adjacent to the trailhead, has restaurants, parking and restrooms.

 Pay admission and pick up a trail map at the **FAI entrance booth**, reached through a signposted gate uphill from Assisi's basilica. A broad path switchbacks down into the forest, with staircases and **wooden railings** easing your progress.

 Beautiful views open up back to the basilica as the trail levels out at the base of the hill. Shortly, an optional detour to the left leads to **Ponte dei Galli**, an arched medieval bridge named for the passage of Charlemagne's troops through here in the 8th century. Continue north on the main trail through olive trees to the gardens of the **Monastero di Santa Croce**, a harmonious ensemble of cypresses, grapevines, fruit trees and stone walls draped with

Bosco di San Francesco

trailing rosemary. The restored stone buildings of this 13th-century Benedictine convent now serve as FAI's headquarters and info centre, while the **12th-century stone mill** just across the river has been converted into a restaurant.

03 East of the convent walls, take the path marked 'Terzo Paradiso'. A short jaunt up the riverbed brings you to the *calcinaie* – wood-fired kilns historically used to process limestone. Continue upstream, soon arriving at the **Terzo Paradiso open-air art project**. In the clearing before you, 10 dozen olive trees arrayed in three rings spread across the grassy slopes. Artist Michelangelo Pistoletto envisioned this 'Third Paradise' as a sanctuary for contemplating the bonds between humanity and nature. Curving paths run between the rows of tightly interwoven olive trees, inviting you to enter this calming refuge.

04 For a view of it all, climb the **Torre Annamaria**, a stone tower at the northeastern end of the clearing.

South of Terzo Paradiso, the main trail continues to an inviting picnic area near a more traditional olive grove. Cross the Torrente Tescio on stepping stones to return along the river's eastern bank to Santa Croce. From here, you can either retrace your steps uphill through the Selva di San Francesco, or climb the slightly steeper paved road, Via Ponte dei Galli, to re-enter Assisi via the Porta San Giacomo gate.

☕ Take a Break

Housed in a converted mill on Assisi's outskirts, **Osteria del Mulino** (*fondoambiente.it/luoghi/bosco-di-san-francesco/visita*) makes a tasty halfway break on a walk through the Bosco di San Francesco. Specialities such as *umbricelli al boscaiolo* (Umbrian-style spaghetti with wild mushrooms) are a delight, and carnivores will rejoice at Il Mulino's meat grilled on the open fire, from local lamb to Black Angus beef with salt and rosemary.

Also Try...

Lago di Pilato

Above the Piano Grande

DURATION	DIFFICULTY	DISTANCE
3hrs	Moderate	10km

This hike climbs high into the hills above Castelluccio, affording views of the Monti Sibillini and the Piano Grande. It's beautiful year-round, but uncommonly so in June, when the *infioritura* (wildflower bloom) is in full swing.

Just north of Castelluccio's main crossroads, turn left (northwest) onto a side road past Agriturismo Valle delle Aquile. Sheep pastures and pretty stands of beech trees alternate for the next hour as you follow the unpaved road west. Pass a blue EU sign on the left, and continue uphill, soon bypassing a right-hand junction marked only with a cairn. Climb 20 minutes through a high grassy meadow to a T-intersection with a major dirt road, and turn left. A long, winding hour-long descent brings you to a junction with the signposted E13 trail; turn left, enjoying phenomenal Piano Grande views all the way back to Castelluccio.

Traversata del Conero

DURATION	DIFFICULTY	DISTANCE
4hrs	Moderate	11km

This delightful hike south of Ancona skirts the slopes of Monte Conero (572m), affording expansive views along Le Marche's Adriatic coastline.

From the roadside Osteria del Poggio restaurant, head east on trail 301. The broad dirt track climbs gently through shady forest to a viewpoint overlooking the Piano Grande, a coastal shelf beneath Monte Conero's chalky cliffs, punctuated by a Napoleonic fort, Santa Maria di Portonovo church and a pair of lakes. Branch left onto trail 301A, soon reaching the Belvedere Nord, with more fine views north over the Adriatic. From here, the road turns south to the Convento dei Camaldolesi, a historic-monastery-turned-hotel whose bar offers a welcome break. Descend east along trail 301 to the Belvedere Sud for east- and south-facing coastal perspectives, then continue 1½ hours to Fonte d'Olio, the trail's southern terminus near the seaside village of Sirolo.

Castelluccio

Monte Vettore

DURATION	DIFFICULTY	DISTANCE
4–4.5hrs	Hard	10km

Peak-baggers will love this classic climb from Forca di Presta (1550m) to Monte Vettore (2476m), the Monti Sibillini's highest summit.

Ascend the grassy slopes north of the SP477. The gradient is moderate at first but soon steepens, climbing past Monte Vettoretto (2052m) and Rifugio Tito Zilioli to fantastic views over Lago di Pilato. Large switchbacks culminate near Monte Vettore's summit, where the northern Sibillini's great bald summits and ridges are revealed; on a clear day, you can make out the Adriatic coast.

Lago di Pilato

DURATION	DIFFICULTY	DISTANCE
5.5hrs	Hard	12km

This walk leads to Lago di Pilato, a hauntingly remote lake long associated with necromancy and reputed to be Pontius Pilate's final resting place.

The path (signposted as trail 151) begins where the road ends in the village of Foce, 7km southwest of Montemonaco. Elevation gain is 995m, but it's well worth the effort, as you pass through the grassy Piano della Gardosa into the awe-inspiring Valle del Lago, with Monte Vettore (2476m) to your left and the sheer rock walls of Pizzo del Diavolo (2410m) towering to your right.

Manarola (p202)

Liguria

51 Levanto to Monterosso
Epic ramble between two of Liguria's finest beach towns. **p198**

52 Portofino to San Fruttuoso
Deluxe resort meets hidden monastic hamlet on the protected Portofino peninsula. **p200**

53 Manarola to Corniglia
Spectacular meander between two of Cinque Terre's pastel-hued villages. **p202**

54 Sentiero Azzurro
A historic journey along the Ligurian coast on old mule paths. **p204**

55 Porto Venere to Riomaggiore
Wander atop precipitous cliffs and dip down to classic Riviera harbourfronts. **p208**

Explore

Liguria

For centuries an eastern outpost of the Most Serene Republic of Genoa, Liguria's history is written all over its steep-sided cliffs in diminutive chapels, hidden coves, and deftly terraced olive groves. It is also preserved underfoot on an intricate network of narrow paths that have been trodden down by generations of farmers, monks, sailors, townsfolk and – more recently – tourists.

Cinque Terre

Set amid some of the most dramatic coastal scenery on the planet, these five ingeniously constructed fishing villages can bolster the most jaded of spirits. A Unesco World Heritage site since 1997, Cinque Terre isn't the undiscovered Eden it once was, yet it remains a world apart. Sinuous paths traverse seemingly impregnable cliff sides, while a 19th-century railway line cut through a series of coastal tunnels ferries the footsore from village to village. Thankfully, cars were banned over a decade ago. Rooted in antiquity, Cinque Terre's five villages date from the early medieval period. While much of this fetching vernacular architecture remains, Cinque Terre's unique historical draw is the steeply terraced cliffs bisected by a complicated system of fields and gardens that have been hacked, chiselled, shaped and layered over the course of nearly two millennia. The extensive *muretti* (low stone walls) can be compared to the Great Wall of China in their grandeur and scope.

Monterosso al Mare

The most accessible Cinque Terre village by car and the only one of the five settlements to sport a proper stretch of beach, Monterosso, the westernmost village, is the least quintessential of the quintet. Notwithstanding, the village, known for its lemon trees and anchovies, is delightful. Split in two, its new and old halves are linked by an underground tunnel burrowed beneath the blustery San Cristoforo promontory.

Portofino Peninsula

Even the trees are handsome in Portofino, a small but perfectly coiffured coastal village that sits on its own peninsula, 35km east of the gritty city of Genoa. Hotels here are hushed and headily priced establishments, and a walk around the yacht-filled harbour and adjacent designer shops can be a largely vicarious experience unless you have rock-star connections. But you don't

WHEN TO GO

The crowd-shy would be wise to avoid the Cinque Terre during the peak summer months of July and August, when the area becomes inundated with hordes of tourists keen to experience its much-famed beauty first-hand. September and October are arguably the best months. Many businesses close in winter and paths can be wet and slippery.

need to be a Rolling Stone to enjoy the abundant trails. Protected within a regional park, the crinkled hills and indented coast of the peninsula contain 60km of walking paths that link isolated churches, old mills, abandoned WWII coastal batteries and the gorgeous little monastic hamlet of San Fruttuoso.

Beyond Cinque Terre

If you can't stomach the crowds in the Cinque Terre, there are some fine options further afield. Less-crowded Porto Venere has obvious appeal with a dramatic setting at the tip of a peninsula, an island just offshore to explore and some pretty walks right from town. Across the gulf of La Spezia, the villages of San Terenzo, Lerici and Tellaro also make charming bases in the region, with good beaches, dining and walking nearby. Even easier to reach is the seaside town of Levanto, which has a fine beach, and a historical centre sprinkled with medieval sites. Further up the coast, Sestri Levante is another captivating option, and it remains more popular with Italian rather than foreign visitors.

 WHERE TO STAY
Overnighting in Cinque Terre is truly special but note that hotels can book out for the entire April-to-October season and almost all are closed outside of that. Book well ahead and be willing to pay if you want something special. Alternatives are apartment rental or making a base in either La Spezia or Levanto. Hotels in Portofino are stratospherically priced (if beautiful). Nearby Santa Margherita Ligure has cheaper options.

TRANSPORT
The Cinque Terre walks in this chapter are all within steps of the coastal railway line that runs from Ventimiglia through Genoa to La Spezia. Connect in Genoa for Turin, and La Spezia for Florence and Milan. The Portofino peninsula is accessible from Camogli or Santa Margherita Ligure train stations.

Avoiding the Crowds

The glorious Sentiero Azzurro is perennially popular and it gets frustratingly crowded at peak times. To avoid the mayhem, get out early in the morning or later in the day (after 6pm in the summer). Alternatively, take one of the less famous trails in the national park, which see far fewer visitors – though it's still best to get an early start if you don't enjoy hiking with crowds.

 WHAT'S ON

Sciacchetrail
Held in Spring, this challenging long-distance foot race takes to the hills of Cinque Terre, following a rocky path along cliff edges, through terraced vineyards and looping past five iconic villages (sciacchetrail.com).

Resources
parconazionale5terre.it Official website of Parco Nazionale delle Cinque Terre with comprehensive information about hiking trail closures.

cinqueterre.com Route descriptions of all the main Cinque Terre walking paths.

parks.it/parco.portofino Website for the Parco Naturale Regionale di Portofino.

51

Levanto to Monterosso

DURATION	DIFFICULTY	DISTANCE	START/END
2.5hrs	Moderate	7km	Levanto/ Monterosso al Mare

TERRAIN	Mostly firm coastal paths with some undulations

This walk takes in Mediterranean forest, sea cliffs and overlooks. It also offers a window into the past, with stops at a 13th-century castle and the ruins of a medieval monastery. The highlight is the view from atop Punta Mesco, where you'll be able to see all five Cinque Terre villages tucked along this jagged stretch of coast.

Getting Here
Frequent regional trains run along the coast to Genoa (€7.30, one hour) and La Spezia (€4.50, 30 minutes). From late March to October, boats sail from Levanto to Cinque Terre villages.

Starting Point
Begin the walk on the shoreline of Levanto. Walk towards the southern end of the promenade and admire the view from this underrated coastal town. Take the marked stairway just past the stone columns on your left.

01 The stairs go up through an old part of the village and past Levanto's beautifully preserved **13th-century castle**. This hunky fortification, complete with crenellated towers, fulfilled many roles over the years – including as a prison in the 18th century. Today it is privately owned.

02 Beyond the castle, the route joins a paved road before branching off to track the coast. Cultivated land and holm oak forest bisect the ascent to Punta Mesco. Just before arriving, you'll encounter the terracotta-coloured **Podere Case Lovara**.

03 The path ascends along rocky soil, through pines, holm oaks and Mediterranean scrub, with the views becoming ever more majestic

Podere Case Lovara

Less than 1km northwest of the Punta Mesco, the FAI (the National Trust for Italy) is restoring an abandoned agricultural site overlooking the Ligurian Sea. Olive groves, new drystone walls, fruit trees and vegetable gardens, and rebuilt farm dwellings are transforming this ruin into a place of beauty and productivity. If volunteers are around, you're welcome to take a look at the work that they're doing or have a picnic on the property (small donation requested).

Cinque Terre coast

over the cliff faces. You'll soon be at a prime panoramic spot on the **Punta Mesco**. Atop this lofty promontory you'll be able to see both the bay of Levanto and the bay of Monterosso.

04 The ruins of a **hermitage dedicated to St Anthony** lie at the end of a short 300m spur off the main trail. The site dates back to the 1300s, and was gradually abandoned over the centuries. The brothers here kept an eye out for pirate ships on the horizon and lit signal fires to warn nearby villages of approaching corsairs.

05 You'll have fabulous **views** as you begin the descent towards Monterosso. After many stairs, the **beach** comes into view, with Fegina, Monterosso's modern half, just beyond.

06 Before rejoining civilisation, walk to the beach and check out the huge statue known as **Il Gigante** set into the cliff face. The 14m statue, which depicts the sea god Neptune, dates from 1910 and once adorned a picturesque villa, though storms have removed his arms and trident.

07 End your walk in **Monterosso's historic centre**, reached by taking the **car-pedestrian tunnel** located a few hundred metres past the train station.

☕ Take a Break

Just below the train station, Il Massimo della Focaccia is a strategically placed takeaway firing up the best focaccia in all of Cinque Terre. You can order that perfectly crisped bread topped with pesto, tomatoes and olives, sweet onions, with cheese or in various other fashions. There's also quiche-like *torta* (savoury pie) and a few sweet dessert items.

52

Portofino to San Fruttuoso

DURATION	DIFFICULTY	DISTANCE	START/END
2hrs	Moderate	4.5km	Portofino/San Fruttuoso

TERRAIN	Stone steps and well-marked coastal and forest trails

The Portofino peninsula, just east of Genoa, is a pocket of ruggedness on the otherwise elegant Italian Riviera. This short coastal rollercoaster dips into both its wild and deluxe sides.

Follow Via del Fondaco away from Portofino's small harbour. The town quickly disappears behind you as the street turns to steps. Head up, go left at a fork and pass through a couple of gates to reach the cluster of buildings known as **Cappelletta**.

Go right here and head down the dirt road forking left after 300m in the hamlet of **Olmi**. This trail, marked by two red dots, zigzags around a scattering of houses and quickly enters a wilder domain with **epic coastal scenery**. This is the **Parco Naturale Regionale di Portofino**, where pines and Mediterranean *macchia* dominate the headlands, and broad-leaved vegetation abounds in the gullies.

The next landmark is a park junction known as **Base 'O'**, which served as a military post in WWII. Soon after this you'll cross a concrete helipad and begin the descent through forest to **San Fruttuoso** nestled in a cove below. The hamlet's sensitively restored **Benedictine abbey** was built as a final resting place for Bishop St Fructuosus of Tarragona, martyred in Spain in AD 259. It was rebuilt in the mid-13th century with the assistance of the Doria family. Today, its calm simplicity and charming everyday collection of ancient monkish things feels touchingly close and human. The hamlet has several restaurants, a sheltered pebble beach and regular boats back to Portofino.

San Fruttuoso

53

Manarola to Corniglia

DURATION	DIFFICULTY	DISTANCE	START/END
2.5hrs	Moderate	5km	Manarola/Corniglia

TERRAIN	Narrow hillside paths and many steps

A more-than-adequate substitute for the closed section of the Sentiero Azzurro between Manarola and Corniglia, this spectacular walk links the Cinque Terre towns via the lofty village of Volastra, passing through terraced vineyards and lush forest along the way.

Getting Here

Manarola is on the main train line for the Trenitalia Cinque Terre Express trains.

Starting Point

Reach the start of the trail by walking uphill along Manarola's main street, Via Discovolo. Just around the bend – and before you reach the church – take the ramp leading off to the left, with a makeshift sign indicating 'Volastra'.

01 After about a 20-minute climb, the path intersects a set of stairs. Take these up to the left, following the red-and-white blazes for the rest of the hike. You'll get a serious workout as you walk up hundreds of steps, passing **fig trees**, **olive groves**, **blackberry brambles** and **old stone fences**.

02 The path continues uphill for another 1km before arriving in the peaceful hamlet of **Volastra**. Older than Manarola, Volastra was founded by the Romans in 177 BC as a staging post for changing horses. Settlers quickly realised the agricultural potential here; the town's name comes from 'Vicus Oleaster' – the land of the olive trees.

Best for

QUAINT VILLAGES

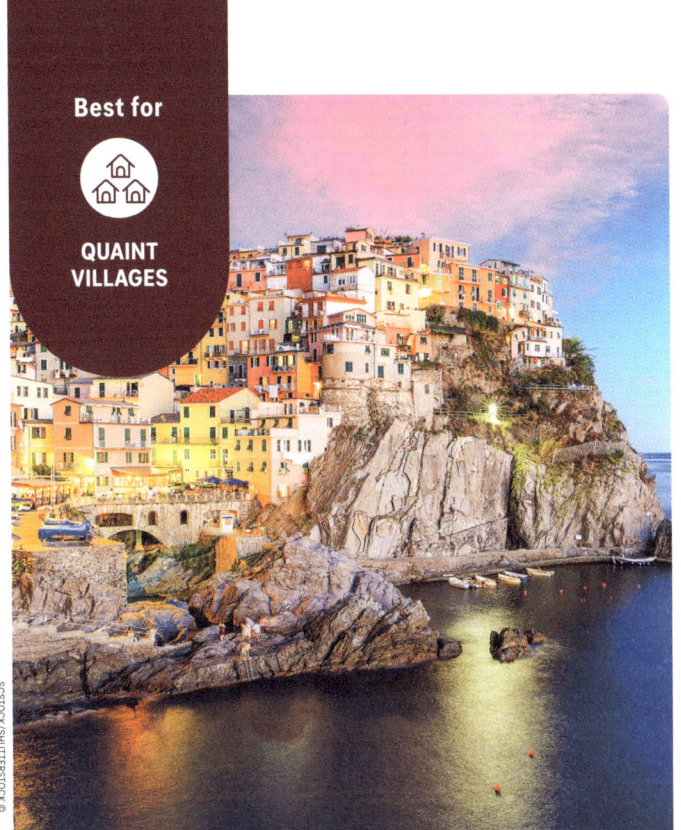

Manarola

Manarola

Bequeathed with more grapevines than any other Cinque Terre village, Manarola is famous for its sweet Sciacchetrà wine. It's also awash with priceless medieval relics, supporting claims that it is the oldest of the five. The spirited locals here speak an esoteric local dialect known as Manarolese. Due to its proximity to Riomaggiore (852m away), the village is heavily trafficked, especially by Italian school parties along with the regular tourists.

03 The **village church** was likely built in the late 12th century, and has a plain gabled facade, and an image of the Madonna that is particularly venerated. According to legend, the church bells were hidden during a time of Saracen raids, and never recovered. It is said that the bells still toll on stormy nights.

04 You'll leave the village by following signs to Corniglia along trail 586. This stretch offers **views over land and sea**, and passes right through a patchwork of terraced vineyards. Volastra has an ideal microclimate for winemaking. As you leave town, you might see locals hard at work in the surrounding fields – cultivating the DOC Le Coste, one of Cinque Terre's best wines.

05 As you descend, you'll enter a forest of **maritime pines**. This lush area was once cultivated – you'll see abandoned terraces, rusting water tanks and moss-covered stone walls which have now been reclaimed by the forest.

06 The descent gets steeper and rockier as you near **Corniglia**, Cinque Terre's 'quiet' middle village that sits atop a 100m-high rocky promontory surrounded by vineyards. Trail 586 intersects with 587 (signed 'Corniglia'), which you'll take into the village. You'll arrive at a T-intersection, practically behind the Chiesa San Pietro. Turn right and follow the lane onto Via Fieschi, Corniglia's main street – and a fine place to find refreshments.

Take a Break

The casual **KM0** (facebook.com/KM0Corniglia) on Corniglia's main drag serves simple but delicious market-fresh fare. Think well-balanced seafood risotto, tomato and mozzarella salad, hearty plates of ravioli, and good beers and wines. You can dine in the flower-fringed courtyard just across the lane from the restaurant.

54

Best for

COASTAL SCENERY

Sentiero Azzurro

DURATION	DIFFICULTY	DISTANCE	START/END
3hrs	Moderate	7.5km	Monterosso al Mare/Corniglia

TERRAIN	Narrow but well-used coastal trails with steep ascents and descents, including steps

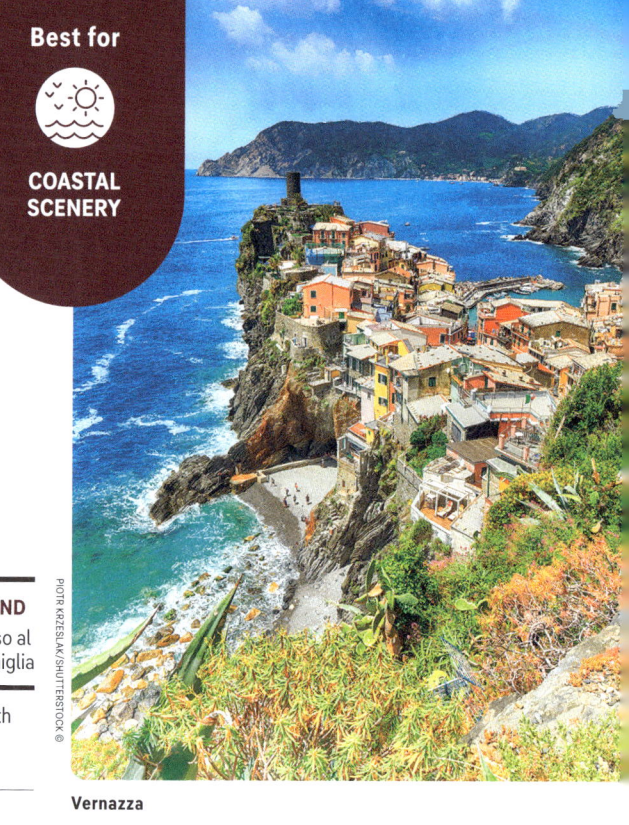

Vernazza

Cinque Terre's most emblematic and popular walk follows the course of an age-old path that theoretically connects all five villages. However, due to weather damage, only the two sections between Monterosso and Corniglia remain open to independent walkers. Short but steep in parts, the trail is a conveyor belt of fabulous scenery, with views over terraced vineyards, olive groves, steep mountains and pastel-hued villages.

Getting Here

Monterosso is on the main train line for the Trenitalia Cinque Terre Express trains. It also has the largest parking area of all the villages.

Starting Point

Exit Monterosso train station and turn left, passing through the shared pedestrian-car tunnel. After the tunnel, stick to the main road that parallels the beach. About 400m from town, you'll reach the staffed entrance to the trail where you'll need to purchase a trekking pass.

01 The ascent begins gently, passing by **vineyards** to your right and left, with **periodic lookouts** back to Monterosso. Soon, the climbing begins in earnest as the route incorporates copious flights of steps (there are over 1000 throughout the walk). Keep an eye out for the sign announcing **Vétua**, a small family-run vineyard of just 6000 sq metres. Here Bosco, Albarola and Vermentino are cultivated to create classic varieties of Cinque Terre DOC white wine. Aside from grapes, Vétua also grows lemons, artichokes, capers and herbs – all nurtured sustainably.

204 BEST DAY WALKS: ITALY

Weather-Beaten Trail

The 12km-long Sentiero Azzurro is an old mule path that dates back to the Republic of Genoa in the 12th and 13th centuries. Until the opening of the railway in 1874, it was the only practical means of transport between Cinque Terre's five main villages. Owing to bad storms and landslides, only two sections of the trail remain open to independent walkers: from Monterosso to Vernazza and Vernazza to Corniglia. The trail between Riomaggiore and Manarola (the Via dell'Amore) reopened in 2024 after renovation, but is now accessible only by guided tour. The path between Corniglia and Manarola has been so badly damaged by landslides that it will likely never reopen.

02 About halfway between Monterosso and Vernazza, the trail winds its way back to the coast, affording **dramatic views** over the seaside. In contrast to the manicured lands you've just passed through, the landscape here is wild and untouched, with a view stretching far off into the distance to the steep mountainsides that intersect with the foaming waters surrounding the wave-battered shore. In parts, the drop-off is sheer, so watch your footing and keep children close.

03 The worst of the climbing is now in the bag, with only a few gentle ups and downs over the rest of the walk. A mesmerising **perspective of Vernazza** comes in and out of view as the cliff-side trail winds down. At first glance, the seaside village seems like something from a fable: tiny pastel-coloured buildings nestled amid the imposing mountainsides rising above at near-vertical angles. The details come more into focus as you round the final bend: the harbourfront buildings standing tightly together, with the geometric block of a medieval tower set on the sea cliff just behind them. The tiny **beach**, watched over by the bell tower of the **church**, sits beside the small **waterfront piazza**, hardly visible beneath the yellow, red, blue and green umbrellas of the square's al fresco restaurants and cafes. And behind the waterfront, **terraced vineyards** rise steeply above the village.

04 Nearing the village, cultivated fields materialise once more. Olive groves, vineyards, lemon trees and vegetable gardens grow just beyond the rock walls skirting the trail. Soon you'll pass the ticket booth for Monterosso-bound hikers, and a popular panorama of Vernazza dominated by the cupola of **Santa Margherita d'Antiochia**. People not up for doing the full hike often come up to this viewpoint for the inspiring perspective.

☕ Take a Break

One of the only places where you'll find refreshment on the Sentiero Azzuro sits alongside the trail (on the Mediterranean side) in Prevo. **Il Gabbiano** serves up cold drinks (smoothies, iced coffee, granite) as well as panini and other snacks. Perched right over the cliff, the shaded outdoor tables have magnificent views.

05 After passing the church, the path turns into Via Ettore Vernazza. Take the first set of stairs leading down to the right. These put you right onto the waterfront **Piazza Guglielmo Marconi**, where you can have a drink or a meal, or refresh over some gelato while sitting on the breakwall. Be sure to take a peek inside the **Chiesa di Santa Margherita d'Antiochia**, a few steps from the waterfront. The atmospheric Ligurian-Gothic church is one of the finest in all of the Cinque Terre.

06 To rejoin the Sentiero Azzurro, head away from the waterfront along Via Roma, and take the first right just before the pharmacy. Look for the small sign with red arrows labelled 'Sentiero per Corniglia' on the wall. Head up the steps and follow this *carruggio* (narrow street) as it winds up through the back parts of town. Veer left up the stairs at the first T-intersection; after another 200m, you'll see a well-worn stone staircase up to the right, with a 'Corniglia' sign pointing the way beside a red-and-white blaze (these are used everywhere in the Cinque Terre as trail markers).

07 The stairs take you up to a **lookout** with a stop-in-your-tracks view over Vernazza. From here, it's possible to peer over wildflowers and cacti clinging to the hillside just below your feet, down to the tiny **beach** below the cliffs.

08 Continue on the path to reach the checkpoint for the next section of the hike. The walk starts off with gentle ascents, following the cliff edge along the sea with superb views at every turn. You'll start out above the open train tracks. Around 500m up the track, you'll begin climbing up uneven stone steps which zigzag past **olive trees** and stretches of **bushy forest**. You'll also pass **terraced gardens** that have long since been abandoned. The path is compacted dirt or flat stones in places, with plenty of stairs throughout. Along the cliffs, wooden railings provide added protection, but the trail suffers significant wear and tear during the rainy months.

09 Soon you'll reach a wild part of the coast with **views** of densely forested slopes of distinct Mediterranean vegetation stretching ahead, and the cliffs to the right thick with Indian fig opuntia and agave plants.

10 At around the midpoint between Vernazza and Corniglia, the path skirts the hamlet of **Prevo** off to your left. According to tradition, the tiny settlement was founded in the 16th century by families of mountain shepherds who migrated here in the winters to shelter with their flocks. Protected by dry stone walls, the terraces here nurture **vegetable gardens**, and **lemon** and **pomegranate trees**, as well as **cherries** and **quince**.

11 It's worth slowing down to admire the view here: this is one of the highest points of the Sentiero Azzuro, at an elevation of 208m. On clear days, the fine vantage point affords **views over the distant islands of Corsica**, **Elba**, **Gorgona** and **Capraia**. There's also a spectacular **view of Corniglia**, a jumble of soft-hued buildings huddling tightly together atop the steep, seemingly vertical cliffs above the sea. Terraced gardens have modified the hillside just behind the village; while farther along the coastline, the village of Manarola is partially visible.

12 The **knee-killing descent** into Corniglia begins at the outskirts of town with a seemingly endless stretch of stairs. After this you'll cross several bridges over mountain streams before reaching the main road into town.

13 Cross the pavement and look for the connecting path, which continues a few metres up on the left. The path winds its way into the village, past **vineyards** to right and left, eventually reaching the top of Via Fieschi, near the steps of the **Chiesa di San Pietro**. Turn right onto this lane, which will lead into the heart of **Corniglia**.

Cinque Terre Card

If you plan to hike between villages, the best way to get around Cinque Terre is with a **Cinque Terre card**. Two versions of the card are available: with or without train travel. Both include unlimited use of walking paths and electric village buses, as well as cultural exhibitions. The basic one-/two-day card for those aged over four years costs €7.50/14.50. With unlimited train trips between the towns, the card costs €27/49. A one-day family card for two adults and two children (under 12) costs €70/20 with/without train travel. Both versions of the card are sold at all Cinque Terre park information offices and each of Cinque Terre's train stations. You can also purchase trail admission at each of the trailheads.

Vineyards, Cinque Terre

55

Porto Venere to Riomaggiore

DURATION	DIFFICULTY	DISTANCE	START/END
4.5hrs	Hard	13km	Porto Venere/ Riomaggiore

TERRAIN	Mountain paths with some dirt tracks and paved sections

Just a few kilometres shy of a full-blown marathon, the 38km Alta Via delle Cinque Terre from Porto Venere to Levanto is beyond the capabilities of most day-walkers. A less-demanding option is to partake in the first epic third of the walk. For every 100 people you see on the Sentiero Azzurro, you'll spy only one or two up here.

Getting Here

Porto Venere is served by daily buses from La Spezia. From late March to October, Consorzio Marittimo Turistico Cinque Terre Golfo dei Poeti (*navigazionegolfodeipoeti.it*) sails from Porto Venere to Cinque Terre villages.

Starting Point

Find your way to the Piazza Giacomo Bastreri in Porto Venere and take the stairs leading up to the Castello Doria.

01 Ascend alongside the castle walls to emerge onto a narrow rocky path that skirts the coast. Behind lies the castle and the island of Palmaria. Leaving the views temporarily behind, enter a scrubby forest and continue up the rocky path which skirts the ruins of **Forte Muzzerone**, a 19th-century fortification used in both world wars.

02 Leaving the fort behind, the Alta Via steepens as it passes a **marble quarry** above the Muzzerone cliffs. There are some steep drop-offs in places. Keep climbing and you'll reach one of the most striking lookouts over Porto Venere. Known as **Pitone**, this ledge juts out above the hilltop, providing a natural balcony high above the sea. Here, one can admire the islands of **Palmaria**, **Tino** and **Tinetto**.

Best for

AVOIDING THE CROWDS

Riomaggiore

Local Marble

The stone found on this part of the coast with its valuable black marble and goldish-yellow streaks is called *marmo portoro* (portoro marble). Marble extraction near Porto Venere dates back to the Roman era, and in the 1860s there were 30 active quarries throughout the region (including five on the island of Palmaria). Today, however, the quarry at Muzzerone near the start of this walk is the only one still in operation.

03 The ascent continues, at times crossing over boulders and jagged rocks, and through dense Mediterranean vegetation. It's another 40 minutes or so of climbing to reach the small village of **Campiglia**, passing the ruins of a **17th-century windmill** on the way. Several other paths intersect in the village. Look for the AV5T signs and continue straight through.

04 Up is the only way to go as the route climbs past orchards and vineyards. **Views over La Spezia bay** offer some cool relief as the path enters a forest of pine, chestnut and oak. Around 2.3km from Campiglia is the Valico di Sant'Antonio, another trail intersection. Here, there's a **chapel**, a **fountain** and a wooded *Palestra nel Verde* (open-air gym).

05 It's a fairly flat stretch up to **Colle del Telegrafo**, so named for the telegraph wires that used to be strung here. You'll know you've arrived when you reach the restaurant named after the spot.

06 From the Colle, take trail 593 (SVA3) down to Riomaggiore. The path descends first through scrub and, later, cultivated gardens to the 18th-century **Santuario della Madonna di Montenero**. From the church, continue on 593 as it crosses the provincial highway, contours a wide gully and deposits you in the top end of **Riomaggiore**.

 Take a Break

You can refuel with plates of bruschetta and cold drinks, while relaxing on the terrace overlooking the sea, at **Colle del Telegrafo**, a walker's favourite located two-thirds of the way into this walk.

Also Try...

Santuario della Madonna di Montenero

Camogli to San Fruttuoso

DURATION	DIFFICULTY	DISTANCE
2.5hrs	Moderate	8.5km

The Portofino peninsula is littered with trails – 60km of them. Many are absolutely remote and a galaxy away from the sinuous sports-car-lined roads inland.

From the fishing town of Camogli, one of the more popular routes leads over the coastal escarpments to the road-less fishing hamlet of San Fruttuoso. The trail, initially marked with two red circles, heads south, climbing copious steps to the chapel of San Rocco. From here it divides: the red-dot path takes a vertiginous 'expert-only' route around the cliff sides to San Fruttuoso, while an easier inland path, marked by a single red ring, journeys through chestnut, pine and olive trees to a path junction called Pietre Strette. Here, a rockier path switchbacks down to the hidden hamlet with its Benedictine abbey and sheltered pebble beach. You can catch a boat back to Camogli.

Alta Via delle Cinque Terre

DURATION	DIFFICULTY	DISTANCE
4.5hrs	Moderate	13.5km

The antidote to the Sentiero Azzurro, the Alta Via traverses the Cinque Terre coastline at a higher altitude. It is thus more isolated from the historic villages and a lot less crowded.

Due to its length (38km), the path is often tackled in smaller chunks. The middle section from Colle del Telegrafo to Foce Drignana is a sizeable bite for a day walk, although you'll need to get on and off the trail by using public transport or other trails. The scenery oscillates from open, scrubby terrain to dense forest, with the Mediterranean just a blue suggestion through the thick foliage. Along the way, you'll pass the ruins of an old fortress, a weathered menhir signed just off the path and the lofty slopes of Mt Malpertuso, the highest point of Cinque Terre at 815m.

Camogli

Monterosso to Santuario della Madonna di Soviore

DURATION	DIFFICULTY	DISTANCE
1.5hrs	Moderate	2.5km

From Monterosso, follow trail 509 up through forest and past the ruins of an old hexagonal chapel to an ancient paved mule path that leads to Soviore, the Italian Riviera's oldest sanctuary, dating from the 11th century.

Here you'll find a bar, a restaurant and views as far as Corsica on a clear day. It's a 1.5-hour walk to get there. Reach the trailhead by taking Via Roma up through town; just after the roundabout, take the stairs (signed with trail markers) off to the left.

Riomaggiore to Santuario della Madonna di Montenero

DURATION	DIFFICULTY	DISTANCE
1hr	Moderate	1.5km

You'd better like stairs to tackle the short, sharp uphill grunt to Riomaggiore's hilltop chapel.

Trail 593V starts harbourside in Cinque Terre's most easterly village and ascends well-worn steps past walled gardens to a restored 18th-century chapel with a frescoed ceiling, which sits atop an astounding lookout high above the coastline. The walk includes a short 400m stretch along the main SP370 coast road. The total 300m of ascent is condensed over a short distance.

The Matterhorn (Cervino, p222)

The Western & Maritime Alps

56 Tour du Mont Blanc
Explore the Italian side of Europe's most majestic mountain. **p216**

57 Sella-Herbetet Traverse
Visit a royal hunting lodge in Italy's oldest national park. **p220**

58 Gran Balconata del Cervino
Glimpse the iconic Matterhorn from meadows along the Italian–Swiss border. **p222**

59 Vallone di Grauson
Walk upriver amid waterfalls, high pastures and stone villages. **p226**

60 Rifugio Garelli
Climb to an alpine refuge high in the Maritime Alps. **p228**

Explore
The Western & Maritime Alps

Sweeping up to spectacular alpine summits along the French and Swiss borders, northwestern Italy is a paradise for mountain walks. This region is home to world-renowned icons like Mont Blanc (Monte Bianco) and the Matterhorn (Cervino) – but it also shelters plenty of lesser-known natural attractions. Tucked into the northern region of Valle d'Aosta, Italy's oldest national park – Parco Nazionale Gran Paradiso – presents a landscape of rushing rivers, high pastures, stone huts and snow-capped peaks, while further south, the Mediterranean-influenced Alpi Marittime offer equally enticing walking opportunities at slightly lower elevations.

Cogne

Gazing up at the 4061m summit of Gran Paradiso (Italy's seventh-highest peak), Cogne (1534m) is the main stepping stone into Parco Nazionale Gran Paradiso. It's a low-key place with a dependable collection of hotels, restaurants and shops catering to outdoors-oriented tourists. The adjacent national park was created in 1922 after Vittorio Emanuele II gave his hunting reserve to the state, ostensibly to protect the endangered ibex. The park preceded the rise of the modern ski resort and has so far resisted the lucrative mass tourist trade. Its tangible wilderness feel is rare in Italy.

Courmayeur

Flush up against France and linked by a vertigo-inducing cable-car ride to its cross-border cousin in Chamonix, Courmayeur is an activity-oriented Aosta village that has grafted upmarket ski facilities onto an ancient Roman bulwark. Its pièce de résistance is lofty Mont Blanc, Western Europe's highest mountain – 4810m of solid rock and ice that rises like an impregnable wall above the narrow valleys of northwestern Italy. In summer, the Società delle Guide Alpine di Courmayeur is bivouacked here and the town is an important staging post on the iconic Tour du Mont Blanc (TMB) long-distance hiking trail.

Breuil-Cervinia

One of the Alps' most architecturally incongruous resorts, Breuil-Cervinia is a rather dull collection of high-rise hotels and

TRANSPORT

This large region is serviced by airports in Turin and Genoa, and is convenient to Milan Malpensa, too. Frequent trains run from Turin, Genoa and Milan to mountain gateways such as Cuneo, Aosta and Courmayeur. Buses serve many side valleys, including SVAP (*svap.it*) to Cogne in Valle d'Aosta, *Arriva Italia* (*aosta.arriva.it*) to Breuil-Cervinia in Valtournenche and Grandabus (*grandabus.it*) around Cuneo. Even so, having your own wheels is advantageous for reaching the region's more remote trailheads.

ski lifts redeemed only by its gorgeous mountain backdrop, smack at the foot of the Matterhorn. Less than 10km from Zermatt, Switzerland, as the crow flies, it crowns the far end of Valtournenche, a side valley running north off the Valle d'Aosta. Ugly or not, Cervinia's facilities are second to none, with a plethora of accommodation and restaurants, and gondolas that can whisk you up to trails in the surrounding high country.

Cuneo

Sitting on a promontory between two rivers, stately Cuneo provides excellent mountain views framed by the high pyramid-shaped peak of Monte Viso (3841m) in the Cottian Alps. There are a raft of reasons to visit this pleasant provincial capital, not least being the food, the bike friendliness, the hiking possibilities nearby and, last but certainly not least, the city's signature rum-filled chocolates.

WHEN TO GO

Summer is prime time for exploring the Western and Maritime Alps, though conditions vary widely from year to year. While most high-country walks should be accessible from June through September, snow can remain above 2500m until mid-June, or even later. From mid-July until late August, the area is very busy and accommodation is at a premium. Public transport services are more frequent during summer; camping areas and *rifugi* are generally open from late May to mid-September. Thanks to their lower altitude and proximity to the Mediterranean, the Maritime Alps become free of snow somewhat earlier than more northerly parts of the Alps, though heavy snow cover in winter is a certainty.

 WHAT'S ON

Festa delle Guide Alpine

At this annual mountaineering festival in August, alpine guides demonstrate their climbing skills at locations throughout Valle d'Aosta.

Terra Madre Salone del Gusto

Hosted by the locally based Slow Food Movement in October, this biennial gathering in Turin celebrates sustainable agriculture and regional cuisine, drawing chefs and producers from 150 countries.

Resources

Parco Nazionale Gran Paradiso (*pngp.it*) Website for Italy's oldest national park, founded in 1922.

Parco Naturale delle Alpi Marettime (*parcoalpi marittime.it*) Info about this well-run regional park near the French border.

Parco Naturale del Marguareis (*parcomarguareis.it*) Info about the Alpi Marittime's other most important park.

 WHERE TO STAY

There's a big variety of places to stay in this diverse region, from luxury hotels to *agriturismi* (farm stays) – but for many hikers, nothing compares to the romance of overnighting in a trailside *rifugio* (mountain hut). Hotels in Valle d'Aosta range from rustic family-run places to the ultra-luxurious. Most of them utilise the vernacular architecture of the region, with stone and wood playing an atmospheric part. Piedmont does pared-back, quiet elegance with aplomb and tends to be better value than elsewhere in the north, with a host of welcoming B&Bs and farm stays.

56

Tour du Mont Blanc

Col de la Seigne (p218)

DURATION	DIFFICULTY	DISTANCE	START/END
9hrs	Hard	20km	Rifugio Maison Vieille

TERRAIN	Dirt roads and trails, some very steep

Europe's highest mountain, Mont Blanc (Monte Bianco in Italian) exerts a magnetic appeal over hikers, who flock here every summer to complete the 170km Tour du Mont Blanc. The long day hike described here (easily split in two with an overnight at Rifugio Elisabetta) focuses on an especially scenic section of the TMB, all on the Italian side of the mountain near Courmayeur. It's a memorable way to feel the excitement of this legendary loop and rub shoulders with through-hikers, without committing to the entire multiday trek.

Getting Here

In July and August a *funivia* (gondola) and *seggiovia* (chairlift) run from Courmayeur up to Maison Vieille (*courmayeur montblanc.com*). Otherwise it's a two-hour walk.

Starting Point

Rifugio Maison Vieille has restrooms, a bar-restaurant and dormitory accommodation, making it an ideal stopover before hitting the trail.

01 Bid farewell to the red plastic cow and Tibetan prayer flags outside **Rifugio Maison Vieille** and lace up your boots for an exhilarating adventure. From the low saddle of **Col Chécrouit** (1956m) the trail starts climbing instantly, heading straight uphill past ski lifts and meadows full of grazing horses. Diamond-shaped TMB symbols and triangular signs for trail 2 regularly appear alongside the route, letting you know you haven't lost your way.

Hiking the TMB

If hiking a one-day segment of the TMB just whets your appetite for more, perhaps it's time to join the 30,000 souls who pass through Courmayeur each summer on the unforgettable 170km odyssey around the base of Mont Blanc. Most people spend one week to 12 days circumnavigating the mountain, passing through Italy, France and Switzerland and stopping to sleep and eat at *gîtes* and *rifugi* at the nine hiker-friendly villages en route. It's possible to do the hike solo, but if you're unfamiliar with the area, hooking up with a local guide is a good idea, as the route traverses glacial landscapes. The Società delle Guide Alpine di Courmayeur is a great place to arrange a trek.

02 Half an hour up the mountain, pass sparkling **Lac Chécrouit** (2165 m) on the left. The **views** – north into the forested depths of Val Vény, west to the hulking massif of Mont Blanc and southwest to the undulating outwash of the Lex Blanche glacier – just keep getting more majestic as you climb the now treeless slopes.

03 After 1¾ hours of steady climbing from Maison Vieille, a set of switchbacks leads up to **Arête du Mont-Favre** (2435m), where the trail levels out, revealing **grand views** into the next valley south, with the Lex Blanche glacier looming on the far horizon.

04 For the next hour or so, the trail heads down, down, down through a broad side valley off Val Vény, initially tracing a zigzag descent from the pass, with a creek on the left-hand side, to reach the stone huts of **Arp Vieille Dessus**. On the outskirts of this mountain outpost, watch for black-on-yellow trail symbols for the TMB and trail 2 painted on rocks. Another 10 minutes of walking brings you to a bridge across the creek, and 15 minutes further on, with Val Vény now in plain view ahead, you'll pass a decaying shed on the right, its roof beams overgrown with grasses and wildflowers. From here it's another 15 minutes to the valley floor.

05 The trail flattens out at a prominent signposted junction beside the milky grey-blue glacial meltwaters of **Val Vény**. Signs here point southwest to Rifugio Elisabetta, northeast to Rifugio Monte Bianco, and northwest to Cabane du Combal (1968m, a lakeside *rifugio* 10 minutes across the valley). Take the left fork and emerge into the blissfully flat **Plan Vény**, with wonderful close-up views of Mont Blanc's pinnacles reflected in the wetlands to your right. To your left, a curious bilingual (French-Italian) placard on a tree commemorates the September 1975 disappearance of a 23-year-old gem collector, last seen near here with his orange Volkswagen

BEST DAY WALKS: ITALY 217

☕ Take a Break

For a memorable lunch with front-row views of Mont Blanc and the Lex Blanche glacier, head for the ample sun terrace at Rifugio Elisabetta (*rifugioelisabetta.com*), high on the mountainside near the French–Italian border. The menu features a mix of Italian and alpine specialities, followed by local desserts such as chestnuts with homemade whipped cream.

and never heard from again. After half an hour of flat walking along a wide dirt road, begin climbing again via a series of switchbacks towards Rifugio Elisabetta, now visible on a dauntingly high hillside directly above you.

06 After a 25-minute climb, the dirt road levels off at a right-hand turnoff for **Rifugio Elisabetta**, marked by a sign on a nearby building (La Lex Blanche, 2282m). It's well worth the 10-minute uphill detour to the *rifugio*, where hearty lunches come accompanied by amazing **Mont Blanc views** from the outdoor deck. If you prefer to split the journey over two days, there are reasonably priced dorms and private rooms upstairs.

07 The main TMB trail continues straight ahead (southwest) from La Lex Blanche junction towards the French border at Col de la Seigne (2516m). A few metres ahead, near a **freshwater spring** pouring into a log trough, trail 2 forks to the left, marked by a yellow-and-black triangle and signs for Col de Chavannes/La Thuile. Branch off here, almost immediately crossing a simple wood bridge across a creek and beginning a gradual climb up the opposite slope.

08 Trail 2 continues relentlessly uphill for the next 1¼ hours, revealing ever more **expansive views** of the grassy slopes of Mont Fortin dropping into the braided gravel riverbed below, with the hulking backdrop of Mont Blanc dominating the northern horizon. The terrain gets more rugged as you climb, switchbacking up into a forbidding world of scree and boulders as you near the summit. Identified by a trail marker, **Col de Chavannes** (2592m) is a high saddle at the foot of a long ridgeline. Pause to admire views in all directions, then turn left here along trail 2 towards Courmayeur, following the eastern edge of the ridge.

09 After about 10 minutes, take a left fork onto the smaller trail 11B (signs for Mont Fortin). You'll soon pass **Lac du Mont Percé**, a high mountain lake backed by stark peaks on the left side of the trail. Following circular black-on-yellow symbols for trail 11A painted on stones, continue climbing another 40 minutes to a promontory just below the summit of **Mont Fortin** (2753m). From here, the north-facing perspectives across deep Val Vény to Mont Blanc's *aiguilles* (needle-sharp pinnacles) are truly awe-inspiring.

 Following signs for trail 9 to Ponte Combal, branch left over the edge of the ridge and begin a steep descent into the valley below. Take your time navigating the scree and boulder fields along the trail's higher reaches. Far below you lie the stone huts and meadows of Arp Vieille Dessus, which you passed on your earlier descent towards Val Vény. The trail gets less steep as you near the valley floor, ultimately joining up with the TMB trail after about an hour.

11 Turn right on the TMB and retrace your steps to **Rifugio Maison Vieille**, about 1¾ hours to the northeast.

Melting Glaciers

Global warming has started to hit close to home in Italy's western Alps. In recent years, scientists have been alarmed to see a massive chunk of ice beginning to detach from the Planpincieux glacier on the Grandes Jorasses peak north of Courmayeur. In 2019, daily ice movements of up to a metre a day (vs the normal daily rate of 10cm) spurred Italian authorities to order the evacuation of homes and roads in the area. In 2019, daily section of the glacier was in danger of collapse. While the glacier in question poses no threat to the section of trail described in this guide, it's a sobering wake-up call to the real-world implications of global climate change.

Tour de Mont Blanc

57

Sella-Herbetet Traverse

DURATION	DIFFICULTY	DISTANCE	START/END
7.5hrs	Hard	15km	Valnontey

TERRAIN	Dirt trail; steep, tricky sections

This incredibly exhilarating and scenic traverse follows the precipitous slopes high above Valnontey, with plenty of wildlife to keep you company.

Getting Here

Several daily buses run from Aosta to Cogne (50 minutes), from where you can walk (3km) or catch a free shuttle (five minutes) to Valnontey.

Starting Point

Tiny Valnontey offers restaurants, bars, restrooms and paid parking at a lot in the village centre.

 01 Head west across the bridge from **Valnontey village** and follow signs for trail 18 towards Rifugio Sella. After half an hour climbing through evergreen forest, cross a bridge and emerge into a meadow with a collapsed farm structure and a water trough. Zigzag another 15 minutes uphill to reach **Pascieux** (2224m), where a stone hut sits astride sloping pastureland, commanding **amazing views** over distant mountains. About half an hour above Pascieux, the trail dips to cross a rushing creek above a waterfall, then continues up the opposite bank.

 02 The trail switchbacks relentlessly up the creek canyon, traversing rugged treeless slopes. About 30 minutes along, the clustered stone houses of Alpe Gran Lauson appear across the creek. Soon thereafter you'll reach a signposted junction opposite the old stone **Casotto del Lauson** (2588m), in

Best for

MOUNTAIN VIEWS

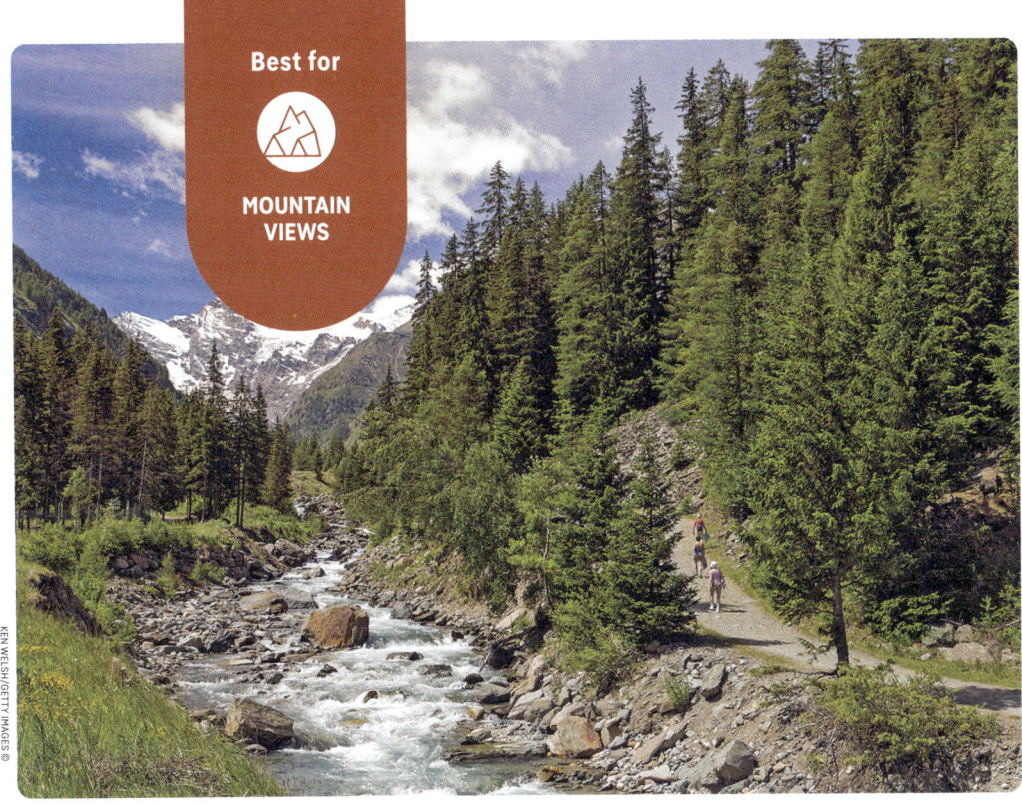

Parco Nazionale Gran Paradiso (p226)

a mountain bowl ringed by rocky slopes. Before you stands **Rifugio Sella**, a perfect lunch stop.

03 Continue through the open high country, following black-on-yellow markers for trail 18B. The sinuous route climbs through stone-strewn pastures, passing a mountain lake and affording **ever more amazing views** into the Valnontey valley. About 45 minutes past the *rifugio*, a series of rope handholds, metal steps anchored in the rock and a short ladder help you navigate a steep section. You're soon rewarded with **magnificent vistas of the towering snow-capped peaks** at the valley's far end. After veering right to cross a creek, the trail doubles back through a boulder field with painted arrows indicating the way. Ethereal views of the valley far below continue for another hour as you emerge on a high rocky shelf and pick your way towards the mountain meadow of Herbetet.

04 Massive slate roofs crown the **Casolari Herbetet** (2437m), a cluster of stone houses flanked by a spring where you can replenish your water supply. Trails 18B and 22G converge here; follow the latter towards the valley floor (signs for Alpe Money), switchbacking steadily down the mountainside for the next hour to reach another crossroads. The day's final stage back to Valnontey is a meandering, relatively level 1½-hour walk downstream along the verdant banks of the Torrente Valnontey, traversing a wonderland of enormous boulders, rocky spires and deep green forest.

Take a Break

The high country's uncontested lunch pick is **Rifugio Sella** (rifugiosella.com), King Vittorio Emanuele II's former hunting lodge. Set on a plateau at the hike's midpoint, surrounded by mountain walls, it offers lunches of homemade minestrone, followed by polenta served with fontina cheese or *carbonada* (veal stewed with onions and white wine).

58

Gran Balconata del Cervino

Best for

QUAINT VILLAGES

Cheneil

DURATION	DIFFICULTY	DISTANCE	START/END
6hrs	Moderate	15km	Chamois/Breuil-Cervinia

TERRAIN	Dirt trail, meadows and rocky slopes

Spellbinding views of the Matterhorn – seen from the less-familiar Italian side – are the star attraction on this 15km section of the 73km Gran Balconata del Cervino, one of the Alps' classic loop hikes. For most of the walk you'll be traversing rocky ridgelines and grassy meadows high above the pastoral Valtournenche valley, with the shapely 4478m triangular peak (known to Italians as Cervino) towering high above it all.

Getting Here

From Buisson on the SR46, the year-round Funivia Buisson-Chamois cable car (*funiviachamois.it*) climbs to Chamois in five minutes. At trail's end in Cervinia, Arriva Italia (*aosta.arriva.it*) runs buses back to Buisson (€3.30, 30 minutes).

Starting Point

Near the upper cable car station in Chamois are a couple of bar-restaurants with restrooms, but no parking (cars are prohibited in Chamois).

01 From the **upper cable car station**, walk straight ahead (east) through **Chamois village** – also known as Corgnolaz. Shortly after passing Bar Chamois on your right, yellow-and-black signs for trail 107 point you left up the hill. Opposite the turnoff, a fountain with a cute ibex-head spout makes a good place to fill your water bottles.

02 Zigzag up the hill on a mix of stone steps, paved road, dirt road and single-track trail. Signposts are frequent along this stretch, but make sure to stick to trail 107, as several other trails branch off here. Pass a kids' playground and a variety

BEST DAY WALKS: ITALY

Climbing the Matterhorn

Some 3000 alpinists summit Europe's most photographed peak (4478m) each year. You don't need to be super-human to do it, but you do need to be a skilled climber in tip-top physical shape and have a week in hand to acclimatise beforehand to make the iconic ascent up sheer rock and ice. No one attempts the Matterhorn without local know-how: mountain guides charge around €1500 per person for the eight-hour return climb. Client:guide ratios are 1:1. Mid-July to mid-September is the best time of year to attempt the ascent. You'll probably be required to do training climbs first, just to prove you really are 100% up to it. The Matterhorn claims more than a few lives each year.

of stone houses on Chamois' outskirts, then merge onto a wide **larch-shaded path**, ignoring signs for Rifugio Ermitage as you cross a road and continue straight uphill between low stone walls.

03 After a 35-minute climb from Chamois, arrive at **Lago di Lod**, a mountain lake flanked by ski lifts. The small lakeside park here offers picnic tables, drinking water and restroom facilities. Note that between late June and early September you can reach this same point via chairlift from Chamois. At the three-way junction to the right of the lake, trails 3 and 34 branch right and left, respectively, while you take the narrower central route marked 107 in black-and-yellow paint on a pylon. Starting as a faint path running parallel to the ski lift, the trail passes briefly through larch forest, then opens onto a wider dirt road climbing steeply up the ski slopes, with pretty **views over the lake and mountains** below.

04 You've reached the 'no pain, no gain' part of the trail – but rest assured, Matterhorn views are coming soon! At the top of the ski slope, as chairlift pylons disappear off to the right, trail 107 branches left off the grass-covered dirt road onto a narrow, steep path with signs for Cheneil. The trail continues climbing steadily, eventually levelling out a bit as it passes through low juniper scrub, meadows and larch forest.

05 Sunlight floods in as the trail leaves the forest, re-enters a meadow and bears left to reach the summit at **Col Cheneil**. Follow signs for **Cheneil village** along a broad, grass-covered road to your left. Begin a gentle descent, with **fantastic views** of the Matterhorn to the north and a mountain ridge framing the deep valley of Valtournenche to the west. A bench surrounded by wood railings makes a pleasant spot to

☕ Take a Break

Conveniently placed opposite the bus stop on Breuil-Cervinia's lower traffic circle, **Birdy Bakery** (*facebook.com/BirdyBakery*) is a perfect trail-ender. This friendly corner bakery and all-around local hangout serves tasty homemade pizza, sandwiches, focaccia and pastries, along with great cappuccinos. At lunchtime, check out the daily specials such as homemade pasta or delicious Swiss-style *rösti* (pan-fried potatoes with cheese, prosciutto and/or a fried egg).

take it all in. From here it's mostly downhill to the village of Cheneil, where the **Hotel Panorama al Bich restaurant** makes another welcome rest stop.

06 Exit Cheneil to the north, following signs for trail 107, and climb through the forest to the tiny **hilltop church of Notre Dame de la Guérison**. Tantalising glimpses of the Matterhorn reappear as you continue beyond the church into the high country, weaving through meadows and stands of larch forest. About 40 minutes past the church, pass a left-hand turnoff for Champlève (trail 28) and continue straight on trail 107, following the clear indications painted in yellow on the rocks.

07 After cresting a ridgeline, the trail descends to cross the ski slopes around **Dzandzoevé** and **Cime Bianche** (also shown as Desert on some maps). A couple of bar-restaurants offer refreshments here, including **Willy Bar** at the top of the Salette gondola, and **La Roisette**, in an old stone house near the base of the Motta chairlift.

08 Trail 107 continues north through high open country for the next half-hour, passing occasional stone houses and widening from a single-track path to a dirt road. Just beyond the picturesque **lichen-covered ruins** of an old stone house on the left, at a T-intersection signposted Tramail di Mande (2310m), turn right onto a paved road. About 10 minutes further on, turn left at a **long stone barn** (**Alpe Manda**) to stay on trail 107.

09 Five minutes beyond the stone barn, at a Y-intersection of two dirt roads, branch left (signs for Breuil-Cervinia) and begin an hour-long descent to the valley floor. Pass a **pretty stone building** backed by fabulous **mountain views**, cross a **wooden bridge** over an old funicular railway, then snake your way across a large rockslide. Bewitching **glimpses of the Matterhorn** framed by trees greet you for the next 15 minutes as you descend more steeply through larch forest.

10 The trail levels out at a clearing signposted Layet (2045m), where you'll find a **natural spring** with drinking water and the two-storey **Baita Layet restaurant**. From here, it's all downhill to **Lago Blu** (Lac Bleu, 1981m), just 10 minutes below. This piercingly blue mountain lake is one of Valtournenche's **most photographed spots** thanks to the perfect reflections of the Matterhorn mirrored in its waters.

11 You've now reached the valley floor, where a 25-minute walk parallel to the main road leads past a picnic area to the ski village of **Breuil-Cervinia** – home to a plethora of restaurants and a bus stop where you can hop a ride back to the base station of the Buisson-Chamois cable car.

Lago Blu

59

Vallone di Grauson

DURATION	DIFFICULTY	DISTANCE	START/END
3.5hrs	Moderate	10km	Gimillan

TERRAIN	Dirt trail, some steep sections

Reaching deep into the mountains northeast of Cogne, the beautiful Grauson valley shelters small meadows, larch woodlands and thundering cascades in its precipitous lower reaches, while its grassy highlands are dotted with stone huts, some still used by herdsmen during midsummer grazing.

From **Gimillan's village centre**, follow signs for trail 8 towards Grauson Desot. Climbing past electrical pylons, the trail reaches a meadow with fine **views** over Gimillan's wooden chalets and slate rooftops.

Trail 8 soon branches right, descending to cross the **Torrente Grauson** at Tschezeu junction (1910m). Begin climbing the opposite side of the valley, with views ahead to a **dramatic waterfall (Cascate di Pila)**. Beyond the falls, the trail climbs a steep embankment and passes through larch forest to reach a hilltop shrine with a cross about 1¾ hours from your Starting Point.

From here, a gentle stroll of less than 10 minutes descends to the tumbledown stone chalets of **Grauson Desot**. Refill your water bottles at the freshwater spring on your right just before the village bridge, and consider a picnic on the stone benches along the town's lone thoroughfare.

Return via trail 8E along the opposite side of the river, making sure not to miss the picturesque views back to the village as you leave. After initially climbing high above the Grauson valley, with **splendid long vistas** towards the snowy peaks of Parco Nazionale Gran Paradiso, the trail spends the next hour descending parallel to the river gorge. Beyond a large meadow, turn left at a junction for trail 3C, which reconnects with the path you came in on (trail 8) about 20 minutes outside of Gimillan.

Grauson valley

60

Rifugio Garelli

DURATION	DIFFICULTY	DISTANCE	START/END
5hrs	Moderate	12km	Rifugio Pian delle Gorre

TERRAIN	Dirt roads and trails, sustained climbs

Experience the primeval essence of the Marguareis range on this delightful day hike into the wide-open high country surrounding Rifugio Garelli. This fleeting taste of the Maritime alpine wilderness gets you up and back in five hours, with an optional lunch stop at the midpoint.

Getting Here

Grandabus (*grandabus.it*) runs buses from Cogne via Chiusa di Pesio to Certosa di Pesio, 3km north of the trailhead. Drivers can park at the trailhead.

Starting Point

You'll find paid parking, restrooms and a bar-restaurant at Rifugio Pian delle Gorre, directly adjacent to the trailhead.

01 From **Rifugio Pian delle Gorre**, head uphill on a broad unpaved road signposted for Rifugio Garelli. The going is easy and pleasant, traipsing through forest and past a waterfall on the left to reach a clearing with a large signboard in about 30 minutes. Leave the dirt road here, branching left onto trail H8 (marked Gias di Sestrera/Rifugio Garelli) and zigzagging up through giant evergreen forest. In about 20 minutes, emerge from the trees at **Gias Sottano di Sestrera** (1331m), a gloriously green meadow with a natural spring pouring into a stone trough. Trail H1 to Laghetto del Marguareis (your eventual return route) branches right here; continue left instead on trail H8 to Rifugio Garelli.

02 A sustained climb ensues, as you make your way into open high country. After an hour or so, you reach the stone barn of **Gias Soprano**

Rifugio Garelli

di Sestrera, where a plaque relates the WWII history surrounding this outpost. A further 15 minutes of climbing brings you to **Pian del Lupo** (2000m), a wind-swept summit made hospitable by the sleek, solar-powered **Rifugio Garelli**.

03 Leaving the *rifugio*, follow signs for Sentiero F Sordella, a narrow trail that leads gradually downhill to the frigid waters of **Laghetto del Marguareis**. At the next trail junction (about 20 minutes past the lake, 40 minutes from Rifugio Garelli), ignore the trail straight ahead for Passo del Duca, turning right instead to follow signs for Rifugio Pian delle Gorre. Begin steadily descending a long valley running parallel to a creek on your right, traversing a rugged, treeless high country landscape. Occasional stone shepherds' huts painted with red-and-white blazes offer the only hint of civilisation. About half an hour into the descent, ignore a trail junction on your left marked 'GTA' (Grand Tour des Alpes) and continue descending straight ahead through the sheep pastures.

04 An hour or so after leaving Laghetto del Marguareis, the trail finally drops back below the tree line, first passing through a **maple-fringed meadow**, then following the rushing creek into a full-fledged **deciduous forest**. Cross a bridge over the creek, and you'll soon find yourself back in the clearing at Gias Sottano di Sestrera. Turn left at the familiar water trough and retrace your steps down the hill to Rifugio Pian delle Gorre.

☕ Take a Break

Perched in a mountain meadow at 1970m, **Rifugio Garelli** (*rifugiogarelli.com*) makes a welcoming spot for a hearty mountain lunch, with specialities including mushroom risotto and grilled trout. If you're wiped out from your long climb, you can even spend the night!

Also Try...

Cascate di Lillaz

Lago di Valscura Circuit

DURATION	DIFFICULTY	DISTANCE
6hrs	Moderate	21km

Near the French border, this superb walk to glacial lakes at the head of a picturesque alpine valley affords fine Alpi Marittime views.

From Terme di Valdieri, climb an hour to Piano del Valasco, a rock-strewn high plateau where you can refuel with snacks at a historic royal hunting lodge. Continue up through a glacial valley to reach Lago Inferiore di Valscura (2274m) within 1½ hours, then follow the GTA (Grand Tour des Alpes) – here an old military road built between the world wars – towards Lago del Claus. Passing some lakelets, the trail enters the cliff-fringed glacial basin of Lago del Claus (2344m), then zigzags down to a signposted junction for Rifugio Questa, which serves home-cooked lunches and offers accommodation. Red-and-white squares mark the GTA as it descends to rejoin your earlier route. Go right, descending two hours back to Terme di Valdieri.

Alpe di Money

DURATION	DIFFICULTY	DISTANCE
5.75–6.25hrs	Hard	15km

This outstandingly panoramic walk through Parco Nazionale Gran Paradiso leads to alpine grazing huts below the edge of a glacier.

From the bridge in Valnontey village, follow trail 22 upstream along the rushing Torrente Valnontey. Turn left after about 50 minutes onto trail 22C and weave up through a series of cliffs, enjoying magnificent valley and mountain views. The trail levels off after another hour, crossing huge rock slabs to Alpe di Money (2325m), where several slate-roofed stone farm structures contrast picturesquely with the stunning backdrop of Gran Paradiso and its glaciers. The path continues south through the high country, then descends to a bridge over Torrente Valnontey about two hours from Alpe Money. Bypass a left-hand junction with trail 22G and continue downstream on trail 22 all the way to Valnontey, with the Torrente Valnontey rushing beside you and cliffs soaring above.

Inferiore di Valscura

Cascate di Lillaz

DURATION	DIFFICULTY	DISTANCE
1hr	Easy	3km

This short climb from Lillaz village leads to a series of gorgeous waterfalls at the edge of Parco Nazionale Gran Paradiso.

Cross a pedestrian bridge from the village parking lot, turning left past Bar Cascate to reach the Parco Geologico. Signs for 'Cascate' lead onto a flat, paved riverside path, then up stairs to the lower falls. Continue uphill to two more waterfalls before rejoining the main path, crossing a bridge over the falls and paralleling your original route back down to Lillaz.

Torrente Valnontey

DURATION	DIFFICULTY	DISTANCE
3hrs	Easy	10km

The river is your constant companion on this easygoing ramble through the valley of the Torrente Valnontey.

From Valnontey village, follow signs for trail 22 south. Beginning as a broad track, the level trail parallels the rushing river through conifer forest and cow pastures, narrowing as it continues upstream. About an hour into the hike, cross the river at Ponte dell'Erfaulet and continue 30 minutes up the forested, boulder-strewn valley, turning around at a junction with trail 22G and returning downriver.

Arriving

Italy's major cities are well-connected by air to the EU, the UK and the rest of the world. Efficient, dependable train service links northern Italy with neighbouring France, Switzerland and Austria, while ferries run from France, Croatia, Greece and Tunisia. Most Italian airports have their own train stations, providing convenient access to other destinations via Italy's extensive national rail network.

Travelling with Hiking Gear

It's generally easy to transport everything you need for a walking vacation in standard luggage such as a suitcase or backpack. If checking a backpack under the plane, avoid tying items such as hiking boots or sleeping pads to the outside, and help prevent damage by securing all belts and straps and enclosing the pack in a plastic bag (often available at the airport check-in counter). Depending on your airline and point of departure, metal objects such as hiking poles, tent stakes and camp stoves may be considered hazardous and subject to confiscation if transported in carry-on baggage; play it safe and check these items under the plane. Note that flammable materials such as camp stove fuel can never be transported by plane, even in checked luggage. When travelling by train within Italy, overhead luggage racks make it easy to stash your gear above your seat.

Travelling from the Airport

	Milan	Rome	Palermo
TRAIN	50 mins €13	30 mins €14	35 mins €7
BUS	60 mins €10	60 mins €7	50 mins €6.50
TAXI	40 mins €110	40 mins €50	30 mins €50

BORDER CROSSINGS

Entering Italy from most other parts of the EU is generally uncomplicated, with no border checkpoints or customs formalities, thanks to the Schengen Agreement.

SIM CARDS

You'll find free wi-fi throughout Italy. Pay-as-you-go (*prepagato*) SIM cards are available from the main telecom providers, including TIM, WindTre and Vodafone. Prepaid eSIMs offer affordable data.

CASH

ATMs (known locally as *bancomat*) are widely available throughout Italy. Most will accept cards tied into international banking networks such as Visa, Mastercard, Cirrus or Maestro.

VISAS

EU citizens can enter Italy with a valid ID. Citizens of Australia, Canada, New Zealand, the UK and the USA only require a passport, while some nationalities may need a visa; see *vistoperitalia. esteri.it*.

Getting Around

PUBLIC TRANSPORT OPTIONS

Public transport is generally the most convenient way to get around Italy, though a rental vehicle can be handy for groups and remote destinations. Trenitalia (*trenitalia.com*) operates express trains (*frecce*) that ply the north–south corridor between Naples, Rome, Florence and Milan at 200 to 300 km/h. Slower regional trains and buses run to other destinations. Ferries serve offshore islands and the Italian Lakes region.

TO DRIVE OR NOT TO DRIVE?

Having your own vehicle can be convenient (sometimes indispensable) for reaching remote trailheads in rural regions. But if you're walking in an area well-served by public transport, consider ditching the car. Downsides of driving in Italy include high petrol prices, tolls, limited urban parking, narrow one-way streets and traffic-free zones marked ZTL (*zona a traffico limitato*), where unauthorised entry will incur a hefty fine, most likely charged directly to your credit card by the rental company.

DRIVING INFO

Drive on the right.

Speed limit 130 km/h (motorways); 90 km/h (secondary roads); 50 km/h (towns)

.05

Blood alcohol limit is 0.5g/L.

Car Hire

International and Italian car hire agencies are well-represented at airports and some train stations. Reserve in advance for the best rates. Note that credit card companies typically don't offer complimentary CDW (Collision Damage Waiver) coverage for rentals in Italy.

Parking

During business hours (9am–1pm & 4–8pm Mon–Sat), parking spaces designated with blue stripes require prepayment (€1–2 per hour). Free or reduced rates apply on evenings, Sundays and during lunch hours. Spaces marked with white stripes are always free.

Low-Carbon Travel

Electric car rentals and charging stations are increasingly available, especially in northern Italy; EnelX and BeCharge operate the most extensive charging networks. For hassle-free travel between urban centres, the train is the most convenient low-carbon option.

TRAVEL COSTS

Train
Florence to Rome €45

Ferry
Naples to Stromboli €82

Car rental
From €225/week

Petrol
Approx €2.10/litre

LEFT: TREK6500/SHUTTERSTOCK ©, RIGHT: ROUTE66/SHUTTERSTOCK ©

Accommodation

HOTELS

Hotels in Italy are known as *alberghi* and *pensioni*. A *pensione* will generally be of one- to three-star quality, while an *albergo* can be awarded up to five stars. Quality ranges widely, from simple one-star *pensioni* with minimal amenities and shared bathroom facilities to luxurious five-star hotels with perks including room service, laundry and dry cleaning.

HOW MUCH FOR A NIGHT IN…

Bunk in a *rifugio*
From €30

Agriturismo double with half-board
€125

City-centre *pensione* double
From €100

Camping

Campgrounds in Italy, known as *campeggi*, are graded according to a star system. Most are major complexes with a full range of amenities including swimming pools, restaurants and supermarkets. Charges typically vary according to the season, peaking in July and August. Note that some places offer all-inclusive pricing, while others charge separately for each person, tent, vehicle, and/or campsite. Reserve in summer..

Hostels

Italy is no longer affiliated with the worldwide Hostelling International (HI) network, but the country has a growing contingent of independent *ostelli* (hostels), many barely distinguishable from budget hotels. Italian hostels

B&Bs

B&Bs are a burgeoning sector of the accommodation market and can be found throughout the country in both urban and rural settings. Options include everything from restored farmhouses to city *palazzi* (mansions), seaside bungalows and rooms in family houses. In some cases, a B&B can also refer to a self-contained apartment with basic breakfast provisions included.

Agriturismi

Long a booming industry in Tuscany and Umbria, *agriturismi* (farm stays) have spread throughout Italy. Options range from rustic country houses with a handful of olive trees to fully functioning farms and elegant country estates. All are required to grow at least one of their own products, and some serve farm-to-table meals. To search for *agriturismi* by region, see *agriturismoitalia.gov.it*.

RIFUGI (MOUNTAIN HUTS)

Italy has a vast network of *rifugi* (mountain huts), ranging from rudimentary shelters to cozy alpine chalets. Many are operated by CAI (Club Alpino Italiano). *Rifugi* typically open from June to late September and offer dormitory accommodation. Many also serve hot meals and/or provide communal cooking facilities. Blankets, mattresses and duvets are usually provided, though you may need to bring your own sleeping bag or travel sheet. Prices start around €30 for a bunk with breakfast, or €50 with half board. Book CAI huts online at *prenotarifugi.cai.it*.

Hiking

> **RESOURCES**
>
> **CAI**
> (Club Alpino Italiano) *cai.it*
>
> **Trekking Italia**
> trekkingitalia.org
>
> **Escursionismo**
> escursionismo.it

Gearing Up for the Trail

Finding quality hiking supplies is a breeze in Italy, especially in destinations such as the Alps and Dolomites where walking is a key focus for visitors. In hot spots like Courmayeur, Cogne, Bolzano and Cortina d'Ampezzo, outdoor gear stores such as Sportler and Decathlon sell everything from topo maps and clothing to tents and sleeping bags. Italian hiking boot manufacturers including La Sportiva, Salewa and Zamberlan also have factory stores where you can buy at the source. Rental gear is occasionally available at sports shops, tour agencies and some hotels. For example, if you want to climb Stromboli without lugging gear from home, it's easy to rent boots, helmets, hiking poles and headlamps affordably at the trailhead.

Via Ferrata

The *via ferrata* is a type of fixed-protection high-altitude climbing route with origins in northern Italy. During WWI, Italian and Austrian forces who engaged in mountain combat developed a system of ropes and ladders to help navigate the Dolomites' impregnable crags. After the war, some routes were retrofitted for recreational use with steel rungs, iron bridges and heavy-duty cables. The resulting network of *vie ferrate* (plural) allows adventurous souls to safely engage in an exhilarating mix of hiking and high-altitude climbing. To tackle one of these trails you'll need a climbing harness and a *via ferrata* kit including carabiners, a lanyard and a shock-absorbing device. For a map showing hundreds of vie ferrate throughout Italy, see *ferrataguide.com/ferratas/map*.

TRAIL ETIQUETTE

When walking in Italy, abide by the hiker's mantras: 'pack it in, pack it out' and 'take only photos, leave only footprints'. Don't build fires, pick wildflowers or leave rubbish in the wilderness, and refrain from disturbing cairns (piles of stones marking trails in areas with minimal vegetation).

LEFT: AISHE/SHUTTERSTOCK ©, RIGHT: MAKASANA PHOTO/SHUTTERSTOCK ©

Health & Safe Travel

INSURANCE

Purchasing tickets with a credit card can sometimes provide limited travel accident insurance and/or cover cancellations or delays to your travel arrangements. However, for peace of mind, it's worth considering a comprehensive travel insurance policy to cover theft, loss and medical problems while you're in Italy.

Drinking Water

In Italy, tap water is generally safe to drink. You can also confidently drink water from *sorgenti* (fountains) in towns and villages, and from taps over troughs in the countryside, unless you see a sign stating 'acqua non potabile' (non-potable water). Avoid drinking water directly from streams and rivers, as it may have been contaminated by animals upstream.

Blisters

Your footwear should fit comfortably, with enough room to move your toes. Boots that are too big, too small or not worn in will cause blisters; so will wet or muddy socks – always pack a spare dry pair. If you feel a blister coming on, apply a sticking plaster such as Moleskin, which will protect against excess friction.

Dehydration

Dehydration is a potentially dangerous condition caused by sweating combined with inadequate fluid intake. Initial symptoms – weakness, thirst and dark-coloured urine – can progress to drowsiness, dizziness and fainting. It's easy to forget how much fluid you're losing to perspiration while walking, particularly if a breeze is drying your skin. Stay hydrated by drinking 3L of water per day.

IN CASE OF EMERGENCY

Police
112, 113

Ambulance
118

Fire
115

SUN & HEAT EXPOSURE

Protection against the sun is paramount, particularly when walking near water, sand or snow. Avoid sunburn by applying sunscreen and wearing a broad-brimmed hat, and protect your eyes with UV lenses. When walking in warm weather, heat exhaustion from dehydration and salt deficiency is also a concern; symptoms include fatigue, lethargy, headaches, giddiness and muscle cramps.

Responsible Travel

Climate Change & Travel

Lonely Planet urges all travellers to engage with their travel carbon footprint, which will mainly come from air travel. While there often isn't an alternative, travellers can look to minimise the number of flights they take, opt for newer aircrafts and use cleaner ground transport, such as trains.

One proposed solution—purchasing carbon offsets—unfortunately does not cancel out the impact of individual flights. While most destinations will depend on air travel for the foreseeable future, for now, pursuing ground-based travel where possible is the best course of action.

The UN Carbon Offset Calculator shows how flying impacts a household's emissions:

The ICAO's carbon emissions calculator allows visitors to analyse the CO2 generated by point-to-point journeys:

Slow Food
slowfood.com
Italy-based organisation supporting sustainable food.

Fundazione Campagna Amica
campagnamica.it
Maps farmers markets throughout Italy.

Trenitalia
trenitalia.com
Low-impact travel by bicycle and train.

SUPPORT LOCAL

Embrace Italian culture, delight your taste buds and support the local economy by purchasing direct from producers at local markets and dining at family-run restaurants that specialise in regionally sourced, seasonal cuisine.

REUSE & RECYCLE

Reduce plastic waste (and expenses) by bringing your own water bottle, which you can safely fill at village fountains and springs along many trails, or with tap water at your accommodation.

TRAVEL GREEN

Walking is a wonderful way to engage with Italian culture while minimising negative impacts on local communities. Bike rentals are also widely available throughout Italy, and Trenitalia allows bikes aboard their trains for a small surcharge.

Nuts & Bolts

GOOD TO KNOW

Time Zone GMT +1 hour

Country Code +39

Population 59 million

CURRENCY: EURO (€)

Opening Hours

High-season hours (April through September) are as follows.

Banks 8:30am–1.30pm & 2.45–4.30pm Mon–Fri

Bars 7pm–2am

Cafes 7.30am–8pm

Clubs 10pm–4am

Restaurants noon–3pm & 7.30–10pm

Shops Shops 9am–1pm & 3.30–7.30pm Mon–Sat

Cash

In cities and at major tourist venues, many businesses welcome card and contactless payments. When shopping at independent stores, you may get a discount if you pay in cash. In villages and rural areas, it's advisable to carry cash, as many family-run businesses don't accept digital payments. Try to pay as close to the price as possible, and avoid large denominations, as smaller establishments often have insufficient change.

Tipping

Tipping is appreciated but not mandatory. In restaurants, service (*servizio*) is generally included; otherwise, a euro or two is sufficient in pizzerias and trattorias, or 5% to 10% at higher-end establishments. Many cafe patrons leave small change (€0.10 to €0.20) if drinking at the bar. Most round taxi fares up to the nearest euro.

Smoking

Smoking and vaping are banned in Italy in enclosed public spaces, including restaurants, bars and public transport.

Toilets

Public toilets in Italy are mostly limited to museums, department stores and train stations.

ELECTRICITY 220-230V/50HZ

Type F 230V/50Hz

Type L 220V/50Hz

HOW MUCH FOR A...

Cappuccino €2

Pizza From €5

Gelato From €3

Glass of wine From €3

By Difficulty

EASY

Castellina to Radda 92
Certaldo to San Gimignano........... 94
Greenway al Lago di Como 26
Oasi Faunistica di Vendicari 124
Orrido di Sant'Anna........................... 24
Panzano to Radda............................. 90
Passo del Lupo.................................180
Percorso delle Segherie.................152
Pragser Wildsee 150

MODERATE

Above Pescasseroli........................... 68
Adolf Munkel Weg 154
Around the Pian Piccolo................ 188
Bosco di San Francesco................ 190
Cala Goloritzé...................................162
Cala Sisine to Cala Luna 170
Campo Imperatore Ridge............... 70
Chianti Classico................................. 96
Fossa di Vulcano 126
Gola dell'Infernaccio......................182
Gola di Gorropu................................162
Gran Balconata del Cervino 222
Hans & Paula Steger Weg 136
La Rocca di Cefalù 118
La Strada del Ponale........................30
Le Tre Marine..................................... 54
Levanto to Monterosso................. 198
Manarola to Corniglia 202
Medieval Towns & Villages........... 104
Monte Corrasi 172
Monte Isola Loop 32
Monte Subasio 184
Necropoli di Pantalica.....................116
Passegiata del Pizzolungo............. 44
Portofino to San Fruttuoso 200
Punta Campanella............................. 46
Punta Troia 128
Rifugio Garelli................................... 228
Riserva Naturale
dello Zingaro.................................... 120
Santa Maria
del Castello Circuit.......................... 58
Santo Stefano di Sessanio
to Rocca Calascio 66
Sassolungo Circuit...........................142

HARD

Alpe di Fanes....................................146
Monte Baldo:
Sentiero del Ventrar........................ 42
Monte Mileto......................................76
Passo Gardena to Vallunga 138
Porto Venere
to Riomaggiore............................... 208
Rocca Ridge 72
Sella-Herbetet Traverse 220
Sentiero della Libertà 80
The Slopes of Monte Grona......... 34
Tour du Mont Blanc....................... 216

Sentiero Azzurro.............................. 204
Sentiero degli Dei 48
Stromboli..114
Tiscali 166
Tre Cime di Lavaredo 144
Tuscan Hill Crests 100
Valle del Sambuco 52
Valle delle Ferriere 56
Vallone di Grauson.........................226

Index

A

Above Pescasseroli 68-9, **68**
Abruzzo 63-85, **62**
   accommodation 65
   festivals & events 65
   resources 65
   transport 65
   travel seasons 64
accessible travel 7
accommodation 16, 234
   Hotel Pragser Wildsee 151
   Lido Palace 31
   Pensione Tranchina 122
   Rifugio Elisabetta 218
   Rifugio Garelli 229
   Rifugio Menaggio 35
   Villa della Quercia 49
activities 16-17, 77, 79, 185, *see also individual locations*
Adolf Munkel Weg 7, 154-5, **154**
agriturismi 88, 100, 106, 192, 234
air travel 232
airports 232
Alicudi 130
Alpe di Fanes 14, 146-9, **147**
Alpe di Money 230
Alps, the 10
Alta Via delle Cinque Terre 210
Amalfi 43, 56
Amalfi Coast 8, the, *see also* Campania & the Amalfi Coast
Ancona 179, 192
Apennines 64
Aquilegia 165
Arco di Lupiru 171

Walks 000
Map Pages 000

Arco Naturale 44
Arête du Mont-Favre 217
Around the Pian Piccolo 13, 188-9, **188**
Arp Vieille Dessus 217
arriving in Italy 232
Assergi 85
Assisi 178
astronomy 70
Atrani 61

B

Baunei 160
beaches 8, 205
   Baia di Ieranto 47
   Cala Berretta 122
   Cala Capreria 121
   Cala della Disa 122
   Cala dell'Uzzo 122
   Cala Fuili 174
   Cala Goloritzé 6, 162
   Cala Luna 8, 170, 174
   Cala Sisine 8, 170
   Cala Tonnarella dell'Uzzo 122
   Calamosche beach 125
   Marina di Praia 54
   Positano 50
Bilichinzos 168
boat travel 13, 233
Boccaccio, Giovanni 95
Bolzano 134
Bomerano 48
books 19
borders 232
Bosco di San Francesco 190-1, **190**
Bottaccio 98
Bozzanigo 28
Breuil-Cervinia 214-15, 224
budget 238
business hours 238

C

Cadenabbia 28
Cala Goloritzé 6, 162-3, **162**
Cala Sisine to Cala Luna 8, 170-1, **170**
Calascio 67
Camogli 210
Campania & the Amalfi Coast 41-61, **40**
   accommodation 43
   festivals & events 43
   resources 43
   transport 43
   travel seasons 42
Campiglia 209
camping 74, 234
Campo 78, 83
Campo di Giove 82
Campo Imperatore Ridge Walk 70-1, **70**
Campocecina 109
Cannobina 24
Cannobio 39
Cansano 81
Cantaru Orruos 164
Capo d'Acqua trail 58
Capo Testa 175
Cappelletta 200
Capraia 206
Capri Town 44
Caramanico Terme 85
Carmine Superiore 39
car rental 233
car travel 233
Carzano 33
Casa Campore 106
Casa di Reclusione 101
Cascate di Lillaz 231
Casolari Herbetet 221
Casotto del Lauson 220
Castellina 92
Castellina in Chianti 92

Castellina to Radda 92-3, **92**
Castello di San Polo in Rosso 98
Castelluccio 178, 192
Castelpoggio 109
Castelvecchi 90
Catania 112
cathedrals, *see* churches & cathedrals
caves
   Grotta del Biscotto 48
   Grotta dell'Uzzo 122
   Grotta di Matermània 44
Cefalù 113
Celts, the 12
cell phones 232, 238
Certaldo 7
Certaldo to San Gimignano 7, 94-5, **94**
Chalet Margherita 142
Chamois 222
Cheneil 223
Chianti 88
Chianti Classico 14, 96-9, **97**
Chiosco Sa Barva 164
churches & cathedrals
   Basilica di San Francesco 190
   Chapel of St Johann (San Giovanni) 155
   Chiesa di San Giuseppe 28
   Chiesa di San Pietro 206
   Chiesa di Santa Margherita d'Antiochia 206
   Chiesa di Santa Maria delle Pietà 67
   Chiesa di Sant'Anna 24
   Chiesa Parrocchiale 68
   Chiesa Santa Maria della Misericordia 78
   Collegiata di Santa Maria 52
   Notre Dame de la Guérison 224
   Parrocchia di Sant'Abbondio 28
   Pieve di Cellole 95
   Pieve di San Giusto in Salcio 97
   Pieve di Santo Stefano a Campo 108
   Sacro Monte di San Francesco 39

Walks 000
Map Pages 000

   San Giacomo church 27
   San Gimignano cathedral 101
   San Lorenzo 106
   San Rocco 33
   San Rocco chapel 27
   Santuario della Madonna del Soccorso 27
   Santuario di Monte Tranquillo 73
   Santuario Madonna della Ceriola 33
   St Johann 155
   Volastra village church 203
Cime Bianche 224
Cinque Terre 13, 196-7, 207, **196**
Cisternulo 49
Ciuciano 101
climate 16-17
clothing 18
coastal walks 8
coasts 8
Cogne 214
Col Chécrouit 216
Col Cheneil 223
Col de Chavannes 218
Col de Locia 147
Colle del Telegrafo 209
Colle Mitra 81
Colle Savente 81
Collemucioli 95
Colma di Malcesine 36
Colonno 26
Compaccio 136
Compatsch 136
Conca dei Marini 55
Conero Riviera 180
Convento San Nicola 53
Corniglia 7, 202, 206, 208
Corno Grande 84
Corsa degli Zingari 77
Corsa dei Ceri 185
Corsica 206
Cortina d'Ampezzo 134
Corvara in Badia 134
Courmayeur 214, 217
credit cards 238
Croce della Conocchia 60
Cuneo 215

D

da Vinci, Leonardo 10
dangers 236
disabilities, travellers with 7
Dolomites, the & Stelvio 134-57, **133**
   accommodation 135
   festivals & events 135
   resources 135
   transport 135
   travel seasons 134
Dorgali 161
Dreizinnenhütte 145
drinks, *see* food & drink
drinking water 236
driving 233
Due Sorelle 181
Dusler Alm 155
Dzandzoevé 224

E

Elba 206
electricity 238
emergencies 236
etiquette 235
Etna 131
Etruscans, the 12
events, *see* festivals & events

F

family travel 7, 79
festivals & events 16-17, *see also* individual locations
films 18
Fiordo di Furore 55
Fiume Calcinara 116
Fiume Era Morta 106
Fonte Bregno 186
Fonte Ramarozzo 81-2
Fonte Sulmonita 81
food & drink 14, 17, 99, 139
   Agriturismo Nuraghe Mannu 171
   Baita Layet 224
   Bar Dante 98

Bar Su Porteddu 163
Birdy Bakery 224
Caffè Sicilia 125
Capanna Alpina 146
C'era Una Volta 59
Colle del Telegrafo 209
Da Armandino 55
Dolceria Corrado Costanzo 125
Dreizinnenhütte 145
Durnwald 151
Gelateria Dondoli 95
Gostner Schwaige 137
Gschnagenhardt 155
Hotel Panorama al Bich 224
Il Duca degli Abruzzi 74
Il Gabbiano 206
KM0 203
La Capannina 37
La Fabbrica del Gelato 28
La Forgia Maurizio 127
La Roisette 224
La Scarpetta di Venere 82
L'Incontro 106
Lo Scoglio 47
Locanda al Lago 33
Locanda Sotto gli Archi 67
Mandralisca 16 119
Ostello Lo Zio 71
Osteria del Mulino 191
Osteria delle Catene 102
Osteria Sara 181
Panino allo Scarafischio 189
Plattkofelhütte 143
Ponale Alto Belvedere 31
Relais Villa Miraglia 130
Rifugio Fanes 148
Rifugio Menaggio 35
Rifugio Puez 140
Rifugio Sella 221
Ristorante Ispinigoli 165
Ristorante La Rocca 186
Ristorante-Pizzeria Majella 78

Walks 000
Map Pages 000, 000

Ritrovo Ingrid 115
Sal de Riso 53
Sicilian cuisine 125
Su Gologone 168
Trattoria Il Veliero 129
Trattoria Santa Croce 50
Willy Bar 224
Zi Peppe 59
food walks 14
Forato 108
Forca Canapine 189
Forcella Cir 139
Forcella Col de Mezo 145
Forcella de Ciampei 139-40
Forcella de Crespëina 139
Forcella Lavaredo 144
Forcella Rodella 142
Forte Muzzerone 208
Fossa di Vulcano 7, 126-7
Fosso delle Carceri 187
Francis of Assisi 184-6

G

Galenda 97
Geisler Alm 155
Gias Soprano di Sestrera 228
Giro dei Laghi 157
Giro del Bullaccia 157
glaciers 219
Gola dell'Infernaccio 182
Gola di Gorropu 164-5
Gorgona 206
Gorropu gorge 164-5
Gran Balconata del Cervino 7, 222-5, **223**
Gran Paradiso 11
Grauson Desot 226
Greeks, the 12
Greenway al Lago di Como
Greve in Chianti 108
Gschnagenhardt Alm 155
Guado di Coccia 82
Gubbio 185

H

Hans & Paula Steger Weg 6, 136-7, **136**
health 236
highlights 8-15
hiking 18, 235, *see also individual locations*
historical sites 198
   Anàktoron 116
   Apennine castle-fortress 67
   Caldora Castle 78
   Castel Mancino 68
   Castelvecchio 105, 107
   Ercole Curino 84
   Necropoli di Pantalica 116
   Podere Case Lovara 198
   Santo Stefano di Sessanio 66
   Segesta 123
   Tempio di Diana 119
history 71
history walks 12
hostels 234
Hotel Supramonte 165
hotels 234
Hütte, Jimmi 139

I

insurance 236
internet access 232
Iscala 'e Pradu 172
Ischia 60
Isola Comacina 27
Italian Lakes, the 21-39, **20**
   accommodation 23
   festivals & events 23
   resources 23
   transport 23
   travel seasons 22

J

Jëuf de Frea 138

L

Lac Chécrouit 217
Laghetto del Marguareis 229
La Rocca 73
La Rocca di Cefalù 12, 118-19, **118**
La Spezia 209
La Strada del Ponale 30-1, **30**
La Tese trail 59
lakes
   Lac du Mont Percé 218
   Lago Blu 224
   Laghi dei Piani 145
   Lago di Biviere 130
   Lago di Braies 150-1
   Lago di Como 7, 22, 26-9
   Lago di Garda 22-3, 30-1
   Lago di Lod 223
   Lago di Pilato 193
   Lago di Valscura Circuit 230
   Lago D'Iseo 23, 32-3
   Lago d'Orta 39
   Lago Lagazuoi 148
   Lago Maggiore 22
Langalmhütte 145
language 19, 147
L'Aquila 64
Laranzer Schwaige hut 137
Lé de Limo 148
Le Marche, *see* Umbria & Le Marche 177
Le Tre Marine 54-5, **54**
Levanto 197
Levanto to Monterosso 198-9, **198**
Liguria 195-211, **194**
   accommodation 197
   feativals & events 197
   resources 197
   transport 197
   travel seasons 196
Lipari 112

Walks 000
Map Pages 000

M

Maiori 61
Malcesine 36
Malga Gran Fanes 147
Malga Sassopiatto 143
Manarola 7, 203
Manarola to Corniglia 7, 202-3, **202**
marble 209
Marettimo 128-9
Marguareis 228
Marina di Furore 55
Marina di Praia 54
Maritime Alps 13
Massa 33
Matterhorn the, 7, 223, 224
Medieval Towns & Villages 12, 104-7, **105**
Mezzegra 28
Minori 53
Minuta 57
mobile phones 232, 238
Molino di Foci 101
Monastero di Santa Croce 190
money 232, 238
Mont Blanc 11, 216-17, **216**
Montauto 102
Monte Baldo: Sentiero del Ventrar 36-7, **36**
Monte Corrasi 172-3, **172**
Monte Grona 6, 34-5, **34**
Monte Isola Loop 32-3, **32**
Monte Mileto 11, 76-9, **77**
Monte Oliveto Convent 100
Monte Subasio 184-7, **185**
Montepertuso 50
Monterosso 198-9, 204, 211, **198**
Monterosso al Mare 196
Morrone di Pacentro 77
mountain walks 11
mountains 17
   Mont Blanc 11, 216
   Mont Fortin 218
   Monte Baldo 37
   Monte Conero 192
   Monte Corrasi 172
   Monte delle Croci 67
   Monte Entu 174
   Monte Grona 34
   Monte Isola Loop 32
   Monte Mileto 76
   Monte Mottarone 38
   Monte Pietroso 73
   Monte Porrara 82
   Monte Portella 71
   Monte San Costanzo 47
   Monte Sant'Angelo 58
   Monte Subasio 184
   Monte Tranquillo 73
   Monte Tuoro 44
   Monte Vettore 193
   Monte Voltraio 106
   Monti Sibillini 192
museums 92
   Casa Chianti Classico 92
   Centro di Visita di Pescasseroli 73
   Museo della Carta (Paper Museum) 57
   Museo della Cultura Contadina 122
   Museo della Manna 121
   Museo delle Attività Marinare 122
   Museo dell'Intreccio 122
   Museo Etrusco Guarnacci 105
   Museo Naturalistico 121
music 19
Mussolini, Benito 71

N

national parks & reserves
   Castelvecchio Nature Reserve 107
   Centro di Visita di Pescasseroli 73
   Majella National Park 80-1
   Parco Naturale Fanes-Sennes-Braies 146-9
   Parco Naturale Puez Odle 138
   Parco Naturale Regionale di Portofino 200
   Parco Nazionale d'Abruzzo, Lazio e Molise 64-5
   Parco Nazionale del Gran Sasso e Monti della Laga 65
   Parco Nazionale della Majella 65
   Parco Nazionale Gran Paradiso 230

Parco Regionale del Conero 180
Necropoli di Pantalica 12, 117
Nerano 47
Nocelle 49
Noto 112
Nuoro 161
Nuraghic, the 12, 167

O

Oasi Faunistica di Vendicari 8, 124-5, **124**
off-the-beaten-track walks 13
Olzano 33
Orfento Gorge 85
Orrido di Sant'Anna 7, 24-5, **24**
Orta San Giulio 39
Ossuccio 27

P

Pacentro 76, 78
palaces
    Brentano 28
    Lido Palace 31
    Pala Úporo 168
Palazzina 106
Palena 82
Palmaria 208
Pancole 95
Pania della Croce 108
Pantalica 116
Panzano in Chianti 90, 92
Panzano to Radda 90-1, **90**
parks & gardens, *see individual locations*
parking 233
Pascieux 220
Passeggiata del Pizzolungo 8, 44-5, **44**
Passo del Lupo 180-1
Passo Gardena 138

Walks 000
Map Pages 000, 000

Passo Gardena to Vallunga 11, 138-41, **139**
Passo San Leonardo 78
Percorso delle Segherie 7, 152-3 **152**
Pescasseroli 72
Phoenicians, the 167
Pian del Lupo 229
Pian Piccolo 188-9, **188**
Piano Grande 189, 192
Piazza Guglielmo Marconi 206
Pieralongia 156
Pignano 106
Pitone 208
Piz da Uridl 143
Piza Nord 147
Plan Vény 217
planning 16-19
Plattkofelhütte 143
podcasts 19
Podere Case Lovara 198-9, **198**
Pogerola 56
Poggio San Polo 98
police 236
Ponale 30-1
Ponale Alto Belvedere 31
Ponte dei Galli 190
Pontone 57
population 238
Pornanino 92
Porta dei Cappuccini 184
Portofino 6, 196
Portofino to San Fruttuoso 6, 200-1, **200**
Porto Venere 197
Porto Venere to Riomaggiore 13, 208-9, **208**
Positano 50-1, 58-9
Pragser Wildsee 7, 150-1, **150**
Pregasina 31
Prevo 206
Procinto 108
Punta Campanella 46-7, **46**
Punta Corrasi 172
Punta La Marmora 175

Punta Mesco 199
Punta Troia 13, 128-9, **128**

R

Raccicano 105
Radda in Chianti 89, 90, 92, 96
Ranza 101
Ravello 53, 61
responsible travel 233, 237
rifugi 234
    Rifugio Celidonio 78
    Rifugio Colle le Cese 189
    Rifugio della Difesa 73
    Rifugio di Lorio 74
    Rifugio di Monte Tranquillo 73
    Rifugio Duca degli Abruzzi 71
    Rifugio Elisabetta 218
    Rifugio Emilio Comici 143
    Rifugio Fanes 148
    Rifugio Friedrich August 142
    Rifugio Garelli 13, 228
    Rifugio Lavaredo 144
    Rifugio Maison Vieille 216, 218
    Rifugio Pian delle Gorre 228
    Rifugio Puez 140
    Rifugio Salei 142
    Rifugio Sandro Pertini 143
    Rifugio Scotoni 148
    Rifugio Sella 221
    Rifugio Vallonica 187
Rifugio Garelli 13, 228-9, **228**
Riomaggiore 208, 211
Riserva Naturale dello Zingaro 14, 120-3, **120**
Riva del Garda 23, 30
Rocca Calascio 7, 66-7, **66**
Rocca Minore 184
Rocca Ridge 14, 72-5, **73**
Rocchicciola 185
Roda de Pütia 156
Roman history 27
Romans, the 12, 67, 167
running 77, 185

S

Sacro Monte di Ossuccio 27
Sala Comacina 26
Sa Sedda 'e Sos Carros 167
Sambuco 53
San Donato 102, 105
San Fabiano 108
San Fruttuoso 6, 200, 210
San Gimignano 7, 89, 94-5, 100, 102, 104
San Matteo gate 95
San Pierto della Lenca 85
San Silvestro 140
Santa Margherita d'Antiochia 205
Sant'Amate 35
Sant'Angelo a Tre Pizzi 60
Santo Stefano di Sessanio 7
Santo Stefano di Sessanio to Rocca Calascio 7, 66-7, **66**
Santuario della Madonna di Montenero 209, 211
Santuario della Madonna di Soviore 211
S'Arcu 'e Dispensa 164
Sardinia 8, 12, 159-75, **158**
   accommodation 161
   festivals & events 161
   resources 161
   transport 161
   travel seasons 160
Sass Corbée 38
Sasso Piano 186
Sassopiatto 142
Sciliar 143
Sassolungo Circuit 142-3, **142**
Scopello 113, 120
Seceda 156
Segheria Veneziana dei Bègoi 152
Seghja Di Braghje 152
Seiser Alm 136-7
Sella di Monte Aquila 71
Sella Ronda 141
Selva di Val Gardena 134
Selvaggio Blu 171

Walks 000
Map Pages 000

Sella-Herbetet Traverse 11, 220-1, **220**
Sentiero Azzurro 8, 204-7, **205**
Sentiero degli Dei 8, 48-51, **49**
Sentiero della Libertà 12, 80-3, **81**
Sentiero del Ventrar 3, 37
Serra Carpineto 82
Serra di Monte Aquila 70
Sestri Levante 197
Sicily 8, 111-31, **110**
   accommodation 113
   festivals & events 113
   resources 113
   transport 113
   travel seasons 112
skiing 74, 82
Slopes of Monte Grona, the, 6, 34-5, **34**
slow food 59
smoking 238
Sorrento 43
Spiaggia del Fornillo 50
St Anthony 199
Stelvio, see Dolomites, the & Stelvio 133
Strada del Ponale 30-1, **30**
Stresa 38
Stromboli 6, 114-15, **114**
Strombolicchio 115
Su Balladorzu 164
Su Porteddu 162
Su Ruvagliu 166
Sulmona 64
sustainability 237
swimming 27

T

Tenne, river 182
Terme di Rabbi 152
Termini 46-7
Terzo Paradiso 191
time zone 238
Tinetto 208
Tino 208
tipping 238
Tiscali 12, 166-9, **167**
Toblinger Knoten 145
toilets 238

Torraccia di Chiusi 101
Torre Annamaria 191
Torrente Grauson 226
Torrente Rabbies 152
Torrente Valnontey 231
Tour du Mont Blanc 11, 216-17, **216**
train travel 232, 233
Tratto Spino 36
travel seasons 13
travel to/from Italy 232
Traversata del Conero 192
Tre Cime di Lavaredo 11, 144-5, **144**
Tremezzo 28
Tuònes 172
Tuscan Hill Crests 13, 100-3, 101
Tuscany 87-109, **86**
   accommodation 89
   festivals & events 89
   resources 89
   transport 89
   travel seasons 88
TV shows 18

U

Umbria & Le Marche 177-93, **176**
   accommodation 179
   festivals & events 179
   resources 179
   transport 179
   travel seasons 178
UNESCO World Heritage sites 12

V

Vagliagli 98
Val de Chedul 139
Valle delle Ferriere 56-7, **56**
Valle del Sambuco 14, 52-3, **52**
Valle Dentro 77
Valle di Lanaittu 167
Valle d'Orta 78
Vallone di Grauson 226-7, **226**
Vallunga 140
Valnontey 220
Val Vény 217

Vernazza 205
Via dei Monti Lattari 42
Via Ferrata 235
Via Francigena 109
Viale dei Platani 94
villas
  Casalecchi 92
  Villa Balbianello 29, 51
  Villa Balbiano 27
  Villa Carlotta 27
  Villa del Monte 95
  Villa Dievole 98
  Villa Miranda 96
  Villa Palagione 106
  Villa Rufolo 53
  Villa Vistarenni 96
vineyards 90
visas 232
Volastra 202

volcanoes 10
  Mt Etna 10, 131
  Mt Vesuvius 10
Volterra 106
Vulcano 126

W

waterfalls 31
weather 16-17
websites
  Abruzzo 65
  Campania & the Amalfi Coast 43
  Dolomites, the & Stelvio 135
  Italian Lakes, the 23
  Liguria 197
  Sardinia 160
  Sicily 113
  Tuscany , 89
  Umbria & Le Marche 179

Western & Maritime Alps, the 215
Western & Maritime Alps, the 213-31, **212**
  accommodation 215
  festivals & events 215
  resouces 2150
  transport 214
  travel seasons 215
wildlife
  tours 75
wine 88, 99, 105, 203, *see also* food & drinks
World War II 71, 81, 82

Z

Zans 154-5
ziplining 79

Walks 000
Map Pages 000, 000

THE WRITERS

This is the 2nd edition of Lonely Planet's *Best Day Walks Italy* guidebook, updated with new material by Gregor Clark. Writers on previous editions whose work also appears in this book are included below.

Gregor Clark

Gregor is a US-based writer whose love of foreign languages and curiosity have taken him to dozens of countries on five continents. Since 2000, Gregor has regularly contributed to Lonely Planet guides, including titles on Italy and France, as well as cycling guides to Italy. Gregor lives with his wife and two daughters in his current home state of Vermont.

Contributing writers

Brendan Sainsbury

SEND US YOUR FEEDBACK

We love to hear from travelers – your comments keep us on our toes and help make our books better. Our well-travelled team reads every word on what you loved or loathed about this book. Although we cannot reply individually to your submissions, we always guarantee that your feedback goes straight to the appropriate writers, in time for the next edition. Each person who sends us information is thanked in the next edition.

Visit **lonelyplanet.com/contact** to submit your updates and suggestions or to ask for help. Our award-winning website also features inspirational travel stories and news.

Note: We may edit, reproduce and incorporate your comments in Lonely Planet products such as guidebooks, websites and digital products, so let us know if you are happy to have your name acknowledged. For a copy of our privacy policy visit **lonelyplanet.com/legal**.

BEHIND THE SCENES

This book was produced by the following:

Commissioning Editor
James Smart

Co-ordinating Editor
Christopher Pitts

Production Editor
Graham O'Neill

Book Designer
Virgina Moreno

Cartographer
Daniela Machová

Assisting Editors
Imogen Bannister, Melanie Dankel, Maja Vatrić

Cover Researcher
Kat Marsh

Thanks to
Ronan Abayawickrema, Dan Bolger, Gwen Cotter, Karen Henderson, Alex Howard, Alison Killiea, Katerina Pavkova

Product Development
Amy Lynch, Marc Backwell, Katerina Pavkova, Fergal Condon, Ania Bartoszek

ACKNOWLEDGMENTS

Cover photograph
Tuscany; AWL Images/Francesco Iacobelli©